KU-522-243

# QUIET IMPACT

SYLVIA LOEHKEN

JOHN
MURRAY
LEARNING

First published in Germany in 2012 by Gabal.

This edition published in 2015 by John Murray Learning, an Hachette UK company.

First published in US in 2014 by The McGraw-Hill Companies, Inc.

Copyright © GABAL 2014

Translation © Hachette UK 2014

Translation by Michael Robinson

The right of Sylvia Loehken to be identified as the Author of the Work has been asserted by her in accordance with the Copyright, Designs and Patents Act 1988.

Database right Hodder & Stoughton (makers)

All rights reserved. No part of this publication may be reproduced, stored in a retrieval system or transmitted in any form or by any means, electronic, mechanical, photocopying, recording or otherwise, without the prior written permission of the publisher, or as expressly permitted by law, or under terms agreed with the appropriate reprographic rights organization. Enquiries concerning reproduction outside the scope of the above should be sent to the Rights Department, John Murray Learning, at the address below.

You must not circulate this book in any other binding or cover and you must impose this same condition on any acquirer.

*British Library Cataloguing in Publication Data:* a catalogue record for this title is available from the British Library.

Paperback 9781444792867

eBook ISBN 9781444792874

*Library of Congress Catalog Card Number:* on file.

1

The publisher has used its best endeavours to ensure that any website addresses referred to in this book are correct and active at the time of going to press. However, the publisher and the author have no responsibility for the websites and can make no guarantee that a site will remain live or that the content will remain relevant, decent or appropriate.

The publisher has made every effort to mark as such all words which it believes to be trademarks. The publisher should also like to make it clear that the presence of a word in the book, whether marked or unmarked, in no way affects its legal status as a trademark.

Every reasonable effort has been made by the publisher to trace the copyright holders of material in this book. Any errors or omissions should be notified in writing to the publisher, who will endeavour to rectify the situation for any reprints and future editions.

Typeset by Cenveo® Publisher Services.

Printed and bound in Great Britain by Clays Ltd, St Ives plc.

John Murray Learning policy is to use papers that are natural, renewable and recyclable products and made from wood grown in sustainable forests. The logging and manufacturing processes are expected to conform to the environmental regulations of the country of origin.

John Murray Learning

338 Euston Road

London NW1 3BH

www.hodder.co.uk

# QUIET
# IMPACT

521 738 12 3

# About t

Dr Sylvia Loehken helps quiet people to achiev
experience as an academic and as manager of a
given her personal experience of her clients' working environments: politics and
administration, teaching and research, management and consultancy, global and
local fields.

Sylvia Loehken lives with her husband and son between Bonn and Berlin, and
between German and American culture – with happy memories of three years working
in Japan. She is always on the lookout for good books, interesting people to talk to
and a little wisdom.

# Contents

# INTRODUCTION

## Extroverts and introverts: two worlds for the price of one

My name is Sylvia Loehken and I am an introvert. Perhaps that's unusual: introverted – the word conjures up an unshaven nerd, locked away with a computer for days on end scattering takeaway pizza crumbs all over the keyboard. But that nerd is just a cliché of a quiet person. There are a lot of us. I like being with people – they are my profession and my vocation – but after a day of chaotic din and random encounters I need time to be alone and recharge my batteries. I love what I do, but unlike my extroverted colleagues I cannot draw all the energy I need from lively, exciting work with seminar members, audiences and tutees. But why is an introverted existence a suitable topic for a book about communication? I had to find that out for myself as well. It started like this:

Further training is seen as part and parcel of my profession, but at some point I started getting fed up with communication training. And it wasn't the subject matter that did it: what happens when people meet each other is one of the things I am most interested in. No, I was beginning to feel uncomfortable with the trainers and trainees – with my own colleagues. They often seemed too noisy and superficial, and I realized that it was primarily my problem. So, I started to think things over (introverts like thinking things over, they do it all the time). What could I put my finger on that upset me about my colleagues? The people standing up at the front were no worse that I am when I'm standing up there. But they were different – so different that their approach often alienated me. A lot of them saw themselves as an élite: 'top dog' I thought, and still think: it was all over the top. The training courses themselves often dropped hints that confirmed how different I was. My gestures: 'More expansive, please!' My speech: 'More aggressive, please!' The way I put things over: 'More vigorous, please!'

All this made me uneasy. Up until then, I had never felt the need when giving a talk to use big gestures, aggressive negotiation or assertiveness. And up until then, that hadn't done me any harm. On the contrary: the 'quiet' clients and seminar members (the ones with calm, controlled gestures and a co-operative approach, who didn't flaunt their emotions so much) were very keen on what I had to offer. And I liked them: most of my clients were very calm, and thought logically. 'I see! You like "blue brains", the quiet solitary types!' said my (very extroverted) coach when I described my favourite clients to her. She was right. My own experience in seminars had shown me that I enjoy working intensively with people who think similarly to me. And it made me realize that there are no communication courses designed for my clients and me – courses tailored to meet quiet people's strengths and needs.

This book aims to fill this significant gap – along with seminars, lectures and coaching directed at introverted people. My starting point was (and is) that good communication has to do with identity. I can only deal with other people successfully if I know myself and can handle myself properly: when putting things over, when negotiating, when networking and also in my private life. But what makes a quiet person? As there was nothing for us quite normal (i.e. neither shy nor hypersensitive) 'quiet people', I took myself as an example and analysed the way I habitually communicate. Self-help literature written in English, and also psychology, were most helpful here. I also started looking at my clients from a very specific perspective.

The result was exciting. I discovered two sets of qualities that introverted people contribute to communication, neatly divided into strengths and obstacles. It is not only quiet people who have all these qualities – but a lot of quiet people have a lot of these qualities. That's enough to be getting on with!

Strengths clearly are advantages, but so are obstacles, in their own way – if you are aware of the obstacles you create for yourself, then you have a better sense of your own needs than people who don't bother about their weak points. For example, for a long time, if I suddenly felt I wanted to be alone while spending time with family and friends, I thought I was being antisocial. I now realize that it makes complete sense to withdraw, as it helps me to regain my energy when I am exhausted. I would not call that a weakness – just as extroverts are not weak if they rely on being reassured about the things and people around them much more than introverts would.

Let me issue a very warm invitation: get to know your strengths and the obstacles you face. Welcome them both as good friends that share your life with you. That will make it much easier for you to influence a situation so that it 'suits' you and makes you able to communicate well.

Here, two questions are particularly useful in terms of different kinds of human behaviour:

1  What strengths can a quiet person in particular use in this situation?

2  What should a quiet person in particular look out for in this situation?

You will find the answers I have found to these questions in this book, and they are presented so that you can use them in your own life.

## What you will find in this book – and how you can read it

The answers to the two questions above are related to a whole variety of situations in the pages that follow: professional and private, formal and anything but formal, close and distant, addressed directly or negotiated. If you see yourself as a quiet person, this book is intended to help you to get along well in a world that is often much too noisy, and to be successful when things matter to you. Every section is written from an introverted person's point of view.

If you are more of an extrovert, you will understand the quiet people you come across better and come to value their strengths after reading the book – whether they are partners, relatives or friends, colleagues or bosses, co-workers or seminar members.

If you are not sure whether you are a quiet person or not, there is a test in the first chapter to help you make up your mind. And in any case, this book is structured so that you can relate the subject matter to your personal situation: you will keep coming across questions that will help you if you answer them with reference to yourself. Take the opportunity – you will really get to know yourself if you do, and that will help you when communicating with others!

The book is constructed in the way that introverts like to think and communicate: from the inside outwards. It starts by looking at personality. In Part I you will find an introduction and a survey of quiet people's typical strengths and the obstacles they create for themselves – and it makes sense for you to read this part first, to put yourself on a sound footing. Part II, containing Chapters 4 and 5, unfolds a panorama of private and professional scenarios – focusing on what is good for quiet people and helps to make them successful. Above all, this section shows how you can handle these scenarios in an 'introvert-friendly' way. All the subsequent chapters, which make up Part III of the book, explain how you can use these strengths and surmount these obstacles when dealing with other people. Here, I have deliberately emphasized the key strengths and obstacles relating to building up contacts, negotiating, and appearing in public and at meetings. After the test and a glance at the summary at the end of Chapter 1 you will be able to assess clearly which of your personal qualities are important in a particular situation.

The chapters will also introduce you to some of my quiet seminar members and tutees whose (anonymous) stories illustrate how introverts can use their strengths in various situations. I hope what you discover while reading will help you to pluck up courage – and make you want to try out introverted communication!

## Quiet people make the world go round!

Many famous personalities were or are quiet people, or so the qualities ascribed to them suggest. Have a quick look at the distinguished list below.

 **A gallery of eminent introverted individuals**

**Woody Allen**, film director, author, actor and musician, USA

**Julian Assange**, journalist and spokesman for WikiLeaks, Australia

**Brenda Barnes**, president, chair of the board of Sara Lee, consumer goods manufacturers, USA

**Ingrid Bergman**, actress, Sweden

**Warren Buffet**, major investor and entrepreneur, USA

**Frédéric Chopin**, composer and pianist, Poland

**Marie Curie**, chemist and physicist, Nobel Prize winner for physics and chemistry, Poland

**Charles Darwin**, naturalist and originator of the theory of evolution, United Kingdom

**Bob Dylan**, musician, poet and painter, USA

**Clint Eastwood**, actor, USA

**Albert Einstein**, physicist, Nobel Prize winner for physics, Germany

**Mohandas Karamchand Gandhi,** known as Mahatma Gandhi, spiritual leader of the Indian independence movement, India

**Bill Gates**, founder of Microsoft, USA

**Sir Alfred Hitchcock**, film director, United Kingdom

**Michael Jackson**, musician, USA

**Franz Kafka**, German-speaking writer from Prague, Czechoslovakia

**Immanuel Kant**, Enlightenment philosopher, Germany

**Avril Lavigne**, singer and songwriter, Canada

**Angela Merkel**, Chancellor of the Federal Republic, Germany

**Sir Isaac Newton**, physicist, mathematician, philosopher and theologian, United Kingdom

**Barack Obama**, President of the USA

**Michelle Pfeiffer**, actress, USA

**Claudia Schiffer**, model, Germany

**George Soros**, investor and businessman, Hungary / USA

**Steven Spielberg**, director, producer and screenplay writer, USA

**Tilda Swinton**, actress, United Kingdom

**Mother Theresa**, nun, winner of the Nobel Peace Prize, Albania / India

**Charles Mountbatten-Windsor**, Prince of Wales, Duke of Cornwall, heir to the British throne

**Mark Zuckerberg**, computer scientist, founder of Facebook, USA

So you see: many of the most successful, powerful, talented, innovative, courageous, clever and interesting people on this planet have quiet personalities. They are not better than extroverts, but they are not worse than them either – though they often think they are. There is one thing above all that makes them successful: they have remained true to themselves, in terms of their introversion and all their other qualities. That is a wonderful recipe, and I commend it to you most warmly: remain true to yourself as an introvert, do what suits you and your needs. You and your strengths will change the world quietly, like the people in the list. As Dolly Parton once said:

'FIND OUT WHO YOU ARE – AND DO IT ON PURPOSE!'

PS: A word to the experts: academic literature tends to write extraversion, rather than extroversion. I have followed current colloquial language and chosen the latter variant.

# PART I

Who you are.
What you can do.
What you need

# 1.
# Why quiet?!

John studies IT (information technology) at a technical college with an excellent reputation. He has two friends he likes meeting – to go to the cinema with, for example, or to play sport with. He uses social media like Twitter and Facebook to keep in touch with school friends and various people he has met on internships. At the moment he's doing a placement with one of the best-known German car manufacturers. But John is less successful when it comes to love and romance: there aren't many women at the college, and John hardly ever goes to parties or concerts – he finds the noise level and the crowds of people too stressful. In the meantime, he's wondering whether he should try out a dating website to find the right girl for him.

John is getting on well with his course: he's passing his exams and he prepares himself well for essay work. But he doesn't like presenting papers to big seminar groups – and he is terrified of oral tests. He likes running in his free time, and sometimes he gets ideas for his second hobby while jogging: he photographs views in which landscape and technology combine to make something new, for example bridges and industrial buildings.

## But what is a quiet person?

### Introversion and extroversion

People can be divided into introverted and extroverted personalities. Almost anyone can make sense of these terms and will associate certain qualities with them. On closer examination – whether in real life or literature – the boundaries between introversion and extroversion become somewhat blurred. The fact is that there is a great deal of flexibility in the manifestations and definition of introversion – or extroversion.

### Personality factor

This quality is first of all *dependent on personality*. We are born with a tendency to be introverted or extroverted – and thus also with certain characteristics and needs that help to shape us. Introvert and extrovert qualities can be seen even in children. The terms are easier to understand if they are not seen as opposites, but as extreme points on a continuum. Everyone displays both introvert and extrovert qualities. And everyone is also born with a certain flexibility, a kind of comfort zone on the introvert–extrovert continuum that suits them. Most people find themselves in a moderate central area but with a tendency towards the introvert or the extrovert end. Everywhere in the spectrum is healthy – only extreme positions can cause problems. This affects people who are placed at the extreme ends of the continuum, regardless of whether it is the introvert or the extrovert end. However, it is extremely unhealthy to live outside your personal comfort zone all the time. If an acoustically sensitive introvert like John, for example, constantly exposes himself to high noise levels, it costs him a lot of energy – and it is not possible to generate new energy either. If he were forced to sell cars all the time, rather than spend his placement in the admin side of the company, he would be unhappy and drained in the long run. In extreme cases, living outside your comfort zone for too long can actually make you ill.

Secondly, introversion and extroversion are *dependent on the situation*: in other words, like the direction of a railway track, where everyone has the ability to turn inwards or outwards to suit the situation. We human beings are wonderfully adaptable – one of our distinguishing features is an ability to flexibly adapt our thoughts and actions to a particular situation. At any point in our lives we can act in one way or another. This has nothing to do with introversion and extroversion, but with intelligence or possibly discipline – for example, when we deliberately decide on an approach that would be quite different if we had acted impulsively. And the part we play in a situation shapes our decisions about how we communicate. Then quite different questions can affect our behaviour: are we strong or weak in relation to other people? What is expected of us? How do we want to present ourselves?

For this reason, on his mother's birthday, John will chat to his younger cousins cheerfully, as a cool older role model. He'll be polite to his elderly aunts and answer their questions patiently. On his placement company's trade fair stand he'll tend to be reticent when he has to deal with people he doesn't know. But he will also make an effort – when all is said and done, it's his professional role. Even a strongly extrovert personality must have moments that leave them speechless or when they deliberately hold back. A lot of extroverts I know enjoy (and even need!) quiet moments at turbulent times. All in all, this flexibility is fortunate: the fact is that the introvert–extrovert track gives us room for manoeuvre and a wealth of different approaches.

Thirdly, *the culture* around us demands more or less the ability to adapt in the direction of introversion or extroversion. A country like Japan sees being quiet, alone and thoughtful as very important. Shared silence is part of a normal conversation between acquaintances. Introverts from other countries find this a very pleasant experience. But in the USA, a classic 'extrovert culture', where silence falling between two people who are talking to each other is usually seen as embarrassing or at least unpleasant, it counts as normal to spend all one's time in groups, both privately and professionally. And so in many European countries introverts will have to worker harder to adapt to their surroundings by behaving more extrovertly than they would have to in Japan, which has an 'introvert-friendly' culture.

## The time factor

And fourthly and lastly, shifts occur with *the passage of time*. As people get older they tend to move towards the middle of the continuum, becoming 'more moderate' in their introversion or extroversion. This makes introversion more accessible to extroverts in the second half of their lives, which is particularly valuable: it helps them to reflect about themselves and their own lives, to think about values and meaning.

But despite the fact that they depend on situation, culture and even age, both introversion and extroversion are relatively stable personality traits evidenced in certain qualities and inclinations. But above all, the answer to one key question is crucial:

THE KEY QUESTION ABOUT INTROVERSION AND EXTROVERSION:
WHERE DOES THE ENERGY COME FROM?

In other words, how do people behave if they are stressed and/or exhausted and have to recharge their batteries?

## Sources of energy for introverts and extroverts

Fundamentally, there are two answers to this question. One is that some people derive their energy from contact with others. My husband is like that: after a stressful day he finds it relaxing to go out with friends, play for his football team or involve himself in a club function. This is essentially extrovert behaviour. Other people 'close up' and regenerate themselves on their own if possible, with minimum stimulus and conversation. I am like that. After a day's seminar I enjoy sitting alone in my hotel room and reading. Without a word to anyone. Or I meet a good friend and draw energy from a relaxed chat between the two of us. After three seminar days I need half a day to myself for my batteries to be fully recharged. You will be starting to realize: anyone who recovers like this is more likely to be on the introverted side.

Too much stimulation burns up energy for introverts. In a work context this could mean a job involving a large number of things that have to be dealt with at the same time. In private life it could be a party with a lot of people I don't know and loud music – a situation that even young introverts like John find stressful. For introverts, excessive stimulation also means that they need to withdraw. But extroverts like stimulation because it energizes them. This is why they often look for variety when they are thrown back on their own resources and are getting too few new impressions: so in libraries, hospitals or firms with private offices they like to find rooms where some social contact is possible – cafeterias, seating areas, kitchens and anywhere that telephoning or electronic communication is easy. In private offices telephones and computers can be a lifeline for the extreme extrovert, simply because they ensure contact with the outside world.

## Need for peace and quiet

This does not mean that extroverts do not need time on their own and some quiet moments. But for introverts 'time alone' is essential to their existence if they are to recharge their batteries after stress and social contact. If they have no peace and quiet, they get irritable and exhausted. Also, generally speaking, introverts tend to require longer without any stimulation before they can throw themselves back into the everyday hurly-burly. Three weeks in a lonely Swedish forest is more of a dream holiday for introverts than extroverts.

? **A question for you**

You will soon be able to test yourself to see whether you are an introvert or an extrovert. How do you see yourself at the moment?

- I am more of an introvert. ❏
- I am more of an extrovert. ❏
- I am about half one and half the other. ❏

Neither of these two types is better or worse. They simply describe where our own inclinations and needs lie. The better you know what you need, the better you can live 'true to type' and do the things that are important for you. One thing is essential here: balancing time on your own and time with other people, so that you are getting the correct quantity of each. Learn to ask yourself: what exactly do I need? You will soon realize that you almost always know the answer.

THE QUESTION OF LIVING TRUE TO TYPE: WHAT EXACTLY DO I NEED?

## Wind turbines and batteries

A comparison from another sphere of energy generation shows the difference even more clearly: an extrovert generates his energy like a wind turbine – he needs outside input in the first place in order to generate it and secondly he has to be actively involved in this process himself and 'spin' dynamically. But introverts are like batteries: they charge themselves in repose without any 'outside' wind and prefer not to involve themselves in any activity at this stage. So introverts, like 'batteries', need more time to replace the energy they have used.

## Extroverted and introverted brains

Neuroscientists can now show that introverts' brain activity uses more energy than that of extroverts. In comparison, introverts' brains show a higher level of electrical activity – and this applies all the time, not just when facing unusual mental challenges. This higher energy level can be seen above all in the frontal cortex, where internal events are processed. This is the part of the brain that deals with learning, decision-making, memory and problem-solving. So introverts use more energy for processing impressions and thus drain their batteries faster than extroverts, who, like 'wind turbines', can also 'recharge' while they are putting energy into something. That is why it is particularly important for introverts to use their inner resources economically.

## Introvert brains are more easily over-stimulated

Introvert brains also address stimuli from the outside more intensely than extrovert brains: they respond more sensitively to stimuli from the world around them, are more easily over-stimulated and need significantly more energy to process impressions. This means, for example, that for an introvert like John even a low sound level can be detrimental for mental activity such as learning. But his extrovert peers can perhaps learn even more easily if there is moderate background noise (radio!) than in complete silence.

This does not mean that an extrovert is 'more lively' than an introvert. On the contrary, introverts are not 'built' to be quieter than extroverts. Even the label 'shy' has nothing to do with introversion. Shy people are above all anxious about social contact. They often do not feel up to meeting other people. Fear is nothing to do with the introvert–extrovert continuum: it can 'attack' both types.

INTROVERT MEANS SOMETHING QUITE DIFFERENT FROM SHY OR HYPERSENSITIVE. 'HYPERSENSITIVITY' IS ALSO DIFFERENT FROM INTROVERSION. IT MEANS THAT THE NERVOUS SYSTEM IS EXTRAORDINARILY SENSITIVE TO EXTERNAL INFLUENCES, WHICH LEADS TO SENSORY OVERLOAD PARTICULARLY QUICKLY, BUT IT CAN ALSO LEAD TO A HIGH DEGREE OF EMPATHY. EVEN THOUGH RELATIVELY MANY HYPERSENSITIVE PEOPLE ARE INTROVERTED, IT IS ALSO TRUE THAT 30 PER CENT OF THEM ARE EXTROVERTS, AS SHOWN BY PSYCHOLOGIST ELAINE ARON. YOU WILL FIND ELAINE'S WEB ADDRESS, WHERE SHE HAS A TEST THAT WILL ALLOW YOU TO ASSESS YOURSELF, AT THE END OF THIS BOOK.

# Extroverts and introverts: discovering them, and new insights

## Freud and Jung

Sigmund Freud (an extrovert) developed modern psychoanalysis about 100 years ago. He saw sexuality as the driving force in the human subconscious. His younger colleague and sparring partner Carl Gustav Jung (an introvert) was critical of Freud's theory. He came up with a more comprehensive model for the subconscious containing elements other than sexuality. These different basic assumptions did not have a very productive effect on the relationship between the two academics. They started working separately and pursued their research independently of each other.

In 1921, in his essay *Psychologische Typen (Psychological Types),* Jung defined introversion and extroversion for the first time as characteristics that contribute significantly to shaping a personality. He identified four functions (sensing, thinking, feeling and intuition) that further affect the personalities of both introverts and extroverts. Jung's distinction between introversion and extroversion can be found in all major personality typologies. The Myers-Briggs Type Indicator (MBTI) in the USA in particular and the Insights Tests stick closest to the original classifications, because they consider all the four functions identified by Jung. But methods like the 'Big Five Test', the Reiss Profile, the Alpha Plus and the Structogram analyses also use 'introvert' and 'extrovert' as characteristics. But they are not uniformly defined, and not exactly the same terms are used. Interestingly, the 'Big Five Test' places 'introvert' and 'extrovert' as subheadings under the generic term 'extroversion' – looked at logically, that is like using 'woman' as the generic term for man and woman.

In her book *The Introvert Advantage* (2002), Marti Olsen Laney points out that Freud, after his dispute with Jung, presented the concept of introversion negatively in his writings as narcissism, while seeing extroversion as healthy and positive. Could it be that the negative image that introversion still has today (and that is clearly present in many of the tests mentioned) goes back to the conflict between an extrovert academic and an introvert colleague?

Wolfgang Roth (2003) identifies a different link: he feels that Jung, when classifying personality traits, was trying to explain his disagreement with the extrovert Sigmund Freud, something that concerned and bothered Jung for a long time.

But one thing is important: Jung did not assess people in terms of degrees of introversion or extroversion. He saw both types and their traits as important and valuable. In Jung's view, introverts and extroverts complement each other and can help each other to broaden their outlook and use new perspectives. For example, an extrovert colleague can easily organize additional help within the firm, while the introvert colleague ensures that any changes of direction are examined thoroughly. An introvert father can gently set boundaries for his extrovert daughter as she grows up, to avoid conflicts that might easily emerge in extrovert–introvert communication.

## The importance of neuropsychology

In the meantime, research has made progress. One area is particularly exciting here in the introversion–extroversion field: the physiology of the brain. This is not a medical work – but insights in the scientific field are an exciting story in their own right. Studies from the 1990s onwards make it clear that in various areas of the central nervous system the introvert–extrovert continuum is not only a psychological assumption but also a biological reality. That is to say: our personalities and actions are governed by physiological details of the brain. But we cannot conclude from this that we *have to* communicate or act in a particular way. The physiological characteristics simply lead to conclusions about our strengths and inclinations.

Here is a short summary of the most important insights.

---

### ! Introvert and extrovert brains are different!

1. It can be shown that there is *greater electrical activity* in the frontal cortices of introvert subjects than extrovert ones. This is where we deal with our inner processes. It is where we learn, decide, remember and solve problems (Roming 2011).

2. An American doctor, Debra Johnson, showed in 1999 that introversion is linked with an increased flow of blood in this same frontal area. She also showed that differences between introverts and extroverts come about because their blood follows different pathways in the brain. Introverts' stimuli have to travel deeper into the brain along the neural pathways than extroverts'. This is why quiet people often take longer to reflect or react.

3. Different neurotransmitters dominate in the brain of introverts from those of extroverts. These are message carriers that affect the activities of the cerebral cortex, conveying messages including contentment and well-being (Roth 2007). The pathways followed by neurotransmitters are

established by repeated actions and shape everything that we do as a matter of habit. Every individual has their own, genetically determined 'level' for different neurotransmitters. Extroverts show considerably more activity in the neurotransmitter dopamine's pathway, while introverts have more acetylcholine (Olsen Laney 2002).

4. These two neurotransmitters have quite different effects: dopamine deals with motor drive, curiosity, the search for variety and the expectation of a reward; acetylcholine is important for concentration, memory and learning (Roth 2007). Susan Cain sums up the consequences of this neurobiological difference: she defines extroverts as *reward-oriented* and introverts as *threat-oriented* (Cain 2011).

   This has consequences for communication: extroverts' biological equipment makes them more inclined to be joyful, excited, exuberant or even euphoric. Extroverts are also more likely to take risks: for example, they have more conflicts, are more inclined to take risky chances when negotiating and are usually more comfortable with a big audience. Introverts do not feel euphoric so frequently, and they feel it less intensively, but they are more likely to look and listen carefully before they act. They like to avoid conflict, and are rarely aggressive themselves. There are even studies suggesting that introverts are more faithful than extroverts ...

5. Neurotransmitters should be placed in a wider context. There are two 'adversaries' in our autonomic nervous system (i.e. in the area in which everything happens 'automatically'). The *sympathetic system* ensures that the body can perform, preparing it for attack, flight or major efforts in relation to the outside world. The sympathetic nerve uses the 'extrovert transmitter' dopamine for transmission purposes. The *parasympathetic system* deals with the exact opposite: it works to ensure calm, relaxation and conservation. It lowers the heart rate and promotes digestion, using the 'introvert transmitter' acetylcholine.

6. Marti Olsen Laney (2002) draws the conclusion from these links (and some other studies) that introverts and extroverts differ biologically above all because the autonomic nervous system is configured differently: in extroverts the sympathetic system's activities are dominant, and in introverts those of the parasympathetic system dominate. As well as this, extroverts seem (according to Debra Johnson in the above-mentioned research in 1999) to need more stimulus from the outside world than introverts, because they cannot stimulate themselves internally to the same levels of intensity. So outward calm and repose are a challenge for extroverts. Researchers Dean and Peter Copeland showed that for

extroverts the lack of external stimuli (e.g. routine activities, few active people, rigid rituals) cause a lack of stimulation (Hamer/Copeland 1998). So extroverts are quick to become restless or bored if the lack of stimulation persists for long: they have dopamine withdrawal symptoms.

7. This provides a biological explanation of why extroverts draw their energy from active, outward-directed behaviour, while introverts find their strength in peace and quiet: the two ways of finding energy relate to the state of the differently equipped autonomic nervous systems.

## The comfort zone as a natural biotope

So much for the academic basis of our decision. It is easier to understand against this background why it is so healthy to move along the introvert–extrovert continuum within our comfort zone as often as possible: it is the nearest thing to our natural biotope, the one we are best suited to – and in which we can organize our lives most easily and pleasantly.

## Are there more introverts or more extroverts?

It is not yet possible to find precise scientific answers to all questions about introverts and extroverts. This can be seen in the answer to an interesting question, and that answer differs greatly according to the point of view: are introverts in a minority as opposed to extroverts?

INTROVERTS ARE OFTEN LESS VISIBLE – BUT THEY ARE EVERYWHERE.

As extroverts communicate more vigorously via the ear and eye, they can often seem like a majority in groups, while introverts often seem to be present in smaller numbers. Marti Olsen Laney's book cites authors such as Kroeger and Thuesen, who work on the basis that 75 per cent of the population are extroverts, while Susan Cain's estimate comes out as 30 to 70 per cent of extroverts. But Laurie Helgoe's (2008) and Devora Zack's (2012) studies of introverts work on the basis of a balanced 50:50 proportion of introverts and extroverts, as does the literature on the Myers-Briggs Type Indicator.

It is probably impossible to ascertain the exact proportions. But one thing is certain: there are very many introverts. The next section addresses a question that is more important to the central theme of this book than any set of figures. How do introverts stand in relation to their fellow citizens when it comes to communication?

# The right mix of people

## Are introverts antisocial?

Quiet people who are reticent in social contexts are easily dubbed 'antisocial'. This is unfair. Introversion and qualities such as friendliness or interest in your fellow human beings are quite different personality traits. Of course we have the unworldly 'nerd', who sustains his main social contacts via the internet. But we also have the introverted communications expert (like Anne, for example, whom you will meet in Chapter 6), who has a great deal to do with a whole variety of people, and enjoys it. There are also different personalities among extroverts: not every extrovert is a charismatic entertainer – and there are plenty of extroverts who are pretty inept socially. All men and women are social beings. We need each other. But 'need' is a broad term. For example, a baby needs other people in order to survive. As adults, we need the company of others – human rights organisations see solitary confinement as torture. Everyone needs to look at other people in order to establish standards of behaviour.

The ability to build up personal contacts with other people requires a range of qualities. These include interest in other people, empathy, respect, sympathy – and even the ability to acknowledge guilt. People have these qualities regardless of whether they are introverts or extroverts.

QUIET PEOPLE NEED ENERGY FOR SOCIAL INTERACTION, WHILE EXTROVERTS DERIVE ENERGY FROM THIS INTERACTION.

## Investment versus reward

Although introverts and extroverts 'need' their fellow men just like all other members of the species. For introverts, meeting other people always represents an investment: as you have seen earlier in the book, communicating with others, above all in large groups, takes a lot of energy out of introverts. But extroverts gain something from the same encounter, and that is a 'reward' from the neurotransmitters and above all that valuable thing called energy. You will also remember, as 'wind turbines', extroverts need wind, in other words interaction with other people, as urgently as introverts (as 'batteries') need time to themselves in order to recharge themselves. Also, extroverts are usually comfortable in the company of others and so can concentrate more easily on external perspective.

Introverts can feel comfortable with other people as well, but there are differences. Introverts need less stimulation; a great deal more goes on in their minds without any outside impetus than in extroverts' minds. This is why quiet people often find social occasions debilitating – and hold themselves back: they make very few firm arrangements, or take up a passive stance rather then deliberately approaching people. Introverts also prefer other communication forms: they like talking to one or two other people, rather than in a large group. They like to lecture in small rooms, and not in large, packed lecture halls. And, however inspiring a conversation may be, the energy invested in it can only be replaced when the stimulation is processed in a period of rest. Alone.

## Intense inner life

This is why quiet people are inclined to shut themselves off from the outside world if they have too many impressions to process. But this can easily give extroverts a false impression: 'She can't treat people like that!' In worse cases, they see introverts as self-centred, not interested in dealing with other people, even as hermit-like. Dear extrovert readers: this is not true! It is just that, compared with you, introverts simply need to work harder on their intensive inner life: external impressions have to be constantly squared up with experiences, attitudes or personal assessments. This means that it makes sense that the 'working memory' is close to being overloaded by these activities.

AS AN INTROVERT, ENSURE YOU HAVE ENOUGH 'TIME OUT' FOR YOURSELF!

## Time needed to regenerate!

It is especially good for introverts to be alone from time to time: for digestion and regeneration. In this way you will avoid over-stimulation, fatigue and the urge to 'shut down' in the middle of a conversation. And anyway, the need to be on your own is absolutely not antisocial as such. On the contrary, quiet people want to understand what is going on around them properly – and that is why they need to digest it particularly thoroughly. In short: a great deal more 'happens' for them than for extroverts – it is just that this is not visible. Extroverts often feel slightly excluded, bored or even rejected when they are with quiet people. Definitely not: this is a false impression!

So, because of the particular way their brains are organized, introverts benefit if they take care to alternate their time with others and their time on their own appropriately. The correct proportions depend on the position of their comfort zone on the introvert–extrovert continuum (see the section 'But what is a quiet person?' at the beginning of this chapter). There are some withdrawn introverts who need a lot of peace and quiet (at the introvert end of the continuum), particularly after social occasions, while introverts placed more towards the middle of the continuum are content with less time out. They like people, and cultivate their contacts in such a way that they could easily pass as extroverts. Helgoe (2008) calls such people 'socially accessible introverts'. I call these quiet people who could easily extrovert themselves 'flexi-introverts'.

These flexi-introverts are often hard to distinguish from extroverts at first glance. Many people with this type of personality like being with people and are often very good at initiating contacts. It is only when it comes to energy management that it becomes clear that they are different from extroverts in one crucial particular: they need periods of quiet and withdrawal in order to be fully able to devote themselves to other people again.

## Acknowledge the need for time out

It is because this type of quiet person seems so accessible that withdrawal is a problem: other people usually cannot see that a flexi-introvert could possibly need to be alone. Even socially accessible introverts often take a long time themselves to learn that they need this kind of peace and quiet and time on their own: when all's said and done, they enjoy being with other people! But their gift for getting on with people has nothing to do with their need for peace and quiet. Flexi-introverts wear themselves out particularly easily because they are slow to notice this need, and enjoy the company of others. They benefit from planning regular rest periods very carefully.

No question about it: introverts are as much social beings as extroverts. They value a manageable network of reliable contacts. Assess your own preferences now. These two questions will help you to do it.

**?  Two questions for you**

What kind of people do you feel particularly comfortable with?

What situations suit you best?

# Are you a quiet person?

## Assessing your own needs

This question about whether you are a quiet person is probably the most important one in the book: now – after you have got to know about quiet people's most important qualities – you have to locate yourself: where are you placed on the continuum between introversion and extroversion? Once you have found this place you will also gain access to certain strengths and obstacles in dealing with yourself and other people. And you will save a lot of energy as well, energy that you have invested (as I have) in living like a person that is actually not you. And, if nothing else, this new knowledge about yourself will help you to make a conscious assessment of precisely what you need in particular situations.

The following test will help you to locate yourself. Pour yourself your favourite drink, put aside a peaceful quarter of an hour, have a pen ready and find out whether you are a quiet person.

---

### ❓ Where do you come on the continuum?

Tick all the statements that are true for you.

1. I quickly get impatient when I am talking to someone if they take too long to respond. ❏

2. I prefer to talk to one other person rather than several. ❏

3. I find I can understand what I am thinking more easily if I talk to other people about it. ❏

4. I like my surroundings to be clean and tidy. ❏

5. I like to act quickly on a 'gut feeling' rather than thinking about things for a long time. ❏

6. If I'm really tired, I most like to be on my own. ❏

7. People who talk quickly wear me out. ❏

8. I have very personal, distinctive tastes. ❏

9. I avoid large crowds of people if I can. ❏

10. I usually find small talk easy – even with people I don't know. ❏

11. If I spend a long time with people, I often get tired or even irritable. ❏

12. Other people usually pay attention to me when I speak. ❏

13. If I have visitors at home who stay for a long time, I expect them to help. ❏
14. I prefer to work at a project in small sections rather than spending a long time on one piece. ❏
15. Sometimes I am very tired after a lot of conversations, or loud ones. ❏
16. I do not need a lot of friends. ❏
17. I don't spend too long thinking about what is in other people's minds. ❏
18. It matters to me to get enough sleep. ❏
19. I find new places and surroundings exciting. ❏
20. I find sudden disturbances and unexpected situations a strain. ❏
21. I believe people often think I am too calm, boring, distant or shy. ❏
22. I like watching closely and I have an eye for detail. ❏
23. I'd rather talk than write. ❏
24. I brief myself carefully before making a decision about something. ❏
25. I am often slow to spot tension between people. ❏
26. I have marked aesthetic sensibilities. ❏
27. I sometimes find reasons for not going to a party or some other social occasion. ❏
28. I am relatively quick to trust people. ❏
29. I like thinking things over and getting to the bottom of them. ❏
30. I avoid speaking to large audiences if I can. ❏
31. Listening is not one of my great strengths. ❏
32. I often let other people's expectations put me under too much pressure. ❏
33. I can usually take personal attacks in good part. ❏
34. I get bored quickly. ❏
35. If there is something special to celebrate, I'm happy for it to be on a large scale: a proper party or a meal with a lot of people. ❏

*Now assess the statements you ticked:*

Introvert statements: 2, 6, 7, 9, 11, 15, 16, 20, 21, 22, 24, 27, 29, 30, 32.

Extrovert statements: 1, 3, 5, 10, 12, 14, 17, 19, 23, 25, 28, 31, 33, 34, 35.

Statements 4, 8, 13, 18, 26 are nothing to do with introversion and extroversion and are there for one reason only: to stop you dropping into an answering routine.

What does your result look like?

**You are an introvert and have ticked at least three more introvert statements than extrovert statements:**

The more introvert statements you ticked, the more markedly introverted you are. This book will tell you how to identify your needs and work to your strengths. Be sure to keep it with you!

**You ticked roughly the same number of introvert and extrovert statements, i.e. no more than two statements different:**

You are in the intermediate zone between introvert and extrovert and as a so-called 'centrovert' or 'ambivert' you can get on well with both personality types. Your behaviour is particularly flexible. This book will show you above all something about the repertoire of your introverted side – in other words about the side that is probably less obvious to you.

**You are an extrovert and have ticked at least three more extrovert statements than introvert statements:**

The more extrovert statements you have agreed with, the more marked is your extroversion. As you read on, you will find out what makes introverts tick – and you will also come to see how you differ from them as an extrovert. You will understand a lot of people around you better and also be able to get on with them better.

## We are strong when we know ourselves

Now you have assessed yourself. As you have ticked the points that fit in with your self-image, the result will not come as a surprise to you. But this little analysis can do two things for you. Firstly, you can compare yourself with other people (and their results). This could lead to a better understanding of each other – for example, for you and your partner. Secondly, the statements give you hints on how to handle your strengths and needs in life as an introvert or an extrovert. And it is precisely this that makes a crucial difference. We are at our strongest when we know ourselves, acknowledge our own qualities and take responsibility for our strengths and needs.

# The extrovert–introvert table

## Typical extrovert, typical introvert

Those of you who prefer a systematic survey are going to get another comparison here: what makes a typical extrovert or a typical introvert tick?

The key word is *typical:* as has been said, it is rare for personalities to be markedly introvert or extrovert.

---

## ❓ A question for you

Assess yourself again with the aid of the lists below: what introvert and what extrovert characteristics do you have?

- More introvert characteristics overall ❏
- More extrovert characteristics overall ❏
- Both sides about the same. ❏

| Typical extroverts ... | Typical introverts ... |
|---|---|
| regenerate themselves through contact with other people ('wind turbine') | regenerate through peace and quiet and being on their own |
| draw energy from activity and communication | need time to rest after activity and communication, ideally alone |
| often speak or act spontaneously, without thinking – and sort out their own ideas while talking | prefer to think before they speak or act – and don't say anything until they have thought things over |
| prefer to act rather than observe for a long time | observe a lot, act appropriately |
| get moving because of pressure of time and deadlines and like quick solutions. | find tight deadlines stressful and like more time to think or before making a decision |
| prefer to work on several projects at the same time | prefer to work thoroughly and on one area of their work |
| need little personal space | like personal space (for example, their own room, distance from other people in a group) |
| think they have a lot of friends | think they are close to a few people they call friends |
| find small talk stimulating and entertaining; make new contacts with a lot of people | find small talk hard work and superficial, prefer deep discussions with one person or a small group. Happy to wait for others to take the initiative and then to be approached |
| are quickly bored | need few external stimuli |
| like working with others in a team | like working on their own or with one other person |
| are easily distracted | are easily put off |

*(Continued)*

| Typical extroverts ... | Typical introverts ... |
| --- | --- |
| need stimulus from people, places, activities | like to think their own thoughts |
| are glad of agreement and positive feedback about what they are doing and bringing off | like to feel accepted personally – it makes them feel secure and less doubtful about themselves |
| would rather talk than listen | would rather listen than speak. But like talking a lot about things that are important to them – particularly in a small group |
| are quick to talk about personal ideas and feelings | are careful how much they say about personal matters and feelings – and say very little about private matters or areas of conflict, and then only to a few close friends |
| often seem restless, touchy, impatient, hyperactive | often seem quiet, abstracted, withdrawn, arrogant |
| usually feel in their element in large groups, in unexpected situations or under pressure; like communicating with big groups | almost always feel inhibited in large groups, unexpected situations or under pressure, and black out in extreme cases. Prefer one-to-one conversations, or with a small number of people |
| often seem aggressive | sometimes seem distant |
| are interested in a lot of things and know a little about each of them | are interested in a small number of things and know a great deal about them |
| like uncomplicated, readily accessible information | value detail |
| don't easily take things personally and deal well with conflict | are quick to take things personally, find conflict oppressive |
| find it an effort to 'keep at it' when there are complicated developments or difficult decisions are being made | keep at things tenaciously and with concentration even if developments and decisions take a long time to be resolved |
| often talk loudly, emphatically and rapidly. | often speak quietly and with no particular emphasis. |

So? Are you an introvert or an extrovert? Different surroundings offer niches to both personality types in which they can flourish. There are also situations in which it is difficult to live according to type. Subsequent chapters will deal with situations of this kind.

## The world needs introverts and extroverts

One thing needs to be said: whatever your result was – the world needs both introverts and extroverts. The human species (and the animal and vegetable kingdoms) benefit from complementary contrasts. Mankind needs men and women, intellectuals and emotional people, sedentary people and nomads, extroverts and introverts. Extroverts offer introverts something they do not have: surges of energy, spontaneous action, motivation. Conversely, introverts show their extrovert contemporaries some things they tend to lack: for example, keeping quiet when it makes sense to do so, profound relationships, reflection and a ready ear. These and other strengths shared by quiet people form the focus of the next chapter.

---

## ✱ Key points in brief

- Introverts and extroverts differ above all in the way they **gain energy**: introverts need peace and quiet, extroverts gain energy from contact with people and from activities.

- Introversion and extroversion are **two poles on a continuum**. Everybody has a place on this continuum where they feel their best. Ideally they can pass most of their time in this place – otherwise it starts to get unhealthy. **Fluctuations and shifts** between introversion and extroversion are normal and can be due to the prevailing culture, the specific situation, the role, age and even mood.

- **Introversion, shyness and hypersensitivity** are three different qualities that are not necessarily connected.

- We owe the distinction between introvert and extrovert personalities to Carl Gustav Jung. Extrovert characteristics sometimes used to be presented in literature as 'healthier' than introverted characteristics – which is just as indefensible as the opposite.

- Introverts and extroverts differ in the way their brains are organized and in their mental activity.

- The better introverts and extroverts are familiar with each other's needs and inclinations, the easier and pleasanter they will find it to get on with themselves and others.

- The world needs the qualities shown by both personality types!

# 2.

# Introvert strengths: the hidden treasure

## Strong men's treasure chest

This chapter is intended to be something like a treasure chest: in it you will find a survey of all the strengths that quiet people particularly often have. This section is especially important to me. In a world in which the greatest worth is laid on communication between extroverts as something to strive for, it is easy for the things that quiet people can do, achieve and have to offer to slip into the background. But quiet people are just as capable of using their strengths to achieve what they are interested in, to motivate other people, to make and maintain contacts, to resist attacks confidently – in short, they can manage to communicate just as well as extroverts on every level. In their own way. Using their own resources.

## Introverts are inclined to be self-critical

It is these resources that I am going to focus on in this chapter. I have put them all together over my years working with quiet people and sum them up here. The people involved are often entirely unaware of their strengths. Quiet people are inclined to be especially critical of themselves, and often have to make a conscious effort to discover their good sides. On the one hand, it is good when introverts judge themselves strictly and set standards for what they want to be, do and achieve. On the other hand, treating yourself too critically can easily reduce your self-esteem – self-esteem that people who are less strict with themselves have at their disposal and flaunt. In the worst case, self-criticism can even mean self-sabotage.

## Quiet strengths are often missed

If you don't want this to happen to you (any more) you need to take a good look at your strengths – and your ability to see what those strengths are worth. The next few pages are there to help you take this look and then to value what you see. This could mean that you will have to dig deep: things that are available are often taken for granted. And it is also the case that quiet people's strengths are just that – quiet – and so it is easy to overlook them. And yet introvert strengths can be enormously effective in communicating with oneself and others. By the end of this chapter you will have discovered your advantages step by step – and that's a promise!

You already know from Chapter 1 that neurobiologically quiet people tick differently from extroverts. Their brain circuits and their autonomic nervous systems are particularly tuned to concentration, learning, self-reflection and memory, while extrovert brains are more directed towards being proactive and to stimuli from the outside world.

The particular strengths of both types are also to be found in this distinction. This does not mean that *all* quiet people have *all ten* strong characteristics. And still less does it mean that the strengths mentioned are the exclusive province of introverts: extroverts can be also be strong analytically and be able to write well. But quiet people very often have the ten strengths you will find in this chapter – in terms of my own observations and according to the results of studies on introverts. The best thing is for you to keep this question in mind as you read the chapter:

CAN I SEE THIS STRENGTH IN ME?

## Summary of the strengths

You can bring your answers together in a summary at the end of the chapter. This will then be something like your own personal treasure chest. Here is a first summary of the strengths – with a few keywords that will start to put things in place.

---

 **Summary: introvert strengths**

**Strength 1: Caution**

Proceed carefully, avoid risks and adventures, observe attentively, show respect, think before you speak, be unobtrusive, hand out information about yourself sparingly

**Strength 2: Substance**

Draw on the depths of your own experience, emphasize essentials, convey subject matter that is significant, profound and of high quality, have meaningful conversations

**Strength 3: Concentration**

Be able to focus, direct energy accurately at an internal or external activity, persist with things intensely and steadily, be alert

**Strength 4: Listening**

Filter information, attitudes and needs out from what someone says to you, create a dialogue

---

**Strength 5: Calm**

Inner calm as a basis for concentration, relaxation, clarity and substance

**Strength 6: Analytical thinking**

Planning and structuring, subdivide complex issues and derive information, attitudes, solutions and approaches from that systematically

**Strength 7: Independence**

Be able to be alone, be self-sufficient, live inwardly by your own principles, detached from other people's opinions, be able to discount yourself

**Strength 8: Tenacity**

Pursue things patiently and consistently over a long period in order to achieve an aim

**Strength 9: Writing (rather than speaking)**

Aim to communicate more easily in writing as a matter of preference

**Strength 10: Empathy**

Be able to put yourself in the position of the person you are talking to, avoid conflict where possible, place shared interests and qualities in the foreground, be ready to compromise, communicate diplomatically

# Strength 1: Caution

## Careful exchange of views shows respect

At first glance, caution does not seem like a particular strength in terms of communication. But first impressions can be deceptive: cautious people takes things gently when dealing with others, rather than acting heavily and emphatically. They treat the other people involved with understanding, tact and respect and do not take inflexible stands.

As you already know, introverts' and extroverts' different neurobiological equipment means that extroverts will tend to work towards rewards, while introverts are more likely to be concerned with safety. Caution as a strength is a positive consequence of this striving for safety and security: quiet people observe and think deeply before taking risks, if they take them at all …

But risks and adventures are not lying in wait only in the form of bungee jumping and investments, but also in the form of communication. Cautious people prefer to manage without risky comparisons, aggressive suggestions, sudden ideas or even frontal attacks. Two things matter to them when dealing with other people: firstly, they like a respectful distance to be kept. They do not intend to lightly give too much away about themselves. They reserve what makes them tick, what is important to them and what they are enthusiastic about for good friends. Conversely, they also behave respectfully, and like to keep their distance at first. Secondly, cautious people do not say anything half-baked or ill-thought-through or make rapid decisions on the basis of gut feeling. They expect more from themselves: they like ideas to be thought through and examined thoroughly before they are put into words. And they tend to see ill-considered statements by other people in a poor light as well.

## When caution becomes fear

The flip side of caution is the careful reticence with which quiet people pass on information about themselves or enthusiasm about something. An extrovert at the receiving end might see this as distancing or indifference. In extreme cases the caution becomes fear – and, as such, an obstacle. This will be addressed at the beginning of the next chapter.

But people who are in a conversation might begin to feel good about their opposite number's caution: it will make them feel they are being taken seriously, and are not under pressure. What a quiet person says cautiously is unassertive and provides substance. This takes us straight to strength 2.

# Strength 2: Substance

## Communication with a dimension of depth

Introverts are constantly processing impressions. They are continuously concerned with what they are seeing, thinking and experiencing. They reflect throughout their working hours: about themselves and others, about sense and meaning, about what should be and what is. This background activity in a typical introvert brain – and this is one of the best consequences – leads to a capital accumulation of substance. This means that, when quiet people communicate, whatever they convey to others is usually profound: what they say has usually gone through a thorough mental testing and filtering phase, including a check on how important, accurate and fitting it is, and the background to it. This is why things that introverts say are often especially significant, profound and valuable. These are the three spheres implied by substance.

## A preference for deep, genuine friendships

Substance is also crucial to dealing with other people: people with substance will find it more worthwhile and pleasant on a social occasion to conduct genuine conversations with a few people than getting to know a lot of people superficially. They will be more interested in the content of a statement and less interested in the way this content is formulated and presented. They can establish profound, genuine friendships that can last a lifetime – and though there may not be many of these relationships, they will be more important for them than a large but less committed circle of acquaintances.

## The impression of passivity

But substance does have one drawback: like many good things, it takes time to mature. In other words, people with substance are often too slow in a situation involving 'rapid' communication because they need sufficient time for processing things in their minds to achieve the depth they require. This applies particularly when things have to be weighed up or controversy dealt with. Consequently, people of substance are often wrongly seen as passive or ponderous because the intensive activity in their heads cannot be seen.

This is why emphasizing status and the exchange of small talk rarely matter to people of substance, and are even alien to some of them. This attitude is advantageous to quiet people in many situations, for example in good conversation or an academic debate, when reading philosophical articles or at meetings where problems have to be solved.

# Strength 3: Concentration

## Growing by means of concentration

Many quiet people have the gift of being able to concentrate very well. They are able to pursue a matter attentively for a long time. This is easy to explain: unlike extroverts, introverts need less feedback and also fewer external sensations. The beneficial consequences of profound concentration are many and various: people who are able to concentrate will do what they have to more easily and better than people who are easily distracted. In all probability, what they are concentrating on will grow. Nikolaus Enkelmann, a past master in communication, formulated this old principle of growth as one of his 14 life development principles: the law of concentration.

## Concentration makes for strong presence

People who concentrate deal with the matter in hand with all their strength and attention. This means that they radiate an intensity that makes them powerful presences and can profoundly impress their conversation partners. This can be seen, for example, in lectures where quiet people use their quiet resources to captivate the audience. So as an introvert it is not essential for you to be in the spotlight. You do not need to be centre stage to communicate, neither do you need a large number of people listening to you. This has pleasant consequences for people you are talking to: they can tune into you and pay you due attention. Attention is a valuable currency in social intercourse – everybody likes to feel noticed. How about that for capital for someone who can concentrate!

On social occasions, anyone who can give other people real space when communicating will have a lot of good conversations that will be additionally enhanced by strength 2, substance. And the next strength is a big help too …

# Strength 4: Listening

## Monologues instead of real dialogue

Listening is probably one of the most undervalued skills in human relations. If you listen to typical conversations, you will notice, particularly when extroverts are talking, that the dialogue is in fact a sequence of monologues: while one person is saying something, the other is deciding what to say, instead of listening carefully. But when views are being exchanged, being able to listen gives a real chance of creating a genuine dialogue in which the people talking actually address what they are each saying, so that they have heard and grasped each other's viewpoints by the end of the conversation.

## Advantage introvert: real listening

Many quiet people are far better at listening than most other people. They absorb the information as born observers and processors of impressions conveyed, and evaluate them in their subsequent thinking and also in their replies. They know how to filter the essentials out of what has been said: what is important to the other person? Which information is relevant? How does it all fit together? So real listening is a very active, intensive process that is additionally boosted by strength 3, concentration.

The strength of listening is very valuable for the person being listened to: when you are 'all ears', you are giving them your undivided attention. That does everyone good – and works wonders, from establishing relations via the negotiating atmosphere and on to the resolution of conflicts.

# Strength 5: Calm

## The significance of inward and outward calm

Calm has two aspects. *Outward calm* is the absence of external stimuli, while *inward calm* is a mental condition. Both aspects can help quiet people when communicating – but only inner calm can strictly speaking be seen as a personal strength. And yet outward calm is so important for quiet people that it deserves particular attention.

## Outward calm

All quiet people know that outward calm does them good when they want to work intensively or need a new source of energy.

### Calmly taking on energy

So you shut yourself away to reflect or after some tiring phases and let this do its work. In introvert-friendly countries such as Japan, it is seen as courteous to leave space for mutual silence even in conversation. Professional communicators recommend quite deliberately falling silent in certain situations. For introverts in particular this can be a powerful rhetorical resource, in small talk, for example (see Chapter 6), or when negotiating (see Chapter 7). The pleasing thing about outward calm is the lack of agitation. It makes it possible to process information and also to become inwardly calm as well. A quiet person who does not have the possibility of a little peace in relaxing surroundings will soon notice the consequences: tension, irritability and exhaustion are typical symptoms.

### Calm is healthy

Outward peace is a factor that makes a significant contribution to our well-being. A long-term Finnish study of heart disease *(Cardiovascular Risk in Young Finns Study)* showed that women who are sensitive to noise tend to die earlier: it seems to be clear that there is a link between acoustic stress and general physical stress, in the form of raised pulse rate and blood pressure and of proneness to stroke and heart attacks. This is an important finding because introverts are often sensitive to noise. It is not only pleasant to make sure that extensive quiet phases are introduced, but healthy as well. But what is not clear is whether the advantages apply equally to introverts and extroverts.

Carl Gustav Jung also pointed out that introverts seem to need fewer new impressions that extroverts. This is why many introverts find outward calm pleasant, independent of the advantage of gaining energy: their very active 'inner life' provides them with enough stimulation and they are not distracted by the world around them. This gives them more space to reflect and to process their experiences. Introverts' calm is valuable for extroverts because quiet people encourage them to pay attention to themselves and their needs and to think before they act. The ability to create outward calm is therefore definitely to be seen as a strength.

## Inner calm

### The way to clarity

But calm is much more than the absence of external irritants. It is also – and many millennia of spiritual tradition show this – the only way to clarity: about ourselves, about others, about life. But another kind of calm is meant as well: *inward calm*, a condition that causes measurable changes in the brain.

### Inner peace through meditation

Precisely this is shown by people who meditate regularly: neurological studies (for example, the one by Andrew Newberg and Eugene d'Aquili) were able to show that, in people meditating, the areas of the brain relating to happiness, inner peace and the dependence of the ego on the world around us are more active. At the same time, when people are meditating less energy is directed into the areas that activate aggression, an urge to escape or compulsive behaviour.

INWARD CALM MEANS CLARITY, A POSITIVE VIEW OF THE WORLD AND CONCENTRATION.

One other important outcome is good news for quiet people: meditation improves our ability to distinguish between major and minor irritations. This means that the brain functions more efficiently overall because it can reduce its total activity and thus has to use less energy. At the same time, it is capable of concentrating harder on important tasks. In other words, strengths 3 and 5 should be seen as connected: greater calm means better concentration!

## Success through better combination of the strengths

Less energy *and* more concentration – this is not a contradiction in terms. In his book on silence, George Prochnik (2010) compares this apparent contradiction with a top sportsman whose pulse rate is lower than that of someone who plays sport occasionally but who achieves much more in competition because he is able to combine his strengths purposefully and can quickly boost or reduce his energy input.

THE STRENGTHS OF CONCENTRATION AND INNER PEACE ARE LINKED.

People's inner peace provides them with relaxation, just as their surroundings do. The speed at which they talk, pauses and joint reflection introduce calm into their interaction with other people. This means that in casual conversation, for example, or in heated arguments or negotiations, the atmosphere can be made predominantly pleasant and so some degree of stress will be removed.

# Strength 6: Analytical thinking

## More distance from the outside world

Quiet people do not have a monopoly on analytical thinking, but many quiet people achieve a very great deal in this sphere. The constant flow of their inner processes places introverts at a greater distance from their outside world than their extrovert contemporaries: they filter and process all the time, and they also reflect for longer and more carefully than extroverts – in other words, with concentration and persistence (strengths 3 and 8).

## Right-brain or left-brain dominance

There is also a particular group of quiet people who seem particularly gifted analytically. This is a good point at which to introduce a subdivision first used by Olsen Laney in her book in 2002 in order to clarify the difference between different introvert types. It is equally true of both extroverts and introverts that the left- or the right-hand hemisphere of the cerebral cortex is more pronounced than the other, and so there are 'left-brained' and 'right-brained' people. The right-hand cortex is the sphere of intuition and pictorial thinking, while the left-hand cortex deals with skills for processing texts, numbers and logical connections. Here is a summary that will help you to decide which is the dominant side for you.

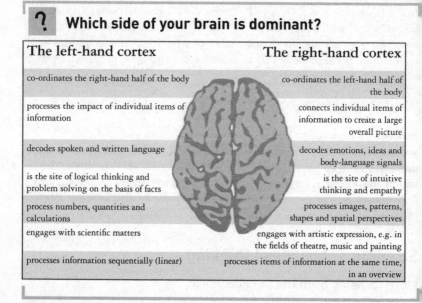

**?** **Which side of your brain is dominant?**

| The left-hand cortex | The right-hand cortex |
| --- | --- |
| co-ordinates the right-hand half of the body | co-ordinates the left-hand half of the body |
| processes the impact of individual items of information | connects individual items of information to create a large overall picture |
| decodes spoken and written language | decodes emotions, ideas and body-language signals |
| is the site of logical thinking and problem solving on the basis of facts | is the site of intuitive thinking and empathy |
| process numbers, quantities and calculations | processes images, patterns, shapes and spatial perspectives |
| engages with scientific matters | engages with artistic expression, e.g. in the fields of theatre, music and painting |
| processes information sequentially (linear) | processes items of information at the same time, in an overview |

This presentation is slightly simplified: both the right-hand and the left-hand cerebral hemispheres are involved in almost all activities, but the summary shows the focal regions for each activity.

## Right-brained introverts

*Quiet people with a dominant right-hand cortex* tend to process information subjectively and intuitively, so more as a 'gut feeling'. They often have artistic talent, react more emotionally than left-brained people and are good at improvisation. They find it easier than 'left-brained people' to handle situations in which they have to deal with several challenges at the same time.

# Left-brained introverts

*Quiet people with a dominant left-hand cortex*, according to Olsen Laney, are closer to the stereotypical introvert: they need fewer social contacts and tend to be object- and theory-oriented. This enables them to distance themselves from their surroundings to a certain extent – a good basis for analytical thinking! 'Left-brained' introverts can keep both their minds and their environment tidy and tend to decide on the basis of reason rather than following their emotions. They are more quickly overwhelmed by too many demands at once than 'right-brainers', and deal systematically with one thing after another. They are particularly endowed with the strength of analytical thinking.

THE STRENGTH OF ANALYTICAL THINKING IS A BONUS GIVEN TO 'LEFT-BRAINED' INTROVERTS IN PARTICULAR.

## Advantages for analytical thinkers

People who think analytically get to the bottom of things. Their strengths lie in researching, comparing and exploring. They can break complex circumstances down into their individual elements and establish categories, then use these as a basis for developing strategies for what they have to say or do. They also arrive at positions for conversations, approaches to solutions or measures to be taken in the same way. Analytical thinkers are excellent planners and are good at processing written matter – even when it includes a lot of numbers.

Analytical thinking is very valuable in areas requiring accurate information, theorizing and categorizing new insights – for example in academic fields, in controlling things and in all spheres in which problem-solving is important: medicine, IT or in handling risky technologies.

## Using rigorous analysis to avoid over-stimulation

Rigorous analysis is also useful for imposing structure on confusing situations, and can, to a certain extent – and this is particularly important for left-brainers – ward off over-stimulation (described as obstacle 3 in the next chapter). If an argument starts up in a meeting, analytical thinkers can ask themselves: what information is important here? Who represents which standpoint? First of all, this attitude cuts pathways through the avalanche of impressions and ensures inner distancing from the situation itself. Both of these approaches greatly reduce the burden, especially for more sensitive introverts.

# Strength 7: Independence

Introverts differ from extroverts in one crucial point: they are, as we saw in Chapter 1, less dependent on responses from other people and impressions of their surroundings. This makes them more independent generally.

## Happy to be alone

Independence shows particularly in the fact that quiet people find it easy to be alone – and in fact they need to be alone to recharge their batteries. Independent people are less concerned with what other people think, and they find it easier to say and do what they see as right and important. (This applies to introverted right-brainers only to a limited extent – see the explanation in strength 6 – because they respond more emotionally to their surroundings.)

The introverted British actress Tilda Swinton is a good example of this: she is married to an older painter and writer and has had twins with him, but she has another relationship with a younger artist and says in interviews that her idea of happiness would be to sleep in her own bed for six months.

So independence means self-sufficiency and inner freedom. It brings the ability to take responsibility for oneself and to make decisions without constantly seeking reassurance from other people. The flip side is that this can detract from communication, from the ability to live with other people and from teamwork.

## Ability to be selfless

I have kept what is probably the highest form of independence until last: the ability to disregard oneself. In the case of a mature, independent character, actions are not driven by personal vanity, ambition or craving for recognition. Other things are central: the whole issue, important and valuable things (strength 2: substance) or other people and their needs (strength 10: empathy). It is interesting that the ability to be self*less* can only derive from healthy self-*confidence*.

# Strength 8: Tenacity

## Purposeful perseverance

Perseverance is the ability to 'keep at' a situation or an idea – even if success is slow in coming or you are resisted. This quality is different from fixation (which you will come across again below as a obstacle): fixation shows a lack of flexibility, which means that the person in question will not shift his or her position when communicating. The strength that is meant here is essentially purposeful patience.

Quiet people also persevere in the way they work: they are more likely than average to be thorough and also prepared to 'crack hard nuts'. They keep at things, are extremely conscientious and are not as easily distracted as extroverts who are more prone to being distracted from something by external stimulation.

## More stamina for more competence

This strength makes it easier to plan and conduct important conversations and negotiations. It makes it easier to decide where it is worth sticking to a position and where there is some room for manoeuvre. It is a strength that leads to the kind of stamina that many extroverts can only dream about – and thus offers a pathway to absolutely optimum performance: research psychologist Anders Ericson concluded from his studies that 10,000 hours of purposeful practice are required in any particular sphere to achieve expert performance (quoted in Cain 2000).

## Marie Curie as an example

One illustrious role model for perseverance is the double Nobel laureate Marie Curie (1903: physics; 1911: chemistry). She devoted herself to science at an early stage – despite numerous stumbling blocks. She was not accepted at the University of Warsaw so went to study in France. She financed her early research by teaching at a girls' school, and her pioneering success in the field of radioactivity often required that certain experiments should be repeated several hundred times. Perseverance seems to be an important prerequisite for extraordinary achievements.

# Strength 9: Writing (rather than speaking)

## The favourite medium for introverts

Many quiet people prefer to communicate in writing – whether it is for themselves (e.g. diary, week planner, book project) or with other people (e.g. texting, email, letter, blog, online network). As they weigh up their thoughts and put them into words before communicating, writing seems to be a good medium for expressing this. Also, writing follows personal rhythms: the written word slows communication down and means that they do not have to respond to the tempo of the person they are talking to. So, when people write, they can proceed at their own pace.

Digital networks (e.g. Twitter, Facebook, online forums and chatrooms) need a chapter to themselves. Many quiet people value this kind of contact-making because the communication takes place in writing and thus guarantees a certain distance. You will find more information about this kind of networking in Chapter 6.

## Advantages of written communication

There are also possibilities at work for people who prefer writing to speaking. Words can be formulated and weighted more precisely in an email than in a telephone call. A written project summary on the intranet means that all team members can see how things stand and contribute to updates whenever they wish to. A short progress report about targets to be set may well be more useful than a report at a meeting. Working party meetings and discussions can be planned with keywords and short written briefings. Then quiet people who favour the written word can go into the group situation feeling more confident: they have thought through the essentials and taken notes to remember them.

There is just one condition that must be met: written communication should be appropriate to the situation – and not serve to avoid a direct exchange of views.

# Strength 10: Empathy

## Intuitive strength

People with empathy are in a position to tune in to their communication partners, and this is done through intuitive strength rather than by using particular strategies. They find it easy to work out what makes other people tick – and so they can decide what matters to them and what is needed. This ability to think yourself into someone else's mind is also called empathy. Right-brainers and highly sensitive introverts are more likely to have this strength than left-brainers. This cortical distinction is explained in the notes on strength 6.

## Mirror neurons make empathy possible

Neurobiologists have shown that it is so-called 'mirror neurons' in the human brain that make empathy possible. Of course, both introverts and extroverts have mirror neurons. So why is empathy an introvert strength? As in strength 7, independence, the answer lies in a typical introvert quality: unlike extroverts, they need less confirmation and assurance from their fellow human beings. It also matters less to them whether they can compare with their opposite number in terms of status, and whether they are as interesting and successful. Most quiet people have an inner 'referee' instead, whom they consult all the time. This independence from other people – combined with a tendency to analyse and categorize – gives introverts a great deal of scope for paying attention to other people, with all their characteristics and needs. They can then act on these insights when communicating. The consequences are positive: what they feel and say treats their opposite number as a real person.

## Establishing trust through empathy

Empathy is supported by another quality found in quiet people: a tendency to pay attention to their surroundings and to process the impressions gained well. Quiet people with empathy find it easy to gain other people's trust. If they also have substance (strength 2) and are good listeners (strength 4), they can be invaluable companions and contacts – for extroverts as well, who feel comfortable, accepted and unburdened by them. And anyone negotiating who deploys analytical focus (strength 6) along with empathy can be simply irresistible.

It is also people with empathy who see possible compromises and can suggest them diplomatically. This is because they are not fixated on a single set of interests but can see all sides of things, and consider ethical aspects as well. They know that the world does not revolve around them. Empathetic people cause few conflicts when they act because they pay attention to other people and look for solutions with them. They are also less aggressive – they clearly understand how much stress aggressive behaviour can cause.

An ability to empathize can be reduced by fear or over-stimulation (see obstacles 1 and 2 in Chapter 3).

## Where do your strengths lie?

### Estimating your own strengths

Quiet people, as already mentioned at the beginning of this chapter, are more likely to be too critical of themselves than to boast about their strengths. You have now found out what strengths a lot of introverts have. Can you identify your own strengths as well? Don't worry if you aren't quite sure, that's not unusual. Here is something to help you: answer the following three questions. They are meant to quieten inner critical voices for you and gradually make you see what your strong points are.

---

### ❓ Three questions for you

1. Think of a role model you admire. Which of this person's strengths do you particularly admire?
2. Think of a person you like and value very much. If I asked this person where your strengths lie, what would be their answer?
3. What strengths do you have? Include the answers to questions 1 and 2 in the list.

Strength 1: Caution

Strength 2: Substance

Strength 3: Concentration

Strength 4: Listening

Strength 5: Calm

Strength 6: Analytical thinking

Strength 7: Independence

Strength 8: Perseverance

Strength 9: Writing

Strength 10: Empathy

Another strength:_____

Another strength:_____

Another strength:_____

I am:

mainly left-brainer ❏ mainly right-brainer ❏

My three greatest strengths are:

1._____

2._____

3._____

## Role model as an identification figure

Did you wonder why you were supposed to include your role model's qualities from questions 1 and 2 in your own strength profile? This is why: a role model is an identification figure. When trying to find this figure, we subconsciously look for qualities that are important and valuable to ourselves. So a person for whom high status and financial success matter particularly will tend to choose Rockefeller rather than Mother Teresa (incidentally an introvert) as a role model, and someone with a passion for science will choose Einstein (an introvert) rather then Lady Gaga (*not* an introvert, I think, but who knows …). This means that there is a good chance that you will have the qualities of your personal role model yourself, to a certain extent.

## Cultivate your strengths

Look at your strengths and be proud of what you find. The next step is to pay conscious attention to your strong sides – ultimately they are your major capital, your personal treasure chest. Positive psychology advises you to rely on your strengths above all when developing your personality and to make use of them. Personality tests and systems like Strengths Finder or the Reiss profile also start by analysing people's strong sides. You will achieve much more by concentrating on your strengths than by laboriously working on your weaknesses, because you are building on what makes you who you are, and what you are good at. You will find it easier to be successful and it will also make you more authentic than chasing after other people's strengths by ironing out your own weaknesses. That leads to more energy chasing less success.

## ? More questions for you

Think back to your schooldays.

1. What was your worst subject?
2. How much were you able to improve with a great deal of preparation and effort?
3. On the other hand, how much could you achieve with the same preparation time and the same effort in your best subject?

## Using your strengths to communicate better

A lot of things we learn at school we learn for life: things we are bad at and don't enjoy will bring relatively little success. So it is better to expand the strengths you have just identified. The first step here is to take a closer look at how you use your personal strengths concretely when communicating. Don't be afraid to include strengths that are not as marked as your three major plus points. Ultimately we are talking here about your development potential when dealing with other people. The top boxes give you an example of what your individual 'treasure chest' might look like.

| My strength: | I can use this strength when dealing with other people: | I can use this strength particularly well in these situations: |
|---|---|---|
| Substance | Shift conversations on to a deeper plane | When I know my opposite number well, when the atmosphere is calm and relaxed |
| _____ | _____ | _____ |
| _____ | _____ | _____ |
| _____ | _____ | _____ |
| _____ | _____ | _____ |

## Look after your own treasure chest of strengths

Now you know yourself a whole lot better. Look after your treasure chest of strengths well: think ahead before talking to other people, and keep in mind what you can contribute to successful communication. Organize situations so that you can make the best of them. You will make – and this is a promise – an amazing discovery: by deliberately using your 'quiet' strengths, you will change the way other people treat you, quite apart from the fact that you will express your aims and interests more successfully.

## * Key points in brief

- Introverts have typical strengths. These help in dealing with yourself and others and when coping with a whole variety of demands.
- The strengths are: caution, substance, concentration, listening, calm, analytical thinking (for 'left-brained' introverts), independence, perseverance, writing and empathy.
- Expanding and using personal strengths improves communication and at the same time makes it possible to live authentically.

# 3.
# Introvert needs: introvert obstacles

## The flip side of the coin

This section is something like the flip side of the previous chapter, which gave you a glimpse of the 'treasure chest' for communication that quiet people are endowed with. Just as there is no light without shade, there is also no treasure without a price. Each strength has a 'weak' flip side. If an introvert's brain has particular strengths, other spheres are therefore less well-developed. Or the strong side has its own special traps that can obstruct communication, or even damage it. Nobody is perfect!

For example, quiet people's inward-looking quality is a strength in relation to concentration, substance and analysis – you have just been introduced to this and some of your other strengths in the last section. The flip side of being inward-looking are the spheres that benefit from outward orientation, such as the stimuli derived from intensive contact with a lot of people – or the ability to show your own achievements at work in the right light and to approach conflicts actively.

## Being aware of your own pressure points

But expressions like weakness and obstacles fall short as useful terms. All quiet people should know their own 'pressure points' because they identify their particular needs. For example, over-stimulation requires clever handling of personal energy resources. Fear of conflict invites analytical treatment of tense situations. In other words, obstacles in the form of needs are outstanding signposts for establishing personal communication.

First, as in the last chapter, comes a summary with brief comments, this time of the weak points and needs that make quiet people vulnerable to attack.

**Summary: introvert obstacles**

**Obstacle 1: Fear**

Reticence and uncertainty when dealing with other people

**Obstacle 2: Too much attention to detail**

Individual pieces of information block the view or priorities and the 'full picture'

**Obstacle 3: Over-stimulation**

Excessive demand from too many, unduly loud or over-rapid impressions

**Obstacle 4: Passivity**

No personal stimuli, stagnation, detrimental perseverance

**Obstacle 5: Escape**

Avoiding situations and things that need doing

**Obstacle 6: Being unduly cerebral**

Neglecting feelings

**Obstacle 7: Self-deception**

Repressing introvert characteristics and needs, or evaluating them negatively

**Obstacle 8: Fixation**

Inflexibility when communicating

**Obstacle 9: Avoiding contact**

Avoiding people

**Obstacle 10: Avoiding conflict**

Giving in or 'shutting off' under pressure

# Obstacle 1: Fear

Fear is a powerful stimulus and it also has its seat in the part of the brain where it is particularly powerful: in the deep parts, the limbic system and the amygdala, where it can easily access the subconscious. We are going into this obstacle in more than usual detail because it is the one that can block you most frequently and persistently.

## Appropriate and inappropriate fear

Fear does not have to be a bad thing. If it is appropriate, it protects us from doing imprudent things, such as jumping off a diving board into the lake without being able to swim. It also protects us from risks that cannot be fully assessed, such as from leaping off a high place with only a rubber ring round our ankle for protection. In brief, fear is life-supporting in *appropriate* places. Its messages follow logically: Don't do it! Don't move! Don't make yourself conspicuous! Keep quiet! Take no risks! And it is very noticeable at business meetings: a lot of people keep to this.

APPROPRIATE FEAR PROTECTS. INAPPROPRIATE FEAR BLOCKS.

## When fear blocks

This brings us to the *inappropriate* places, where fear intrudes, inhibits and even blocks, such as where you are afraid to do things that are actually important and valuable to you: making a speech, for example, making a suggestion in a plenary session at a conference, conducting a confrontational conversation. All very well, you may say, but aren't introverts and extroverts just as afraid as each other? Fear is a general human trait. The answer: yes and no. On the one hand, yes: fear is an emotion that is part of our basic human equipment and that is shared by everyone. On the other hand, no: fear seems to impinge more on communication for people who are more inward- than outward-looking. In other words, fear tends to prevent introverts from dealing uninhibitedly with other people more than is the case for extroverts. I can identify three reasons for this.

Firstly, in comparison with extroverts, introverts need less outward contact and more inward stimuli (there is some information on this in Chapter 1). For this reason, the need for communication cannot counteract the feeling of fear sufficiently and compensate for it. This is different for extroverts: turning to other people is particularly attractive to them, and this means that they can overcome fear more easily.

Secondly, introverts are possibly more susceptible to fear than extroverts. The reason for this is that they are especially able to speculate: on the whole, introverts tend to address their emotions more frequently because they have a higher level of internal activity than extroverts. Fear can make a correspondingly powerful impact, so that the person in question simply does not take on certain activities but prefers to leave them alone from the outset.

Thirdly, introverts are biologically programmed towards safety (see Chapter 1), which means that their brains register potential risks quicker and more clearly, and fear is easily triggered as a result of this. If the fear is so strong that it dominates action, this leads to a quality that can handicap quiet people permanently in their handling of others: shyness.

# Looking fear in the eye

## Deliberately counteracting fear

Now, how can you as a quiet person prevent your fear from putting you off doing things that you feel are important? A big question. You will see quite concrete answers to it in subsequent chapters, always directly linked with a certain situation. But fundamentally one thing is true in all cases: you can quite well counteract it with other parts of your brain – the conscious parts. All the strategies recommended here have one thing in common: they do not steer clear of your fears; quite the contrary!

---

 **Dealing with fear: general strategies**

First phase: be consciously aware of fear.

Young children are often afraid of monsters under the bed. The first phase is anti-monster therapy: light at the fear epicentre (in other words, pointing a torch under the bed) makes the monsters disappear – and a great deal of the fear with them.

Second phase: keep an eye on why what you want to do is important – so important that you want to risk it despite the fear.

This second step means consciously giving yourself the power of decision, and taking this power away from your fear. The seat of fear in your brain is particularly afraid of failure. Here you are deciding to do something so valuable that it justifies the danger of failure.

This is the best way of expanding your comfort zone: you are aware of your fear, and at the same time taking calculated risks that are worth it because what you are aiming at matters to you.

---

## Name your fear out loud

The major obstacle is changing your habits. Every break with habit represents a disturbance at first for every brain, but particularly for an anxious one. If you stop using the well-trodden pathways that make you react automatically, it is stressful and has an uncertain outcome without habitual experience. It is all the more important that you should act purposefully. Seth Godin recommended even more drastic measures in his book *Linchpin*. He says that anyone who says what he or she is afraid of out loud will drive the fear away. Just try it: say 'I am afraid of giving the lecture – because I have opponents in the audience.'

## Laying new pathways in the mind

Seen from a neurobiological point of view, this second phase is the best possible strategy: the cerebral cortex, the seat of conscious thought, is able to soothe the fear centre in the brain (the amygdala). If you can make yourself see why what you are so afraid of is important, then you are helping your brain to lay down new pathways. Once these are established, the fear centre need not be so active any more in the area of the action in question. For lectures, this can mean that, instead of panic, you will just have a mild sense of discomfort.

# Obstacle 2: Too much attention to detail

## Locking on too much to individual items of information

Many introverts are inclined to see individual items of information as the overall whole. This connects up with their particularly powerful powers of analysis and thus applies especially to quiet people with a strong left-hand brain (see the explanation for this in Chapter 2 under strength 6). Analysis means splitting a whole into its individual parts in order to be able to examine it thoroughly. Too much attention to detail – fragmentation – is the opposite side of this coin: observers get lost in the detail instead of constructing an overall picture. A view of what is really important is lost.

This obstacle can be useful in some situations – for example, when an auditor is looking for a mistake in a balance sheet. But in communication situations an inclination towards too much detail often means that an introvert (perhaps when in conversation, speaking at a debate or in negotiations) gets entangled in minutiae rather than paying attention to the full sweep of the subject matter or what his opposite number needs. When combined with perfectionism, too much attention to detail can easily lead to micromanagement and control freakery – and both would be problematic for people with management responsibilities. Too much attention to detail can also become a trap when using small talk as a networking tool. Chapter 6 will show you what you can do to avoid this.

# Obstacle 3: Over-stimulation

## Too much – too stressful

Over-stimulation means that a situation deprives you of energy because the impressions are so diverse. This can happen when too many impressions pour down on you at the same time. But it can also be because your surroundings are too noisy – a lot of quiet people are sensitive to noise and lose their concentration if levels are very high (sound level 3) and their relaxation (level 5).

## Too fast – too stressful

Excessive haste can also cause over-stimulation – for example, if someone is insisting on quick decisions, speaking more quickly than usual or signalling impatience via body language (tapping fingers or feet, looking at the clock impatiently). Over-stimulation tires quiet people regardless of its nature, and it can cast a shadow over encounters with other people. Socializing then becomes stressful. This is why many introverts manage their social occasions carefully and choose them very selectively.

The risk lies in the fact that the prospect of over-stimulation makes quiet people passive (obstacle 4), anxious to escape (obstacle 5) and inclined to avoid social contacts (obstacle 9), all of which hamper communication. Deliberate pressure in negotiations, too much information to process at a social event, a noisy, aggressive argument or a restless audience for a lecture can cancel out a great deal of good preparation and detract from the personal impact made by the over-stimulated individual.

# Finding sources of energy – ensuring downtime

## Downtime to charge the batteries

You already know that quiet people do not charge their batteries in the same way as their extrovert colleagues. They need calm, solitude and reflection in order to regain their energy. At the same time they also use up comparatively more energy in communicating with other people – above all in small talk, in emotionally charged situations such as conflicts and in interacting with large groups. But a normal day with a lot of 'quick changes' can easily exhaust an introvert. This includes constant interruptions, phone calls, passing trade or even small children with their surprising ideas and sudden outbursts.

Anyone who knows this also knows that downtime is a major and non-negotiable need for quiet people. If it is sacrificed to tight deadlines, it will take a considerable toll, and first of all within the situation itself: introverts with no possibility of being alone will 'shut down' if too much energy drains away. They will also join in with fewer conversations and discussions and seek less contact at social events, as all this is very hard work without downtime.

Other people – who cannot always understand the need for solitude – will see behaviour of this kind as aloof, boring or even bored. In a professional context, people who need to distance themselves are felt to be unapproachable, unable to assert themselves or even intellectually challenged. And it is obvious what this can mean for a career …

## Ways to regain energy

If quiet people constantly resist the need to be alone, they will become exhausted. In the worst case they will burn themselves out: constant overexploitation of one's own energy levels comes at a high price. Don't let it come to that! You will be able to avoid these problems if you acknowledge that you need downtime. You will find out the most important strategies here. They are deliberately kept very general in this chapter. You will find concrete help in the thematic chapters under the particular causes.

 **Energy management: general strategies**

1. Analyse what sort of situations and people drain your energy particularly.

Cut down on such engagements and encounters as much as possible. Always plan in downtime from the outset when you have a stressful situation or a meeting with stressful people in the pipeline.

2. Make sure that you have a break from things at regular intervals, ideally every day (at least half an hour), every month (half a day) and every year (a weekend or a week).

It doesn't matter how far away from everyday life you go: what is important is that you can stand back. Use your downtime to do something you really like doing: daydreaming, reading, taking photographs, going for a walk, devising theories, watching a buzzard fly, having a siesta, meditating, solving Sudoku puzzles ... Whatever suits you!

3. Combine exercise and rest.

Find out what kind of movement gives you some energy – and what kind drains your energy. A lot of quiet people like sports that allow them to take short periods of time out while playing them, e.g. hiking, running, cycling, swimming, yoga or Pilates. You will find my suggestions about sport for introverts in Chapter 4.

# Obstacle 4: Passivity

## The difference between calm and passivity

Calm is good, passivity not so much. The fact is that there is a crucial difference between the two terms: calm (in the sense of strength 5) is always a basic inner attitude that makes it possible to concentrate and act purposefully. But passivity suggests an element of denial. Passive people refuse to take initiatives and to exploit stimuli. They sit and wait – without strength, defiant or rigid from shock – in whatever their situation is and prefer to suffer considerably from their plight rather than trying to change something. This includes boredom and even bad relationships.

## Strengthening your voice

Lack of strength can often be detected in the voice: a lot of quiet people speak softly, in other words at a low volume and above all with too little emphasis. A slow, low voice can make a very powerful, high-status impression if the intonation is energetic. But a voice that is too fast or too slow and also soft and uses little emphasis does not have much effect when trying to communicate. It sends out a signal saying 'I am too weak.' And that is how many other people (especially extroverts) respond when listening: they underestimate what is being said, do not hear properly or get impatient.

A SOFT, RELATIVELY UNEMPHATIC VOICE CAN DESTROY THE EFFECT OF WHAT IS BEING SAID — NO MATTER HOW CLEVER OR IMPORTANT IT IS.

## Don't fail to respond when attacked

People who prefer to respond when they are attacked are also passive –
they hope that doing nothing will improve the situation. But that kind of
improvement seldom happens. On the contrary: anyone who allows other
people to break through the boundaries of personal respect is inviting
them to keep on doing it.

But passivity can have its reasons. It has some entirely advantageous aspects
for quiet people, and so it seems to make sense to them: it is comfortable,
helps to avoid over-stimulation (obstacle 3) and thus can be an energy-
saving bulb for introverts. In the worst case this way of saving energy
can lead to a life lived on the back burner, almost literally. Other people
act, passive people are acted against or (when decisions are needed, for
example, or promotion) left by the wayside. Other people offer stimuli,
passive people are set in motion – or they wait around where they are. This
is just as disadvantageous to a career as it is to private relationships, to say
nothing of personal satisfaction. People who allow other people to manage
their lives lose the sense of being able to shape and control a successful life.
What a price to pay! You will find strategies for dealing with passivity in
Chapter 6, which deals with establishing contacts.

## Introverts need time to reflect

It is important to point out another misunderstanding at this point.
Because quiet people like to think things through thoroughly before they
say anything (hence strength 3, substance), they are easily dismissed as
passive, even though in this case they actually aren't. This is because
introverts need more time to digest all the impressions and information
they have acquired. Typical extroverts don't like having to wait a long
time for an answer in conversation, and they keep talking because they
are not expecting an answer any more. And, as a result, they will come to
this conclusion, consciously or unconsciously: their introverted opposite
number must be passive. And this is a case where it simply isn't true. It
is just that the actual activity, reflecting, weighing up and formulating,
happens internally – where you cannot see it happening. If you are on
the phone or talking face to face and need time to think, you should say
that briefly. Here are some examples.

**Sample sentences to gain time to think**

'Just let me think for a moment.'

'Yes, I quite understand that this is urgent. I'll get in touch as soon as possible.'

'You're raising a tricky point. What do you think about it?'

'Hang on, give me a moment.'

'Could I ring you back about it later?'

'I'll think it over and get back to you. Would tomorrow morning be OK?'

And make sure you do what you said. These lines give you time to think, but they promise something that must be delivered: make your point, come up with something – and show your substance and powers of analysis!

# Obstacle 5: Escape

Unlike passivity, escape is an action – but unfortunately it leads in the wrong direction. Escape means avoidance by retreat. A situation becomes too much of a worry – as in the case of passivity (obstacle 4) resulting from over stimulation (obstacle 3), but other things can cause it as well. By escaping, the person concerned is looking for distraction or getting away in the form of a less worrying activity or different surroundings. This suppresses the actual anxiety but possibly what actually needs to be done as well. The latter is know as procrastination – i.e. an inclination to put things off. The dreaded speech to a large audience is suppressed by constantly putting off the idea of preparing it. You don't make an appointment with the boss to discuss a pay rise because you have so many important things to do.

Sometimes escape is the resource of choice for retaining some residual energy. But in the same way it can prevent the person concerned from moving actively and achieving aims. This is because fear or laziness is the key force in the background, blocking meaningful communication. The price is high in this case as well: preparing a speech at the last minute is enormously stressful, particularly for a quiet person who values time to think. And other people with get the pay rise …

# Obstacle 6: Being unduly cerebral

Turning something over in your mind is a good thing in the first place. A lot of quiet people are brilliant thinkers, capable of achieving magnificent things because of their strengths such as substance, calm and analytical thinking.

## Drawbacks of thinking

Being unduly cerebral as an obstacle represents the potentially negative aspect of thinking: it becomes a problem when the mind fails to access or blocks out emotions. Quiet people limit their insights in this way by paying too little attention to their emotional side and too much to their rational side. Being unduly cerebral is no less detrimental when dealing with other people: unduly cerebral people neglect their opposite numbers' emotional worlds, do not try to think themselves into their emotional states and confine themselves to facts when exchanging ideas.

## Don't underestimate the relationship factor

Communication can have unfortunate consequences. Even at work the emotional aspect of an exchange of ideas is immensely important. Exchanging facts is only a small proportion of the impressions involved, whether it is negotiations or a meeting, a conversation in the lunch break or a talk to a small group of colleagues. There are communication psychologists who would put this proportion no higher than 20 per cent. They think that the other 80 per cent is made up of signals about emotions and the way the participants relate to each other.

Have you identified being unduly cerebral as one of your personal obstacles? You will discover in Chapter 7, which deals with intelligent negotiation, how to act so that this trait does not stand in your way.

# Obstacle 7: Self-deception

## When needs are suppressed

This is a special obstacle: it is about introverted people's self-perception in relation to the world around them. Self-deception, or self-denial, means that quiet people either suppress their particular needs and traits or perceive them negatively. This happens particularly frequently when introverts live among people who are predominantly extrovert. This can be a cultural matter in the first place, as in the USA, where most social behaviour is extrovert. In a noisy, outward-looking culture, quiet people can get the idea, directly or indirectly, that that there is 'something wrong' with them. Perhaps this is why most books about introvert personalities are published in the USA!

## Self-alienation or alienation from other people

In the second place, self-deception or self-denial can occur when a quiet person represents a minority in the family or among colleagues because most of the others are extroverts. Such introverts risk two things in circumstances like these, as Laurie Helgoe (2008) points out in his book: either *they alienate themselves socially – in other words, from the people around them*. This can lead to avoiding contact to a very marked extent (obstacle 9), and it will be discussed in more detail later in this chapter. Or introverts *become alienated from themselves*. In our minds, this is exactly what self-denial means.

QUIET PEOPLE WHO SEE THEIR INTROVERSION AS A DEVIATION FROM THE WORLD AROUND THEM RISK SOCIAL ALIENATION, OR ALIENATION FROM THEMSELVES.

Self-deception too appears in various manifestations and guises. Extrovert behaviour can become a measure of good communication for socially approachable flexi-introverts (explained in Chapter 1) if they incline towards self-deception. They will have the impression that they are not in a position to implement this extrovert behaviour fully and completely because they can indeed act like extroverts, but they do not find this a positive experience in the same way. Self-abnegation prevents them from acknowledging and paying attention to their own introvert needs. But even a flexi-introvert is still an introvert. Fine, they like dealing with people in the same way as extroverts. But to a different extent …

# Obstacle 8: Fixation

## When perseverance ossifies

Fixation is the ossified form of perseverance, and it leads to an immobile approach to communication. Many quiet people who come up against this obstacle find it unpleasant if they have to give up their habitual procedures – for example, if they have to work at unusual times or cope with unfamiliar conditions on business trips. Fixation can show up in communication in something like an argument if quiet people take up a rigid position and prefer to look at details to a major extent, rather than the picture as a whole.

## Flexibility required for negotiations

In situations where it is particularly important being able to show flexibility – in negotiations, for example – fixation can prevent you from acknowledging decision criteria, approaches to solutions and your opposite number's needs in your thinking. Chapter 7 will show you how to act in situations like this.

## Fixation is a strategy for saving energy

Like other obstacles in this chapter, fixation is above all an energy-saving strategy. A person who almost always acts in the same way has a kind of internal automatic pilot that seems to make decisions unnecessary. Behaviour patterns and rituals take the place of conscious decisions.

## The advantages of rituals in everyday life

But rituals as such are not necessarily negative. They also have their advantages in communication: they help us to react appropriately and confidently in certain situations, and with a sense of certainty. An everyday example: you introduce two people with whom you have had discussions to each other in a professional context. You will find this easier and tackle it more confidently if you know:

1 who you introduce to whom first (the less important one to the more important one), and

2 what interesting information you can mention apart from name and title to make it easier to get into conversation – perhaps a common interest (e.g. theatre, boxing), similar jobs (e.g. teaching or scientific management) or a new item of positive information about one of the people being introduced (e.g. a recent honour or a new position).

## Being flexible depending on the situation

Rituals like introducing people make life less complicated. They entail experience in dealing with people and establish a stable basis, so that you can go on to concentrate on other things. It is a different matter if an 'automatic pilot' like this robs you of flexibility in dealing with other people, something that is important in non-standard situations.

People who always react in the same way (e.g. by falling silent or insisting on details) in response to a particular setback (e.g. resistance from an opposite number in negotiations) are obstructing successful communication by this inflexibility. And it also makes their reactions predictable for others – and so also for people who have something against them. It is easy to push particular buttons in order to elicit a particular reaction. And what is almost worse than this is the price that quiet people pay for their fixation: they deprive themselves of room for manoeuvre, and thus of the confidence to manage a situation proactively and with an eye on all the important factors.

# Obstacle 9: Avoiding contact

## Reasons for avoiding contact

Quiet people usually prefer to have a limited number of good friends rather than a lot of more superficial contacts. This is perfectly all right. But the more clearly they are placed in the introvert area on the introvert–extrovert scale, the more introverts are inclined to avoid people because they find them hard work or annoying. This is where it gets difficult. People who avoid contact seal themselves off from the outside world and avoid other people. They are quite content if they can get on with their usual activities on their own (additional danger: fixation – see obstacle 8). There can be all sorts of reasons for this: the person concerned is hard work, the aim being pursued by the contact is hard work, or the quiet person has simply had enough of the hurly-burly of human contact.

## Avoiding isolation

This approach means that quiet people are risking getting into an extreme situation: that of social isolation. They are thrown back on themselves, with all their thoughts and emotions. The consequences: important stimuli and also corrections from other people are missing in their professional and private lives. If team work or co-ordination with other people are called for, communication will quickly become difficult – regardless of whether they are planning a holiday with the family or completing a project at work. Other people are quick to see contact avoiders as a little strange.

A classic contact-avoiding stereotype is the introverted husband who takes refuge in his hobby room after a long day at work and restores furniture there or builds model railway layouts rather than talking to his wife. The introverted boss behaves similarly: during the Christmas celebrations she retreats into a corner with her smartphone as an alibi to escape from the general mayhem and particularly from the capricious attempts at small talk made by her colleagues and fellow workers.

## Escaping and avoiding contact

The difference from escaping (obstacle 5) lies in the aim of the avoidance. The person escaping avoids things that should be done or certain situations by putting them off or doing something else. But the contact-avoider tries not to get involved with people he finds hard work. This can have very unpleasant consequences for interpersonal relationships, particularly when combined with the next obstacle, fear of conflict.

Socially alienated introverts (explained above under obstacle 7) can make a career of avoiding contact: they feel misunderstood and rejected by the people around them. This can have a significant effect on communication: in extreme cases contact-avoiding introverts can become embittered loners full of antipathy towards other people.

# Obstacle 10: Avoiding conflict

## Are introverts more peace-loving?

One interesting detail crops up time and time again in the literature about quiet people: even in their younger years, introverts seem to get involved in fewer conflicts than extroverts. Are they more peace-loving? Or more capable of harmony? I think the reason is to be found somewhere else.

## Why introverts avoid conflict

Conflicts are part of human dealings because we differ in our personalities, desires, aims and idiosyncrasies. They happen everywhere, but most people still find addressing conflicts a tricky job: talking about conflicts takes a lot of time, is relatively stressful, and the outcome is predictable only to a limited extent. Consequently, most people talk about conflicts only when it seems worth the energy invested. Here extroverts and introverts seem to have different ways of evaluating things: introverts are quicker to reach the view that addressing a conflict could become too stressful. Also, because they are very bothered about safety, they can easily start worrying that such communication could quickly get out of control. This shows that fear (obstacle 1) has a part to play in resisting conflict. But for outward-looking extroverts the price of investing energy in the same situation is not so high, along the lines of preferring to show a hard line of resistance rather than stewing in their own frustration.

And the resulting disadvantages are different for the two types: when working hard to address conflicts, extroverts can constantly involve themselves in verbal battles in extreme cases, while introverts will toss and turn at night, unable to get to sleep because they are thinking about the conflict they don't want to address but that is nonetheless troubling them a great deal.

In Chapter 7, the example of negotiation will provide a concrete illustration of how you can handle conflicts constructively when they arise from differing sets of expectations.

# What are your personal obstacles?

## Assessing your own obstacles

As in the previous chapter, where you looked at your individual strengths more closely, we are now going to put your obstacles under a magnifying glass. First of all, you need to identify the obstacles that you see as yours.

---

**? Our question to you**

Which of the introvert obstacles you've read about in this chapter apply to you?

Obstacle 1: Fear

Obstacle 2: Too much attention to detail

Obstacle 3: Over-stimulation

Obstacle 4: Passivity

Obstacle 5: Escape

Obstacle 6: Being unduly cerebral

Obstacle 7: Self-deception

Obstacle 8: Fixation

Obstacle 9: Avoiding contact

Obstacle 10: Avoiding conflict

---

My three biggest obstacles are:

1. _____
2. _____
3. _____

## Inferring what your needs are from obstacles you face

Let's go a step further now and use your obstacles to work out your needs: note below where you are particularly aware of a certain obstacle and the consequences this has for you. Then consider the need that lies behind this obstacle – and how you could address this need. Make sure you have plenty of quiet time to look into these questions. I've given you an example again, so that you can see what your list could look like.

### ? What are your needs?

| My obstacle | I am particularly aware of it in these situations – with these consequences: | This shows me that I have this need – and this is how I can do something about it: |
|---|---|---|
| Over-stimulation | On social occasions: too many people, too much background noise. Consequence: stress – which is why I try to avoid occasions like this. | I prefer talking to one person somewhere quiet. In future I can plan in advance who I want to talk to – and perhaps arrange to meet. And I can always try to find 'quiet corners'. |

## Obstacles as signposts for needs

The exercise above has made you aware of an important part of yourself and you now know more about your needs in communication situations.

So, in the same way as you can use your 'treasure chest' of strengths, you should use your obstacles as well, as signposts to point you towards what you need in order to feel comfortable when dealing with other people. A lot of introverts discover that their strengths and obstacles are linked. For example, independence on the strong side can have its flip side of fear as an obstacle, or avoiding contact. Caution and fear are similar siblings, but so are calm and passivity, concentration and over-attention to detail. Look at your notes for the previous chapter again: can you see any connections between your two groups of characteristics?

---

**?** **Another question for you**

Which of your strengths and obstacles seem connected to you?

1. _____ and _____
2. _____ and _____
3. _____ and _____

---

Things get more concrete in the rest of this book: the aim is to shape the way you deal with others so that you play to your strengths and keep an eye on your needs. First we're going to look at your private and professional surroundings.

---

**\*** **Key points in brief**

- Just as they have typical strengths, introverts also have typical obstacles. It is important to be aware of them, so that they do not become weak points in certain situations or make your life more difficult.

- At the same time, quiet people's obstacles are good signposts to their needs.

- The obstacles are: fear, over-attention to detail, over-stimulation, passivity, escape, being unduly cerebral, self-deception, fixation, avoiding contact and avoiding conflict.

---

# Part II

How to have a happy private life and be successful professionally

# 4.

# My home is my castle: shaping your own private space

Christine is an analyst in an international company. At 34, she has achieved a great deal: she has a considerable area of responsibility, she is valued for her expertise and, thanks to her reliability, she is considered indispensable to her department.

Christine puts everything into her work. The downside is that, when she gets home at the end of the day, only her cat is there waiting for her. Occasionally, she meets up with a couple of girlfriends, to cycle or to drink coffee.

Christine thinks that it would be nice to have a partner, but, as a quiet person, she is reluctant to actively look for someone. After a tough day at work, she likes to relax, and she rarely feels motivated to go out and take part in social events. Every now and again she looks at online dating sites, but she's sceptical – after all, there are plenty of untrustworthy people on the internet. She has trouble in imagining that she could make herself attractive to a prospective partner, as if it were some kind of marketplace. In spite of this, she has recently been thinking more and more how nice it would be to spend her life with someone who shares her interests – someone she would be important to.

## The inner social circle

### Introverts among family and friends

Even if we restrict ourselves to the theme of this book – to communication – private life is a very large area to cover. There are plenty of good books about living as a single person, about living as a couple and about family life. This chapter will deal with interactions with family and friends from the perspective of an introverted person. Firstly, there is interaction with a partner (if applicable). There is also a section dedicated to single people, and a section that deals in detail with the different needs of introverted and extroverted children, discussing loving and appropriate parenting strategies for both. You are advised to read the passages that are relevant to your life at the moment!

## Living with and without a partner

People living with a partner and people living without a partner – whether by choice or not – face different challenges. Both ways of life have advantages and difficulties; and this must, inevitably, also be the case for quiet people. Living with a partner is easier in some ways – and more difficult in others. Certainly it's wonderful to live with someone to whom you are important, who understands you and gets you doing new things. Equally, however, it can be exhausting if your partner has needs that are different from yours and as a result you have less time for yourself. Over the next few pages, who will talk about both types of living – but we'll start with the in-between stage of *looking* for a partner, the part that Christine is finding so daunting.

# Finding a partner

## What you will need to invest in this: energy!

Finding a partner – for many introverted people, this is a very big challenge, just as it is for Christine. After all, it means taking the initiative and making the first move, going out to meet unfamiliar people and getting to know them better. This costs energy, and also means that you have to overcome your own resistance to the idea. However, if you have decided that you would rather live with a partner, then, for you personally, it will be worth taking this step in order to arrive at the life you want for yourself. If you are in this situation, I will invite you in the next few sections of this book to do something that, in any case, can't do any harm: to think carefully about the possible options, and then to make a plan – your very own, personal plan!

# An introvert or extrovert partner?

If you are looking for a person to get together with, then, in the light of what you have just read, there's an important question to be answered: as a quiet person, what kind of partner are you better off with – an introvert or an extrovert?

You might respond by saying that there is more to a person's character than their position on the introvert–extrovert continuum. This is very true. And, in theory, a relationship with either type of person might be successful – but in different ways.

## Opposites attract

As partners, extroverts are often attractive to introverts. As Carl Gustav Jung noticed, opposites attract – and that goes for introverts and extroverts as well. Like Plato, he believed that we choose partners who are different from ourselves, that we 'complete' our partners and that they make us whole. The very masculine and the very feminine, the impulsive type and the thoughtful type, the beautiful and the clever, family people and loners: if you look around in your own life, you will find examples of two very different people coming together.

## Extroverts and introverts complement one another

It is easy to see why an extrovert might be attractive to an introvert. Extroverts find it easy to do things that are often far from easy for a quiet person to do, such as making a speech at a family celebration, taking the initiative in planning social occasions or dealing with disputes and making complaints in shops. Diagnosticians using the Myers-Briggs Type Indicator once recommended that couples should be different in as many aspects of their personality as possible – including in terms of introversion and extroversion.

## People who are alike also get along

Perceptions have since changed. New studies show that similarity can also be attractive. In many functional relationships, both partners are similar in terms of their intelligence, their social background and their education and professional careers. However, a similarity of habits in terms of relating to other people and in terms of how you spend your leisure time can also make a partner more attractive and more approachable. You feel more at ease with a 'kindred spirit'.

This makes it understandable that a quiet, intense introvert can be attractive to other introverts. The good part is that, if you are *looking* for a partner at present, you can think it over calmly: how do *you* respond to extroverts and to introverts? What qualities do you find pleasant in a person, and what do you find trying or unattractive? What do you want from your contacts?

But first, we should face the facts: when love strikes, it strikes through the right-hand side of your brain – the side that is concerned with emotion and intuition. You can plan, analyse and think about what you want – that's part of the process – but, in the end, your chosen partner may turn out to be entirely different from what you had in mind. And, after all, isn't that a good thing?

## Looking for a partner: make use of your strengths!

Do you remember the overview of typical strengths of introvert people in Chapter 2? Here it is again: an overview of all the strengths – and how you can make use of them in the difficult task of looking for a partner.

| Strength | Usefulness when looking for a partner |
| --- | --- |
| 1. Caution | One of the best ways to meet someone is to be introduced to them by someone you know, whose judgement you trust. In this situation, you will at least know that one trustworthy third party thinks that the person you are being introduced to is okay. |
| | If you embark on online dating, it is a good idea to take precautions. Here are the most important things to bear in mind: |
| | • Use a computer that is equipped with a firewall and with antivirus programs. |
| | • Only use platforms that allow you to sign up using a username (not your own first name!) plus a valid email address. Do not use a domain email address. |
| | • To start with, do not give your personal information (your name, address, telephone number, email address, place of work) to anyone. |
| | • To start with, take phone calls on your mobile phone, not on a landline. |
| | • Be suspicious if your contact asks for money, talks about marriage too quickly or mentions anything strange in connection with sex. If this happens, break off all contact right away! |

| | |
|---|---|
| | • If you decide to meet up with someone, then arrange to meet in a public place where you will not be out of sight – in a café during the day, for instance. Let at least one person know when you are meeting up and where. The same is true if you meet someone through newspaper ads or a dating agency. |
| | In conversation, reveal information about yourself only gradually. You have all the time in the world. |
| 2. Substance | First, think: what activities do you really enjoy and find worthwhile? Once you know this, you can plan activities that will allow you to meet like-minded people. |
| 3. Concentration | Make time in your everyday life for looking for a partner. You might, for instance, choose, plan and put into action some of the activities from the list you have just made. |
| 4. Listening | Listen carefully: how do men and women talk to each other when they don't know each other well? What parts of this apply to you? |
| | Ask introverted friends who are in relationships how they met their partners. What can you learn from their stories that might be useful to you? |
| | When you meet someone, it is also a good time to do some listening. |
| | What does the other person like to talk about? Is he or she a good listener? |
| 5. Calm | Relax! Expanding your circle of acquaintances should first and foremost be a question of gaining new and interesting experiences – even if you have another aim in mind. This is precisely where being calm can pay off … |
| | Repeat: do not let anyone push you into anything that you don't want to do! |
| | Do not take on too many activities at once. |
| | Make sure you take some time out to recuperate. |

| | |
|---|---|
| 6. Analytical thinking | Once you have answered the question asked under Strength 2, plan some suitable activities. These might include walking the dog, looking around in the library, taking up voluntary work, going to dance classes, visiting exhibitions or taking up a sport. These activities will also keep you occupied – thus making the business of looking for a partner considerably more relaxed. |
| | What activities do you think would be appropriate for a first meeting (dating agency or online dating)? |
| | You should also simply use your powers of analytical thinking to evaluate the people you meet – this is something that can give you confidence. Ask yourself: what qualities can you see in this person? Which of them do you like? |
| 7. Independence | In order to be a good partner, you also have to be good at being alone. The more contented you are with your current way of life, the easier it will be to get to know people. Someone who radiates a sense of need is rarely attractive to anyone looking for a partner who will be their equal – and surely you wouldn't want a relationship on any other terms? Are you independent in this sense? This is something that you should work towards. |
| 8. Tenacity | Looking for a partner can take time. Be aware of this – and make a conscious decision to invest that time. |
| | Don't be too willing to compromise. The second of the two lists included under strength 9 below should help you with this. |
| 9. Writing (rather than speaking) | Make two lists: |
| | • a list of your own attractive qualities (to enhance your self-confidence), and |
| | • a list of the qualities you want in a prospective partner (to help in your search). Examples might include humour, reliability, honesty … Mark the qualities that you think are indispensable. Also think about which differences you feel that you could live with. |
| | In addition to the traditional newspaper ads, use online platforms in your search for a partner. The internet gives you time to think, and is a written medium. |

| 10. Empathy | This is a very useful quality when you are meeting someone, either virtually or in the real world. It helps you to size up the other person – and it also helps you to communicate with them. Do you both feel at ease? What is important to the other person? Take any negative feelings arising within yourself very seriously (this includes annoyance and fear *and* boredom and impatience). You can gain a lot of valuable information by asking innocuous questions – about the other person's leisure pursuits, for instance. |
| --- | --- |
| | Finally: is the other person also asking questions? Is he or she trying to understand you, is he or she able to think beyond his or her own life? |
| | For a first meeting, you will find the tips on small talk in Chapter 6 useful. |

## Christine's case

Christine chooses a traditional strategy. Due to her distrust of online platforms, she places an ad in a respectable weekly newspaper. Having first carefully considered which qualities would be most important to her in a partner, she also gets in touch with a dating agency. She also starts attending a workshop where she can pursue something that has been of interest for her for a long time: she wants to write a crime novel. Who knows who her new hobby might put her in touch with …

# Living with a partner

## Relationships as a challenge

Most people want to be in a relationship. In spite of this, relationships often fail. The Western industrial countries have a divorce rate of 50 per cent – and that figure only reflects the number of relationship breakdowns among people who are actually married. A look at the statistics reveals that, in Europe and much of the world, the number of marriages is consistently decreasing. There is plenty of relationship advice on offer. However, if we are talking about introverted and extroverted people, with their different ways of communicating and different needs, then it makes sense to start by looking at the two possible combinations. How can a relationship between an introverted person and an extroverted person work? And, conversely, what might two introverted people have to offer each other?

> **?** **A question for you**
>
> If you have a partner, is he or she introverted or extroverted?
>
> If you are not sure, use the test and the overview in Chapter 1.
>
> He or she is:_____
>
> Special qualities and needs:_____

## Introvert–extrovert relationships

### When partners complement one another

In this situation, the two members of the partnership are living in different worlds. Once the first, intense phase of being in love has passed, it soon becomes clear just how different the two worlds are. Each person has different values, experiences, talents and personality features – in short, the things that go to make up an extrovert or introvert orientation. The differences resulting from these two different realities are interesting – two worlds add up to more than one world. Often, one partner will be able to do things that the other finds difficult, thereby making their partner's life easier. An extrovert partner will, for instance, find it easy to plan, maintain and keep up the couple's social life.

For example, an extrovert woman might persuade (or push) her introvert male partner to go to parties, and, once the couple are at the party, might make sure that he is not left on his own, and include him in her own activities. Conversely, as the quiet one of the two, he might offer the woman an opposing pole of calmness, balancing out her own personality and offering her substance and stability, like a rock in the storm.

## Differences can be taxing

On the other hand, the differences between an introvert and an extrovert partner can be exhausting. Differences in temperament, needs and ideas can frequently cause clashes and lead to an unequal situation: in the situation just mentioned, the woman, as the extrovert partner, has to carry the entire burden in terms of time and energy associated with keeping up social contacts. At parties, she always has her spouse in tow, although, as an extrovert person, she would be able to have more fun if she could talk to many different people without having to think of including her husband in the conversation. For his part, he finds that living with his extrovert wife makes it difficult to calm down, to relax and simply not to have to be doing *anything* once in a while.

THE DIFFERENCES BETWEEN INTROVERT AND EXTROVERT PARTNERS MAY BE A THREAT TO A RELATIONSHIP, OR THEY MAY ENRICH IT.

## Conflicting needs

When an introvert and an extrovert live together, their irreconcilable differences may, at worst, become a threat to a happy relationship. The introverted partner may feel overshadowed, ignored, misunderstood or pressured. The extrovert partner may find the other member of the partnership weak, inattentive, too compliant or too passive, which in turn may have a negative impact on the introverted partner's sense of self-esteem. In addition to this, extroverts may want more stimulation and a more active social life than their partners. They may also feel emotionally neglected because they do not receive the amount of active affection they require.

Introverted partners, on the other hand, feel more comfortable in a relationship in which they do not have to constantly demonstrate affection or show initiative.

In terms of communication, introvert and extrovert partners often have a different idea of the appropriate speed and volume for an exchange; they will also generally have a different attitude to confrontation and to conflict. What may appear to be too much, too loud, too hard or too fast for an introverted husband may, to his extroverted wife, appear to be a normal way of interacting. Conversely, she, for her part, may have a problem with the way her quieter partner responds to a difference of opinion by becoming withdrawn, instead of addressing the problem. There may also be issues surrounding confidentiality, because extrovert people are more ready to share personal information than introverted people.

## A basis of mutual respect

In spite of all this, introverted and extroverted people may live together successfully and enjoy a very enriching partnership. That's providing that they put into practice something that psychologist Hartwig Hanssen (2008) described as the key to any successful partnership: respect. In a life spent together, respect is, above all, recognizing two things: your own needs and the needs of your partner.

 **Two keys to a successful partnership**

1. **Recognize your own needs!**

   You will only be able to accept the needs of your partner if you also know and respect your own needs.

2. **Recognize the needs of your partner!**

   Recognize that your partner's needs are different from yours and that you may have different views of the same situation. This fact is quite separate from the feelings that you share for one another.

## The advantages of having different needs

It is quite normal to realize that you have different needs. After all, everyone is different. The important thing is how you decide to deal with your differences.

Together, you and your partner make up a team. Any team profits from its members having different qualities and different abilities. You should therefore take a look at the advantages of differing needs in a relationship.

For instance, an extrovert partner:

- has plenty of energy and new ideas to offer to you and to your relationship
- has the ability to initiate activities and social encounters – for you as well – which can be very liberating

- has communication-related strengths that you can profit from where you encounter obstacles: for instance, flexible conversation (see obstacle 8: fixation) or constructive conflict resolution (see obstacle 10: conflict shyness).

## Communicating well with an extrovert partner

For the benefit of introvert partners of extrovert people (after all, this book is for you!) here is a list of the most important communication strategies for interacting with an extrovert partner.

## Strategies for introverts communicating with an extrovert partner

1. **In conversation**
   - Get to the point – express yourself clearly and briefly. Your qualities of substance (strength 2) and capacity for analytical thinking (strength 6) will make this easy for you.
   - When you are speaking, make sure you are speaking loudly and clearly enough. If you talk too quietly or in a monotone, your partner may fail to hear what you say or underestimate the extent of your concern.
   - If it bothers you that your partner speaks too quickly, ask him or her to speak more slowly or to repeat what he or she has said.
   - You have the ability to make the conversation happen slower. You should also be prepared to say that you need time to think about something – before making an important decision that will affect your future together, for instance.
   - Show that you understand your partner's concerns. Active listening (strength 4) and analytical thinking (strength 6) and sensitivity (strength 10) will help you to do this.
   - Prior to any important discussion, write down the most significant things that you want to discuss or to achieve (strength 9).
   - Learn to recognize the messages being transmitted by the other person (irritation, boredom, frustration, fears … ). It's good to learn to understand the other person's 'language', especially when the two of you have different ways of expressing yourselves.
   - You must also express your own feelings, whether they are comfortable or not. This includes regularly showing signs of affection!

- Communicate your needs and ask after the needs of others. In discussions, you should treat both as of equal importance. Demonstrate that you understand that your partner finds some things difficult (and also that you yourself find some things difficult). Ideally, you will both be able to laugh about it ...

2. **When living together**

- Be aware of your needs and arrange your lives accordingly. You must also give your partner sufficient space to live in a way that meets his or her own needs.

- Plan things you do together – holidays, special events and family events – so that, as far as possible, they suit you both.

- Make sure there are plenty of opportunities for withdrawing, and communicate your need to be alone from time to time. It is important that you should make the reasons for this clear: 'I am not getting away from *you* – I need to be alone for *myself*.' Ask for your partner's understanding.

- Respect introversion and extroversion as personal qualities. After all, you know that both personality types bring both strengths and weaknesses with them.

- Show appreciation for the things that your partner can do better and more easily than you can. Thank him or her for doing the things that he or she does for you: creating a contact, registering a complaint or braving the scrum on Easter Saturday to hit the shops.

## Giving each other enough space

In my own introvert-extrovert relationship, I have discovered in what ways my extroverted husband ticks differently to me, and what he needs. Equally important was finding out what I myself need – and that it was okay for our needs to be different. Over the course of our marriage, we have learned to give each other space: my husband needs more social evenings with friends and clubs, more projects and more time on the move, travelling the world. Oh, and he also likes to turn on the radio or the television as soon as he enters the room. I need more peace and quiet, more time alone and, above all, time away from loud noises.

We have gradually discovered ways of living together, in spite of our differing comfort zones and our differing positions on the introvert–extrovert continuum. The time that we spend together is good: we have enough of a sense of humour to be able to laugh about ourselves and about one another.

And, of course, there are always headphones and earplugs! Last but not least, there *are* overlaps in the things that we enjoy doing, things that make us both happy – a pleasant evening meal with friends, or good conversation.

The most important thing to remember is that, if your partner ticks differently from you, then you can't take it for granted that he or she recognizes your different needs. He or she is not a quiet person, after all. Similarly, it may be difficult for you to recognize the needs of your partner, who is an extrovert. This makes it important that you yourself know what you need – and that you communicate this.

# Introvert–introvert relationships
## Reduced potential for conflict

If you are in a relationship with an introverted person, then it is very likely that you feel quite content. After all, you have a companion who understands your needs, and perhaps even shares them. What an ideal start to a relationship!

**?** **Two questions for you**

In what areas do you and your partner have different needs?

**Partner**

_____

_____

_____

_____

**Me**

_____

_____

_____

_____

How can you handle these differences to make them enrich your relationship?

_____

If you are living with an introverted person, you have a partner:

- who is a good listener, with patience and plenty of awareness of your needs

- with a sense of discretion, who understands that you need peace and solitude

- who shares many of your interests

- who offers little potential for conflict.

## The danger of stagnation

This combination, however, also presents obstacles. Perhaps the greatest of these is stagnation: a shared inertia. The risk of this is especially great if both partners tend to be passive (obstacle 4) or to avoid making contacts (obstacle 9). It may result in a lack of friends and too few pleasant, shared experiences, a lack of personal development and too little flexibility in solving problems, conflicts and crises. Understanding each other can turn into fixation and mutual dependency. As you may have guessed, this is not healthy. The overview below shows how you can direct your communication and your life together in such a way that you can enjoy the advantages of this kind of partnership and avoid any disadvantages.

> ## ! Strategies for introverted people communicating with an introverted partner
>
> 1. **In conversation**
>    - Talk about the things that make you different. What do they mean for your relationship?
>    - Communicate your needs and compare them with the needs of the other person. In discussion, treat both sets of needs as of equal importance.
>    - Let the other person know in advance if you want to talk about something important. This will give your partner time to prepare.
>    - You could also choose to communicate in writing, if you both like to express yourself in writing (strength 9). Emails, texts or notes on scraps of paper – you have lots of different media to choose from!

## 2. Living together

Create rituals that will bring a certain amount of variety into your lives. Here are some suggestions:

- Try a new hobby once a year.
- Go out together once a fortnight.
- Once a month, make the acquaintance of an interesting person.
- Every two months, plan something surprising for you and your partner (take turns taking responsibility for this).
- Note your rituals on your calendar.
- Practise difficult discussions and upcoming conferences (Chapter 7) or presentations (Chapter 8) together. This will help to train you both!
- Also pursue your own personal interests on your own, and maintain your own friendships and networks.
- Take on your own share of responsibility for living a balanced life together.

If you are living with an introverted person, now is the time to take a look at your own relationship.

## ? Two questions for you

What do you have in common with your introverted partner?

_____

_____

_____

_____

What obstacles or challenges do you see in your life together and what can you do in order to avoid the negative consequences?

| Obstacles | How to deal with obstacles |
|-----------|----------------------------|
|           |                            |
|           |                            |
|           |                            |
|           |                            |

# Living as a single person who is an introvert

## Being alone without feeling lonely

Living alone has advantages and disadvantages. It may be a lifestyle choice, or it may be the result of losing a partner. Many introverts find that they can live alone without feeling lonely. They pursue various activities that they can do adequately without company, and even find it restful to be able to relax and recuperate in peace and quiet after a hard day's work.

## Risks to singles

The risks are similar to the ones that you have already learned about in the section on introvert–introvert partnerships – with the difference that it is you alone who is finding it difficult to embark on activities or to meet people (and not you and your introvert partner). This is particularly true if you, as a single person, tend to be passive (obstacle 4) or to avoid contact (obstacle 9). Just as with an introvert–introvert couple, this results in a lack of social contacts and too few of the kind of experiences that give you a new perspective and new impressions.

This can quickly result in personal stagnation and a reduced ability to deal with problems, conflicts and crises.

Here is an overview with tips that will help you to enjoy your life as a single person and to avoid the above-mentioned risks.

---

## ! Tips for living happily as a single person

- Create personal rituals to enrich your life. Put them down on the calendar as tasks or appointments. Here are some suggestions:
  - Try out a new hobby once a year.
  - Twice a year, get to know a new place.
  - Once a fortnight, visit an exhibition or a cinema, theatre or dance performance.
  - Once a month, take part in a celebration or a social event.
  - Every two months plan to do something with a friend, taking turns to take on responsibility for this!

- Make sure that you regularly meet people who are interesting and who inspire you. Communicating by telephone or email is fine, but you should also make an effort to plan personal meetings outside of your working life, with friends, family members or colleagues.
- Pursue personal interests that make you happy.
- Engage with your community: keep up friendships and networks. If you are able, help other people out by doing little things for them (watering the flowers, listening, installing a computer program, babysitting ...). It is equally important that you should ask other people for help when you need it.
- If you have a particular cause that is dear to your heart, then consider doing voluntary work outside of your working life. This would allow you to meet like-minded people, which is always interesting – and not only if you are looking for a partner.

Take control of and enjoy your life as a single person, and do things that enrich your own life and those of others. Being a quiet person puts you in a position to do this well.

# Caring for children

If you are living with a partner, then you are a family: instead of living alone, you are living in an association with someone who is important to you. Children and other people may become a part of this family, either on a long-term basis (an elderly father, a widowed mother-in-law) or on a temporary basis (exchange students, friends, au pairs).

For a quiet person, the biggest obstacle to be found in the cheerful hurly-burly of family life is number 3: over-stimulation! The volume and the different sleep rhythms of small children – and the social life of older children – can be extremely trying and exhausting. Possibilities for spending time alone are often limited.

## Tips for a happy family life

The suggestions included in the following list are intended to help you, as an introverted person, to live happily within and with your family.

## ! Strategies for introverts coping with family life

1. **Co-existence on an equal basis**. In most families, extroverts live together with introverts. Within your family, you should make an effort to arrange things in a way that is fair for everyone – regardless of where on the introvert–extrovert continuum their comfort zone is located. You should take care that the needs of both introverts and extroverts are considered equally. It is just as reasonable to want to have a nap at noon as it is to want to visit a fair with friends.

2. **Space to withdraw.** Find yourself a space where you can feel comfortable and can go to be alone – at least for brief moments.

   It might be your bedroom, a basement room, an attic or your own room. The living room is, generally speaking, a room for spending time together in. However, it can sometimes be used for relaxation when the noisy ones are asleep or out of the house.

3. **Noise level**. If you are sensitive to noise, then take active steps to reduce the noise level, which will frequently be too high. One thing you can be sure of is that there will always be plenty of noise! Here are some specific things that you can do:

   • *Insist that everyone talks at 'room volume'!* Establish a rule that everybody talks at 'room volume' at the dining table. You could also use this phrase to remind family members who tend to communicate at high volume in certain situations to moderate their voices.

   • *Get people to take time out alone!* If there is an argument or someone is throwing a tantrum – typical high-decibel nightmare situations – you can remove the stress from the situation by getting those involved to go to different rooms. After all, it is impossible to talk anything over when people are angry. The issue should, however, be discussed later, once things have calmed down a bit.

   • *Make use of technology!* In our family, we have earphones for the television, so that mother, who is introverted and sensitive to noise, can sit next to her husband and son and read her book while they watch *The Simpsons*.

4. **Babysitters**. For introvert parents, babysitters are crucial to survival – whether they are grandparents, teenage neighbours or a kind niece. It is very worthwhile to take time to arrange for someone to babysit, as it relieves some of the burden of parenting. It can also be a good

idea to arrange for a babysitter not because you want to go to the theatre or to an event with your partner, but because you simply want a little peace and quiet. The babysitter could, for instance, take the children to the cinema, to a museum or to a play park for an hour or two. One incidental bonus is that you will be particularly well aware of your love for your children after you have taken a break for a little peace and quiet, and will be visibly more relaxed yourself. If your finances are limited, then you could make an arrangement with other parents involving babysitting their children in return – another kind of successful networking ...

5. **Food for thought**. This is something that, as an introvert, you will need as a kind of compensation to prevent inner life from being overwhelmed by the stress of day-to-day life, particularly in the busy stages of family life. In your place of work, keep up with events. Make sure that you have plenty of good books, interesting films, exciting blogs to read and real conversations about subjects other than measles and choosing a school. You should also make a point of meeting up with people who do not have children.

6. **Sport**. Sport is good for all of us, regardless of who we are living with. Find a sport that suits you – and that you can pursue alone. This has two advantages: it keeps you fit and it charges your batteries! Most of the following sports can also be done together with friends and family if you wish: visiting a fitness studio, gymnastics, in-line skating, jogging, Pilates, cycling, swimming, sailing, surfing, Tai Chi, diving, walking, rambling, yoga.

## An introvert or an extrovert child?

Just like adults, children have personalities – although it should also be said that their personalities change and grow more defined as they mature. Even babies respond to their environment and to people in different ways according to whether they have an introvert and extrovert personality. Children will also have a loosely defined comfort zone on the introvert–extrovert continuum as described in Chapter 1. If you have children or live with children, you will be better able to support them and to promote their development if you know what introverts and extroverts respectively need in order to feel at ease and to thrive. For young introverts in particular, it is of immense value for their own strengths and preferences to be understood, in a world in which it is the extroverts in school and kindergarten classes who are seen as 'cool'. However, it is also good for extroverted children to learn at an early stage what their advantages and difficulties are.

## Assessing your own child

You need only an approximate idea of your child's personality type here and for this you can use the overview in Chapter 1. In children, as in adults, extreme introversion or extroversion is rare – it is more likely that their comfort zone lies somewhere in between, with a mix of qualities and a tendency towards one or the other personality type. Once you have found out whether you have a young extrovert or introvert on your hands, refer to the appropriate section below.

# Bringing up an introvert child

## Personal experience of an introvert child

I have plenty of experience with introverted children: after all, I have one myself! Mr Son (that is what I call him on Twitter and on my blog, so I will stick to it here) is very definitely a quiet person. Ever since he was small, he was noticeably different from his more extroverted contemporaries. He never liked large groups or crowds, and even at an early age he took a lot of convincing to go to a child's birthday party. On the other hand, even when he was attending kindergarten, he impressed me with his rich inner life – and an insight that surpassed that of many adults.

When he was six, my son said politely that he didn't want to go to carnival processions and St Martin's Day parades: the music was loud and bad, and there were too many people. When he was eight, he read that a vegetarian saves the lives of 100 animals a year – and he stopped eating meat on a long-term basis. After school, he would spend a good hour recovering from the hurly-burly of the classroom with his friends Bach, Beethoven, Chopin and Rachmaninov on the piano. He has only a few friends, but they're great. And yes, I am incredibly proud of him …

## Tips for handling an introverted child

The overview that follows is the result of years of research, many discussions and deliberations, and, of course, a lot of love. If there is a part of this book that has been particularly well tested in practice, then this is it!

> **!**  **How to provide support for an introverted child**
>
> 1. **Make sure that your child has the space he or she needs.**
>
>    Quiet children often need a place to be alone and to recover, even at a very early age. Preferably, this should be their own room, or – if this is impossible because of your home or the child's siblings – there should at least be a place without disturbances that 'belongs' only to your child for a sufficient amount of time in everyday life.
>
>    If your child is going on a trip – a class trip, a holiday or a special event – then you could discuss with him or her how he or she might be able to withdraw from time to time if necessary. Let your child have time to observe before taking part in a group activity.
>
>    'Space' also means space away from other people. Respect your child's 'alone time' and always knock before you enter his or her room. Find out how much physical closeness (cuddling and sitting close together in the car) is comfortable for your child, and respect his or her comfort zone.
>
> 2. **Create rituals to make 'taking time out' easier.**
>
>    The more you include regular time-out sessions in the timetable and the more normal they are, the easier it will be for your child to take advantage of them. Rituals – things that are always done in a similar way, for the same reason – can be of great help in this. Here are some examples:
>
>    - *Ritual when on holiday:* plan a restful time to follow an active time – after a visit to the market, plan a day spent reading and, after swimming in the pool, tea and biscuits.
>
>    - *Rituals for events away from home:* get your child there in good time (not at the last minute!) and play a game together: can you find a place where a person could escape from the hurly-burly and relax for a while? Involve your host in this if necessary.
>
>    - *Rituals for everyday life:* when he or she comes home from school or from kindergarten, sit comfortably at the table with your child while he

or she enjoys a glass of his or her favourite drink and something tasty. No barrages of questions! (And I say that as someone who is notorious for asking questions …)

3. **Help your children to discover their own needs.**

Find out what 'feels right' for your child in certain situations – particularly when the usual ideas are more extrovert-orientated. A birthday party, for instance, need not be a big bash with lots of children. It could be a day by a lake with a best friend, a picnic and a cake.

If your child is visibly stressed in a difficult situation, or simply throws a tantrum (which also happens to introvert children!), then try to stay as calm as possible yourself (breathe, and, if necessary, move away). Once your child has calmed down, review events. What happened? What could you do to make sure it goes better next time? It is helpful if you listen accurately ('So, you thought that Mark didn't want to join in with you, and so you …') and ask open questions that ask for an explanation rather than a decision: 'How could you make it so that all the children want to join in the game?' Introverted children are generally good at finding out what they and others need.

As for you personally, be careful not to make judgements concerning your child's needs. This can be difficult if you are a quiet person yourself and find the situation trying. In your own way of living, you should try to show your child how he or she can discover his or her own needs by asking questions like 'What can I do?', 'What do I need now?' If a quiet child holds back in family discussions, then ask for his or her own opinion.

If your child's siblings are more extroverted, then make sure that affection, time spent talking and decisions are fairly divided. The sooner children learn that different ways of communicating and different ways of living can be successful, the better!

You should also show your child that he or she can make contacts in his or her own way. The best way you can do this is by example: if you yourself interact in an easy and relaxed way with family members, friends and acquaintances (and if, when necessary, you withdraw to be by yourself in a similarly relaxed way), then your quiet child, who will be inclined to be observant, will take this on board. If necessary, help your child to find playmates who he or she can get along with.

4. **Acknowledge your child's particular talents.**

This piece of advice goes beyond what has already been said in point 3. 'Recognizing', in this case, means making a conscious effort to put into words the strengths that your child possesses. Have a look at the list of typical strengths of quiet people. Which of these can you see traces of – or the full-blown development of – in your child? To be significant in the long term, recognition of this kind should be specific. Instead of saying 'You're always so sensible!', it's better to say: 'I think it's great that you checked how deep the water was before you got in!'

By doing this, you can also help your child to develop a greater self-awareness and to overcome doubts. Introverted children are more likely to doubt themselves than extroverted children, and are quick to judge themselves harshly ('I'm a loser'). You should therefore try, as far as possible, to avoid transmitting your own stress to an introverted child – for instance, by being impatient or by creating pressure – as he or she will probably feel that it is his or her own fault. If you accept and support your quiet child's individual way of doing things, it will help him or her in the long term: it will help him or her to avoid being stymied by that critical inner voice.

5. **Support your child in his or her school life.**

Quiet children tend to go unnoticed in a school class. On the one hand, this means that they cause fewer difficulties for teachers, but it also means that teachers tend to give them less attention than those of their classmates who are better at making themselves heard. This can be a problem in terms of, for instance, marks given for oral performance, which are less objectively measurable than marks given for written work. A quiet child is easily seen as passive, and also does not contribute as much as he or she might in group work.

You can avoid these problems by keeping up a dialogue with teachers.

The brains of introverted children may take longer to process things, owing to their longer neural 'wiring' (see Chapter 1). On the other hand, they frequently think things through more thoroughly than their more extrovert classmates and tend to concentrate for longer. Simply make people aware of what your child achieves outside of school: in sport, music, reading, socially ...

Last but not least, you should give your child plenty of opportunities to learn the kind of communication required at school in the safe setting of home. This might involve discussions around the dining table, requests for more pocket money, conducting a project about endangered animals in a small group ...

## Are introverts late developers?

Finally, a word of reassurance. In studies concerning quiet people, many psychologists mention that they tend to be disproportionately 'late bloomers'. Much of school life, with its class situations and group pressures, is such a strain on quiet children that they do not always realize their full potential. The good news is that, once young people are able to relate to their own needs and inclinations (in terms of accommodation, study subjects, fields of work and social life), they frequently experience a real 'boost', becoming happy and successful in their chosen activities.

# Bringing up an extrovert child

If you yourself are a quiet person, then an extrovert child may be a challenge. Because this book is intended primarily for quiet people, the following overview gives special emphasis to issues that might cause friction.

 **How to bring up an extrovert child**

1. **Make sure that your child has people to talk to.**

   Extrovert children flourish when they are able to communicate their ideas and impressions to others: this is where they get their energy from! An introvert friend of mine was recently telling me about her son: 'I love him – but when I'm with him it's like having the radio switched on all the time. He just says everything that comes into his head. It drives me mad sometimes!' If you yourself are introverted, the point of this first item is to relieve you personally of some of the pressure. As a mother or father, you should of course be there for your child to talk to – but it is better, both for yourself and for your child, if you are not the *only* one!

   Extrovert people find it easier to develop their thoughts if they are able to articulate them. You will therefore be helping both yourself and your child if you encourage him or her to make friendships and contacts with a number of communication partners: let your child invite friends to the house, let him or her stay the night with friends and relatives and take him or her along to any special occasions and events suitable for children.

   Do not be surprised if even an extroverted child goes through phases of being withdrawn. This is a normal part of childhood development, and it does not mean that your child is turning from an extrovert into an introvert.

2. **Encourage your child to evaluate experiences and impressions.**

Because of the 'short routes' in the brain (see Chapter 2), extroverted people tend to react quickly and impulsively. On the one hand, they can switch quickly from performing one activity to performing another; on the other hand, they are more easily distracted. Use your own strengths to help your child to hold back once in a while and to reflect: what exactly is happening? Who wants what? What possibilities exist for solving the problem? How can this situation be improved?

You should also proceed in this way if you are annoyed by something an extroverted child has done. What is it, from your point of view, that went wrong? (Your child kept ordering a friend around who had been invited over to play.) What should your child do? (Apologize and plan a game for next time that is fair to both of them.)

Your child will gradually learn to collect more information from his or her own actions, modify his or her behaviour and explore his or her freedom to make decisions. These are important steps on the road to maturity.

3. **Find space for differences.**

If you are a quiet person living with an extroverted child, then this may be a strain, or even frustrating: your needs – in terms of favourite activities, intimacy, needing to talk, regulating the day – are probably very different. This makes it all the more important that you learn to cope with your differences – and that your child learns to do this too!

Good communication is an important part of this. Explain to your child that you (and other introverted family members) need some peace and quiet from time to time, and that you are happy with having other children in the house only so long as there are not too many of them and they do not come too often. Conversely, you should also recognize the needs of your child, with his or her own individual temperament. Here are some examples of everyday situations:

- Visiting plan: decide on 'visiting days' and 'peace and quiet days'. If your child has a lot of friends, come to arrangements with the other parents, taking turns and sleepovers or even arranging together for a babysitter for the day so that you yourself can actually go on a quick visit to the library or get a little relaxation ...

- Stimulation: an extrovert child likes to have plenty of material things to do, and thrives on attention and praise. You should simply give your child plenty of challenges: projects or tasks that are in line with his or her interests. This might be a puppet play, a circus, a series of interviews or a home art exhibition ...

- Space: organize quiet times when your child does something that can be done quietly, and when you can take some time for yourself. If your child wants a big birthday party with lots of friends, then it does not necessarily have to take place in your home! You should also set parameters for your own involvement in talking or in activities – that, for instance, you cannot be expected to be on hand all night to answer questions for the school project. Instead, make an appointment lasting an hour. If your extrovert child likes to have the television on as background noise while he or she does homework, turn it off.

4. **Recognize your child's special talents.**

For an introverted child and an extroverted child alike, this piece of advice is the same. Recognizing, in this case, means making a conscious effort to put into words the strengths that your child possesses. What strengths does your child possess? Make them visible! Specific recognition is particularly important for an extroverted child. Don't say: 'You're so good at speaking in front of other people!' Instead, say: 'I heard you explaining to your friends how the game goes. Everyone could play right away because your words were so clear and because you found such good examples!'

Bear in mind that extroverts need recognition from others. For an extrovert child, it is particularly good if you emphasize the positives: how well he or she has done their homework, what a nice Mother's Day gift he or she gave, how much a phone call meant to a friend …

5. **Encourage a longer attention span.**

When it comes to schooling, extrovert children generally have few problems with oral work or with group work. What they do find challenging is concentrating on a subject for a long period of time by themselves, during a quiet working session or a class project, but also when it comes to doing homework.

It is possible to train children to concentrate better. Show your child how to divide larger tasks into smaller steps. Praise him or her when he or she completes an extensive task. Let your child switch between different activities – but only after spending a certain amount of time on an activity, which you should try to gradually lengthen. Alternatively, turn it into a kind of sporting competition: how many maths problems can your child solve in 20 minutes? This kind of friendly challenge is a particularly good way to motivate extrovert children.

## Living with both the strengths and the obstacles

The sooner your children learn to recognize their strengths and obstacles, and the more they feel accepted and loved as they are, the better it will be for their future lives. Growing up in a family where the traits of all family members are given plenty of space and respect is a good preparation for adult life – for social interactions and for living with oneself.

---

### ✳ Key points in brief

- Sharing your life with others is enriching for introverts as well as for extroverts, although introverts may find it easier than extroverts to lead a fulfilling life alone.

- A quiet person can deploy 'introverted person' strengths in **looking for a partner**.

- A **relationship** can be successful with either an introvert or an extrovert as a partner. However, in each case there are different things to take into account and different obstacles to overcome.

- It is essential to recognize and to respect both one's own needs and the needs of the other person – in terms of communication and in terms of living together. When a couple see themselves as a team, it is easier to see the differences as mutually enriching.

- **Quiet people living alone** may be happy with their lifestyle but may also run a risk of becoming isolated, stagnated in their personal development. Choosing the right activities and rituals can be a good way to prevent this.

- Like couple relationships, **living in a family with children** works best when every member of the family has enough space for his or her needs and temperament. On the one hand, this calls for consideration and a willingness to compromise, but it also teaches people how to understand one another.

- **Introvert and extrovert children** have their own special needs in relation to communication and personal development. In bringing up children, it is an advantage for everyone involved if parents know their own personality traits and needs and are able to provide their children with the right support.

---

# 5.

# Public and human: shaping your workplace

Simon is 27 and works in the project team in a large pharmaceutical company. He shares an office with his colleague Boris. Simon is a quiet person and works best and most effectively when he can concentrate on one thing for a long time, preferably without background noise.

One thing is driving him mad, slowly but surely: Boris is completely incapable of sitting at his desk and working consistently, even for half an hour. After a quarter of an hour at the longest he either goes over to the telephone or leaves the office. He usually tells Simon why he is doing this. Simon is also the first person Boris turns to when he is stuck on something: he prefers to solve problems by discussing them with other people. Boris's behaviour regularly tears Simon away from his work, and he finds it difficult to get back into it – all the more so as he is usually frustrated and cross. Does Boris notice that he is creating a disturbance? Even when Simon plucks up courage and raises the matter of working together in the office (as he has tried a few times), it only gets better for a short time. Then Boris slips back into his usual pattern.

## We cannot choose our colleagues

You can only choose who you work with to a limited extent in a professional context. Colleagues, clients, management all have personalities of their own, and their own aims, feelings, interests and foibles. This can be stressful – particularly for quiet people, who work best when they are left in peace. It doesn't affect everyone as badly as the quiet and sensitive Simon, who has to share an office with super-extrovert Boris.

## Introvert success in all sectors

But quiet people are not a minority! This means that introverts are not just analysts, auditors, researchers and IT specialists. It is true in all sectors that introverts are (at least) as successful as extroverts – with their own resources and strengths. They are also significantly more successful in some spheres: for example, the digital revolution and the development of social networks could not have happened without tenacious introvert geeks hammering away at a particular topic. (On the other hand, there would certainly be fewer hackers …)

## Introvert success in the normal working day

This chapter is not intended to replace careers and management or executive manuals. Here, too, the emphasis is on quiet people's strengths and needs, but in a professional context. The subjects we are dealing with here cover the most important questions and pressure points that introverts very often come across in public life. How do you work together professionally in teams? How do you manage people as a quiet person in a way that you are comfortable with? How do you demonstrate your achievements – particularly when you don't like talking about what you can do and what you have achieved? How can you as an introvert use channels of communication in a way that meets your needs? The chapter finishes with a stress factor that is not very visible, but all the more tangible for that, and one that a lot of quiet people have to cope with: how can introverts look after their own well-being on business trips? But fundamentally it is about one big question: how do you design your communication so that it suits you and makes you professionally successful?

The important spheres of professional life such as customer relations, negotiating, lecturing in public and communication in meetings are dealt with in more detail in Chapters 6 to 9.

# Quiet people in teams

## Are introverts incapable of working in teams?

Quiet people like working on their own and are more intensively occupied with internal processes. This arouses the suspicion that they are less good as team players than their extrovert colleagues, who can even derive energy from teamwork. But that is not true. Some projects would fail without introverts, thus seriously limiting some teams' performance. Two other statements are certainly true. Firstly, introverts in teams are easily underestimated and, secondly, introverts often behave differently in teams from extroverts.

# The underestimated team player

Quiet people are quiet – why should they be any different in a team? This quietness can also work very well in a group if the quiet team members' achievements are acknowledged. This depends on various factors: on the professional milieu, the company culture, the attitude of colleagues and managers – and also on the introvert–extrovert make-up of the teams.

Sarah, an acquaintance, worked until a few months ago for the human resources department of a large group of British companies. She and one other introvert colleague were clearly a minority as quiet people among markedly extrovert personalities. Her very extrovert team leader made it clear to her that she no longer wanted her in the team: Sarah seemed too colourless to her, and she felt she showed little initiative. Sarah got the message, applied for a better position, and got the job. Because Sarah did not communicate them emphatically enough, her extrovert boss had completely failed to see her qualities – she was an outstanding researcher, expert in drawing up documents, and had excellent contacts in many areas of the business. The boss did not notice the gap until problems cropped up – information channels had broken off, documents were criticized for lack of clarity. However, in this case her ex-boss was sufficiently fair to tell Sarah this, and to admit that she had misjudged her.

## When qualities go unnoticed

A lot of introverts have the same experience as Sarah: they are underestimated, even though their strengths enable them to perform in a way that considerably enhances the team's achievements. So there is something wrong – extroverts are not aware of their introvert colleagues' qualities. But that is only half the truth: the fact is that these introvert colleagues themselves do too little to ensure that their strengths and achievements are noticed.

# Introvert teamwork

## Making achievements visible

So the key question is: how can you as an introvert work and communicate in your team in such a way that you and your achievements are appropriately visible? And what can you do besides to feel as comfortable as possible with your colleagues – and they with you?

## Strategies for good teamwork

Good answers to this question should meet two conditions: they should consider first your needs and then the needs of the extrovert members of the group (it's simple with the introverts …). The following strategies aim to bring these two points of view together.

 **Communicate effectively in the team: you will then be combining your needs with the needs of others**

1. **Your need: to work alone for a long time without disturbance**

   *Extrovert need*: to work in stages, discuss findings and results and where to go next with others

   *Strategy:* Create rituals for exchanging ideas and information that you and your colleagues can follow, and that will leave you the scope to be able to concentrate on your own work as well.

   *Suggestions:*

   - Get to work earlier, or stay on when the others leave: use this 'lonely' time to stick at a piece of work for longer.
   - Stay on after meetings to talk things over with the others. Build this time in explicitly.
   - Agree with colleagues for a time slot each day in which you can work without interruptions.
   - Divide your work into daily portions and break off after a time to talk to the others about it. Use email and telephone for this as well.
   - If colleagues appear unannounced, you can fix a different time if you can't see them then: 'I'm just working on something urgent. Have you time for a coffee after lunch?' N.B.: This is not appropriate in crisis situations of all kinds!
   - Talk to colleagues about your work. Be specific: 'How that client responded last week …' This kind of attentiveness goes down very well.

2. **Your need: arranging peace and quiet from time to time**

   *Extrovert need:* to arrange discussions with others from time to time

   *Strategy:* At events or even on ordinary days deliberately build in phases when you can talk things over with colleagues. Plan downtime in the same way.

*Suggestions:*

- Treat your work as a theatre stage. Absence requires a certain presence. Make opportunities to leave the stage from time to time in order to rest: this could be a walk in the lunch break, and in especially stressful situations even a mini-break in the toilet cubicle.

- Arrange to meet someone for lunch. A lot of quiet people like lunching with one or two other people. Pay full attention to the people you are with.

- Miss small modules at events or seminars – one lecture, for example. Use the time you gain to relax.

- To make this easier, find out what the team's informal rules are: which social events and encounters are important and which aren't? Act appropriately. This means:

  - Have the courage not to join in with low-priority arrangements – for instance, a drink in the bar after an exhausting day at an event. Make up for staying away by joining in with another activity while your energy levels are still relatively high. For example, go on the first evening, for example, but not on the second.

  - Suggest activities you like to join in with yourself, such as trying out a new café, organizing a present for a colleague's special birthday.

3. **Your need: talk less – work more**

*Extrovert need:* to use communication to show you who you are dealing with and what impression you are making

*Strategy:* Communicate with a clear end in mind.

*Suggestions:*

- Particularly if you like working alone, you should collect together all your success stories. In writing. That is good for your self-confidence and it makes it easier to mention something at a suitable moment, when it will fit in: 'I've just completed a very similar project, namely ...'

- Don't see meetings as a waste of time – use the information in Chapter 9.

- Keep in touch with individuals you admire. Use the tips in Chapter 6 for this.

- Use your powers of observation and analysis: what matters to the people around you? What do they like? Show that you have noticed their interests from time to time: 'Are you still interested in the Botticelli exhibition in Berlin? My sister has just been and says it is really worth the trip.'

- Discover your personal sense of humour. Use it to attract positive attention. Exceptions: sarcasm and irony.

- Help your extrovert colleagues (and bosses!) by summing up key points in conversations or stimulate and support decisions.

- Take responsibility and communicate correspondingly: present the team's results if they are in your sphere. Explain assignments and expectations clearly when you are starting on something new or have a new colleague. Approach people if something is not working out properly.

- Make sure your communication is properly focused – be a *problem-solver* and not a *person with reservations*: so say: 'How can we make sure that the delivery still gets there on time?' rather than 'That will definitely not get there on time!' Both responses are triggered by the same situation ...

- Ensure that milestones are celebrated: by doing this you will reinforce the feeling of working together at a positive moment – and show off the team's good work. By all means invite managers to it ...

# Introvert leadership strategies

Are you a quiet person in a leading position? In that case you are in good company. There are a lot of very successful quiet bosses! There are reasons for this. In her book on introvert bosses, Jennifer Kahnweiler (2009) points out three particular strengths that quiet managers often have: firstly, they can effortlessly look beyond their own egos for the sake of their sphere of responsibility (in this book: strength 7 – independence); secondly, they are calmly self-confident (here strength 5 – calm); and thirdly, they are particularly competent socially because they can consider their colleagues and their colleagues' needs (here: strength 4 – listening, and strength 10 – empathy). Quiet bosses often give active, motivated colleagues the space to implement ideas and develop abilities.

But there are also factors that quiet executive figures have to struggle with: stress, missing networks, lack of self-projection and wrong or inadequate impressions held by others. This is linked up with quiet people's preferred modes of communication – and also the many and various obstacles you are familiar with from Chapter 3.

## Stepping out of the comfort zone

When quiet people take up management positions, it often means a big step out of the comfort zone. Suddenly it is not about tackling a manageable sphere outstandingly: they have to use their own communication skills to make various departments with all the people in them come and work together like an orchestra. If they incline to over-attention to detail (obstacle 2), avoiding contact (obstacle 9) or avoiding conflict (obstacle 10), then the boss's chair can quickly become a nightmare. The new problems and the new responsibility can quickly start to seem diffuse, incomprehensible or chaotic – and as yet they are missing the experience that made a lot of decisions easier, and speeded them up, in their former position.

There are quiet people who firmly decide against a formal executive position (or who prefer to go freelance, so that they can be as independent as possible). That is perfectly all right. However, if you are faced with a decision about whether you want to rise in the hierarchy, please be sure about one thing: it must not be stepping out of your comfort zone that stops you taking the post. As we have already said, there are some outstanding 'quiet' bosses.

Let's take a closer look: what makes these quiet bosses stand out as leadership figures? The answer is to be found in four basic strategies.

## Executive strategy 1: Build up your self-confidence

The background is simple: if you are in an executive position and not convinced about your own strengths and abilities, you will find it difficult to convince your colleagues that you have them. This is because you are emitting too many signals, on various verbal and body-language levels, that send out the message: 'Actually I don't find myself all that convincing.' This is not an invitation to perform some King Kong-like posturing – and as you are a quiet person you surely wouldn't stoop to do it anyway. But you should and could cultivate a sense of healthy self-confidence. Make yourself aware of your strengths and accept your weak points without compunction – regardless of how people around you react. Self-confidence and self-knowledge are closely linked.

YOU WILL REINFORCE YOUR SELF-ESTEEM BY REGULARLY ASKING YOURSELF: WHAT DID I DO REALLY SUCCESSFULLY TODAY? WHAT STRENGTHS WAS I ABLE TO DEPLOY?

## Keep a success diary

A lot of quiet people are very self-critical because they are constantly evaluating their behaviour, the way they communicate and their thoughts, and processing all this internally. Are you one of these? If so, it would help you to direct your thoughts towards furthering your self-esteem by asking some concrete questions. Ask yourself every evening: what did I pull off well today? What strengths was I able to deploy? If you want to reinforce your self-confidence particularly effectively, keep a diary about these successes, and make an entry in it every day. you will soon notice your perspectives changing and your self-confidence increasing.

If you think you should work harder on your self-confidence, it would probably help you to have some specific coaching with a professional expert at your side.

# Executive strategy 2: Pay full attention to the person in front of you

This second strategy is directly connected with empathy (strength 10), but also with strengths such as concentration (strength 3) and listening (strength 4). It shifts the perspective from you to the people around you – to your superiors, colleagues and co-workers.

Introverted superiors can make an increasingly strong impact by concentrating their attention directly on their opposite number. This shows particularly:

• in being able to see your opposite number as a person, not necessarily from a professional point of view (the sick child, the favourite holiday venue)

• by being able to conduct a conversation with substance

• by being able to listen without prejudice (in other words, without instant evaluation or a critical attitude) and to maintain discretion

• by being able to take other people's opinions seriously without taking status or dominance into serious consideration, and to include them in your own considerations.

## Create a strong presence through empathy

An attentive executive can radiate a powerful presence. The first executive strategy is not sufficient for this: people who rely on self-confidence alone and remain inward-looking are not necessarily effectively present – they are not connecting with the world around them, even if they pay attention to the social rituals of the exchange of views and information. We can all sense whether someone is listening to us with genuine interest and giving us undivided attention.

A boss who is attentive to her superiors, colleagues and co-workers in this way has several advantages: she has easier and better access to information because most people like speaking to her and trust her. She finds out what motivates her team members by knowing what matters to them: more time at home, a pay rise or an exciting subsequent project. She knows who is best for a particular job and who could benefit from mentoring or coaching. In short, she is completely in the picture. And the employees feel looked after and noticed.

# Executive strategy 3: Be sure to have a good overview

## Always keep an eye on company aims

Good executives look beyond the next project. They have a comprehensive grasp of their company's aims and of their department's role and capacities. This means that they can distance themselves from everyday business and it enables them to act flexibly and change their plans quickly (because unexpected things happen all the time) and fix priorities (because there is always too much to do).

## Planning: the introvert's forte

People who plan their department's aims and development also gain an overview – even when only part of the plan can actually be implemented. Planning is the forte of many quiet executives, and it fits in with their strengths: it is best done in writing (strength 9), with a detailed analytical review and a division into sub-aims with set priorities (strength 6), and with a clear view of essentials (strength 2). Tenacity (strength 8) also helps to meet the planned targets.

If you follow the third executive strategy, you will notice three things: firstly, you are effective. Secondly, you find it easier to motivate other people, fix aims and targets – especially when you also have executive strategy 2 under your belt. Thirdly, you will find it easier to communicate with your superior about your area of work and to push for decisions or speak up for them: you will start to be seen as an executive who knows exactly what she is doing. Which is true, of course!

## Executive strategy 4: Brush up your ability to conduct dialogue and deal with conflict

### Keep an eye on communication in the team

As an executive, you are not only responsible for meeting productivity targets and making sure that the work is done. Another one of your jobs is to keep an eye on communication: how well are your team members working together? How well are the other executive levels and working units in touch with each other? Who ought to get together with whom? Anyone who doesn't ask questions like these will soon be facing difficult consequences: conflicts escalate, radio silence results in loss of information and possibly resources, people failing to exchange ideas creates misunderstandings or leads to the formation of cliques.

This management strategy relies on your social skills. We shall show next where its opportunities and advantages lie, under the headings 'Dialogue' and 'Conflict'.

### Dialogue

For about 30 years the Americans have had a beautifully vivid term for successful dialogue set up by a management team: 'management by walking around'. The principle is simple: when you are walking around, be sure that you can keep meeting the people who surround you professionally and communicate with them. As a quiet person, you will find it particularly pleasing in this context when you meet just one person, or at least only a few. You will also get to hear more – more can be talked about by just two people or in a small group than in a full team meeting.

So get yourself on the move: meet superiors, colleagues and employees where they work (or even eat). Use business trips, lifts, times when you are waiting with other people and social occasions to get into conversation. Use executive strategy 2 and pay full attention to whoever you are talking to. Be an approachable boss!

PRACTISE MANAGEMENT BY WALKING AROUND.

You will achieve two things by 'management by walking around': firstly, you will find out more. About atmosphere (among other things about conflicts and bullying; see below), news and surprises, confidential and private matters, potentials and problems. Secondly, you will become an astonishingly popular manager – and you will be seen as a person with a finger on the pulse of the business. After all, what is that pulse other than things that concern the people around you?

## Conflict

Conflict is completely normal. People are different – different in what they feel, want or do, in their habits and idiosyncrasies. One thing is absolutely true of all manner of working contexts in which people (in other words, colleagues, clients and business partners) of different generations, traditions and cultures come across each other: personality differences often lead to conflict if there are disagreements. The two office colleagues Simon and Boris that you met at the beginning of the chapter differ in areas that clearly have conflict potential.

## Conflict can mean opportunities

But disagreements alone do not necessarily lead to genuine friction. They can be recognized because they become an emotional burden to the people involved and impact negatively on the workplace. Conflicts carry a risk: if they are not addressed and dealt with, they do not go away, but grow – and so do the sense of burden and the negative impact. Serious conflicts can completely cripple a team's ability to work together. But, if conflicts are addressed and discussed, they also offer opportunities: then a conflict can be a seismograph for trouble, measuring 'communication levels' and thus helping to improve communication, but also situations, processes or general behaviour. And this improvement is another job for management.

## Address conflict actively

For these two reasons – possible damage and possible improvement – executives should be able to deal with conflict actively and to adapt their communication strategies to the personality differences – in other words, to suit Japanese and French people, trainees and senior management, and of course introverts and extroverts. You met Simon and Boris at the beginning of this chapter. Their boss realized that there was tension between them – and defused the situation by giving Simon his own little office when the project section moved buildings, and putting Boris in an office for two with another extrovert.

## Workplace bullying

Conflict management also means dealing with workplace bullying. If you keep up a proper dialogue with your employeesz you will most probably come across trouble in the workplace. Butz as a quiet personz you will probably find it difficult to talk about unpleasant things and to do something about them – particularly if escape (obstacle 5) or avoiding conflict (obstacle 10) are among your characteristics. Don't worry about it too much: conflict is a minefield for extroverts too!

# Making your achievements known

## Why introverts miss out on promotion

However effective and high-powered quiet people may be at work, they usually have a problem in one area: they don't like blowing their own trumpet and are critical of 'drum-beaters and hot-air merchants'. That is one side of the coin. The other side is that quiet people are often overlooked for promotion – simply because the decision-makers do not know enough about their achievements and successes.

**?** **Two questions for you**

What chance do you think you have of implementing the four executive strategies successfully? How can you improve on the individual strategies?

| Executive strategy | My abilities | Approach to improvement |
| --- | --- | --- |
| 1. Building up self-confidence | _____ | _____ |
| 2. Paying attention | _____ | _____ |
| 3. Gaining an overview | _____ | _____ |
| 4. Honing conflict management and dialogue skills | _____ | _____ |

## Principles for successful communication at work

The success strategy obviously lies somewhere in between: you should not beat your own drum or become a hot-air merchant – but you should make sure that your achievements are sufficient and appropriately visible. The following principles will help you to communicate your own strengths and successes.

**!** **Communicating for the sake of your career: five principles for every day**

**Principle 1: Keep your superiors in the picture – and, above all, be sure what you are doing yourself!**

Write down everything you see as an achievement: sales successes, completed projects, solved problems, successful communication with (difficult) colleagues and clients. You can easily forget things you don't write down. Even more important: your list of successes will help you if you are often very self-critical. Think about it: if you are not convinced about your own achievements, how are other people supposed to be? Avoid unduly fierce self-criticism and inappropriate perfectionism by listing your achievements objectively. This will teach you at the same time to take them into account ...

Look at the list every six months, take a sheet of A4 paper and sum up your notable achievements in this period. If you are employed and work to targets agreed with your superiors, these targets form an excellent basis – and provide you with arguments for a pay rise! Perhaps even more important is the fact that you have a complete sense of 'your' portfolio of successes. This makes you pay attention to what you have achieved, something that is all too often neglected. You are also more clearly aware of what you find easy and what interests you. The effect: boosted self-confidence!

You will be most successful in implementing this principle if you know want counts in your professional context:

• What counts as success?

• What is thought to be particularly important?

• What skills are particularly required?

Be sure that the successes you note down fit in with the answers to these questions.

This principle also works very well with superiors who are inclined to micro-manage: make a practice of regularly sending them (at the end of each week or every two weeks, for example) a brief summary of the state of play in current projects, on a single page at the most, and it is fine to divide it up according to a particular pattern. Tried and tested headings are: title, progress (in bullet points), to do, questions to settle. The person who receives this information on Fridays can relax.

### Principle 2: Establish contacts with colleagues and superiors

Achievements reveal themselves typically on professional occasions such as discussions with employees, meetings and lectures. But this 'official' communication does nothing but provide a platform to ensure that you can be seen; you must also establish your own professional network inside and outside your workplace. Go for lunch with selected colleagues. Go to informal events like birthday parties. Make reliable friends. Executive strategy 4 and Chapter 6 will help you to implement this principle.

## Principle 3: Show what you are interested in

If you regularly follow principle 1, you will know what you find easy and what interests you. You base possible career progress on this: the best thing is to head for where you like working and work well.

But the people around you are not clairvoyants. So, if you are interested in a particular project or field of work, you should mention it (casually) to the right people. And you will find that easier if you follow principle 2 ...

## Principle 4: Take responsibility

There are a lot of things you can do that are not necessarily 'your job', but that show what you can do. Make a conscious decision to go for a particular piece of work and take responsibility for it.

This could mean negotiating with a difficult client whom other people avoid. It could also mean speaking to a management committee. Have some points in mind when you go to meetings – have them put on the agenda in your name and pluck up courage to present the situation as it stands or give progress reports, even if your superiors are at the meeting.

Taking responsibility means being visible: other people notice what you stand for and what you are doing. Responsibility also implies risk: you could come to grief with a piece of work, and that will be noticed too. But, if careers were that easy, anyone could bring it off!

## Principle 5: Delegate responsibility

No, this does not contradict the previous principle. You can only take responsibility by delegating certain things that will activate other people and that are no longer a challenge to you. Even if you find it difficult, go ahead – delegate to your employees – give up responsibility if you believe that the person concerned can handle things. The result: good people are motivated when they are challenged – and therefore noticed. So you will find it easier to attract good people to your team. This strategy is beneficial for you personally because it gives you more time for your own areas of responsibility, the ones you classed as important under principle 4.

But be careful: delegating responsibility has its price as well. It could be that you will have to give Joanne some guidance before she can organize the event. This takes time. It could also be that Richard cannot handle the presentation, in which case you are responsible as well, as his immediate superior. The same is true as in principle 4: responsibility also represents a risk. But the possible gains are that your burden is eased once Joanne is in the picture and has gained her first co-ordination experience. And, when Richard has mastered the art of giving presentations, you will be on the winning side as well.

# Make use of communication channels

Telephone and email are by far the commonest communication channels in professional life, along with personal contact. Smartphones that also send and receive emails mean that we are always available even when not in our professional surroundings – or at least a lot of people we communicate with take that for granted.

Most people favour one of the two channels. In my experience, most quiet people prefer email to the telephone – for reasons which will become clear in subsequent sections. But, setting preferences aside, the nature of the matter in hand and the person involved in the dialogue sometimes make email more appropriate and sometimes the phone, so we need both these modes of communication in business life. We are going on to address the question of how you, as a quiet person, can use them in the best way for yourself and other people. But note one thing: there are certain situations in which you should only communicate face to face – for example, if you are notifying someone of a pregnancy, sacking an employee or communicating criticism.

# Telephoning

Quiet people and telephones do not always mix. A lot of quiet people feel interrupted when the phone rings. This applies particularly to people who like to work on a project in long sessions, but it is also true in general: a phone call makes you lose concentration, and energy as well – introverts feel slightly pressurized by a telephone receiver. There are two principle reasons for this: for one thing, the person taking the call has to tune in directly to the caller and what he or she wants. This is more difficult than at a face-to-face meeting because, apart from the information gained from the voice (i.e. pitch, volume, speed and intonation), there is no body language to help with interpretation. Also, an immediate response to what has been said is expected on the telephone; unlike writing an email, there is no time lapse. This means that quiet people often don't just feel interrupted when the phone rings, they feel hijacked by this mode of communication. Extroverts often see a phone call as an opportunity to exchange ideas in the interim and see it less as an interruption than a pleasant stimulus from the outside world.

FOR QUIET PEOPLE, A PHONE CALL OFTEN MEANS STRESS AND A FEELING OF BEING HELPLESS IN THE FACE OF A SITUATION.

## Phone calls as a challenge

Quiet people are also more hesitant when it comes to ringing someone up themselves. There are two particular reasons for this. Firstly, introverts are more likely than extroverts to worry that the call might be inconvenient for the person they want to talk to and be a nuisance – whether it is a client, a boss or a colleague. The background to this must be their own reactions to phone calls: if introverts find the telephone a disturbance, they are likely to feel that other people will react in the same way when rung up. Secondly, a phone call is a leap into the unknown if you are making it yourself: what if the boss suddenly comes up with an additional matter, or if the client you are calling complains about something? What if the colleague wants to chat about this and that and the call goes on for ever? It is a particular 'toughness test' on introverts if they have to ring up someone they don't know: that is a major leap into the unknown. Introverts in call centres are probably genuine rarities …

## Tips for stress-free phoning

Two questions remain for good office communications: when should you ring someone up rather than sending an email? And how do you reduce the stress that phoning and receiving calls can so easily cause for introverts?

 **Telephoning: benefits and stress limitation**

**Ring someone up**

- if you can explain something briefly, directly and rapidly: in that case, phoning rather than sending an email will save you time

- if you want to tell the person you are calling about something 'sensitive' that should not be put into writing beforehand (or that could easily be misunderstood). The tone of your voice provides additional information, and the phone is the most discreet means of communication in this case if you are unable to meet personally
- if you need to negotiate something. For example, if you are trying to reach an agreement about a sales price, a telephone call is more discreet than a written email because of the 'sensitive' subject matter. And you will also spare yourself constant electronic to-ing and fro-ing until you reach an agreement.

## How to take the difficulty out of phoning

*If you are ringing up*

Make notes before the call. Write down headings to help you through the call: unanswered questions, concerns, points of information – whatever will be important in the call. The advantage is that you are making use of strength 7, writing, and thus have a clear line in front of you. If the phone call is particularly important and/or you are particularly uncertain, you can even write down your opening gambit and your conclusion.

You can also use this line if you don't get through to the person in question and so have to leave a message on an answering machine or voicemail. You can't correct or delete a message once it has been recorded. But don't worry: if you allow for the possibility of having to leave a message by formulating headings, then talking to a machine is much less stressful and means less time for thinking things over and fewer unconsidered words, which make you sound as though you are not on top of things.

A good answering machine message should be terse. Put the following information together as full sentences:

- your name
- the reason for your call
- your phone number
- what you want to pass on: what should the recipient of the call do?
- and end up with a friendly goodbye (example: 'Thank you very much in advance for ringing back – Susan Williams').

If you're worried about disturbing someone, say from the outset: 'I need about five minutes. Is this a good moment?' This question is particularly important if you are calling a mobile: you don't know where the recipient is at the moment. If you sense that your opposite number is under pressure, agree on a better time to ring – and a time you can manage and handle with a low threshold of inhibition.

*If someone rings you*

First ask yourself: Can I take a call now, and do I want to? It's sometimes easier to decide if you recognize the caller's number ...

If the answer is 'Yes', keep the call short (unless of course you want to go into something in depth). Establish a time frame straight away ('Can we get through it in five minutes? I've got until ten o'clock.') to give a clear guideline to long-winded people at the other end. If you haven't done this, you can also end the call with an eye on the time: 'I think we've sorted out the most important things. Thank you. I've got a meeting/an appointment now.' And remember that a meeting with yourself is a meeting too. You do not need to be specific ...

If the answer is 'No', let voicemail or the answering machine take a message. Ring back at a time that suits you – or send an email if you would rather deal with things in this way.

This may seem obvious, but I have often found that it is precisely people who don't like phoning who aren't comfortable about letting the phone ring unanswered. Remember this: the telephone is there to serve you, and not vice versa!

# Emails

Quiet people prefer emails as a means of communication for several reasons: first of all they are written, and thus fit in with strength 9. They leave the writer more time to think and formulate than the telephone. It's easy to convey any number of figures to people in a single message, which makes group communication possible even though each individual works alone – a major advantage for quiet people who value working in this way. Emails are more comfortable than any word-of-mouth conversation – energy levels are low because it is possible to communicate and be alone at the same time.

## Email as a speedy medium

And emails have one quality that many introverts can easily overlook: they are fast despite the fact that they are written. What I am trying to say is that many extroverts do not choose their words very carefully and are quick to press 'send' rather than reading through what is on the screen. Also, the choice of words in emails tends to be less formal than letters, and has a great deal in common with spoken communication in terms of style. I am saying this because introverts are inclined to take their own careful approach to formulation as a given for people who write to them. This means that they can be quick to assume that the words in emails mean more than they actually do, so a hastily written, sloppy formulation can easily seem threatening, and an unduly short answer can seem like a put-down.

'Speedy' also means that the sender of an email expects a quick answer, as in spoken exchanges. So anyone who is slow to reply causes corresponding frustration or uncertainty: did my original message get there?

EMAILS ARE WRITTEN, BUT THEY HAVE SOME OF THE ATTRIBUTES OF SPOKEN COMMUNICATION.

## Lack of non-verbal signals

There is one key feature of spoken communication that emails lack: they do not convey any non-verbal messages. Tone of voice is very revealing on the telephone – for example, how important a message is or how seriously people mean what they are saying. If we have a person in front of us, we can also see his or her gestures, movements and physical attitude – and we build the messages that we see and hear beyond the words into our understanding of the speaker's intentions. This is not possible by email. There is only one kind of information category in them: the written word alone. Adding in 'emoticons' does not change very much – but it does show that the writer sees the complete lack of body language as a deficiency, and so puts in some 'smileys': in other words, we seldom express feelings in words – we hear and see them in between the words.

## Tending to over-interpret

Pure text conveys content only, not emotional statements. This makes it all the more likely that reflective (introvert) readers can easily be tempted to 'read something into' a written message: is the reply much briefer than the message sent? This could suggest distance. Did an email written to a client as 'Dear Mr Wilson' get the response: 'Hi Mrs Mason'? That could signal a lack of respect. If not much information is conveyed, even salutations tend to be interpreted in terms of the respect and interest they suggest. This can easily lead to misunderstandings and

alse assessments – the recipient reads into the text what he has in mind
himself; there is absolutely no alignment with the sender's action (in the
form of body language signals).

To sum up: this means do not read too much into an electronic message.
Many users formulate emails like oral statements – quick, sloppy and
without bothering very much about structure and formality.

If the recipient and the message are suitable for electronic communication,
then use it. Just bear one thing in mind: however comfortable an email
might be, it cannot and must not replace direct conversation with
superiors, employees and colleagues. So be careful that electronic
communications do not become a strategy for avoiding personal and
telephone contact with the people who work around you.

## Strategies for using email successfully

The panel below is a counterpart to the summary about telephone use
given above. It will help you to communicate successfully by email.

---

 **The best way to use emails**

**Send an email**

- if you specifically want to have something in black and white: for example,
  an agreed figure, a deadline or the distribution of work in a project. This
  can complement a telephone call, such as a negotiation, if you want to
  confirm a verbal agreement.

- if your own energy levels are low and telephone and email are just as
  appropriate for the matter in hand.

- if you are sorting out a meeting or a deadline and want all the people
  concerned to have the same information. An additional plus is that an
  email can be sent to several recipients and small documents like agendas,
  for example, can easily be attached – or even better, included in the body
  of the email.

- if you are dealing with a recipient you don't know and are not sure how he
  or she communicates verbally. An email gives you greater security (you
  have time to think!) and does not use as much energy.

Benefit from the advantages of emails – but do not let them become a
substitute for direct contact.

---

In conclusion, one last piece of advice: don't be available all the time. Fix times for telephoning and also for reading and sending emails – how frequently depends on your job. You will be surprised how much this simple strategy takes the stress out of your day!

# Business travel

## Travel as a necessary evil

Even though I really love my job, travelling to see my clients is always a necessary evil that I accept in order to be able to do what I like doing. The reason is a simple one: travelling is stressful for quiet people.

Business travel is considerably more energy-consuming for introverts than extroverts. There is often no chance to be alone, and also the large number of impressions and unexpected events drain people's resources. Here I do not mean major disasters. Late trains with uncertain connections are tiring for introverts, and so are crowded waiting or refreshment rooms, all kinds of pushing and shoving, but above all unpredictable noise levels. Doors banging or conversations in corridors, even in good hotels, are among my personal horrors. On trains, earphone wearers playing loud music make me go straight for my earplugs as a reflex action.

## Tips: what makes travelling pleasant

But there's no getting round it: travelling is simply part of professional life for a lot of quiet people. The following recommendations should help to make it easier and more attractive for you. I have been collecting them purely for my own benefit for some time now …

 **Travel tips for introverts**

1. **Look for means of getting away.**

   Means of getting away include everything that helps you to relax and above all to recharge your batteries from time to time.

   • Plan brief escapes to your hotel room at conferences or seminars. Just cut a lecture or a social event for this purpose. Or, alternatively, eat quickly and miss dessert. Pros even get in an occasional snooze.

   • If you can afford it, travel first class on the train (in the quiet coach!) and business class on planes. Just the additional space makes a big difference, and the noise level is (usually) lower.

- Washrooms. I recommend these to nervous readers as places of retreat in strange surroundings. A toilet cubicle is a protected area and thus ideal for deep breathing without an audience. (Especially if it is clean and well ventilated ...)

- Earplugs also offer a way of escape, acoustically. Always have at least one set with you. But I also know some introverts who have gone in for high-tech headphones (you know, those good noise-cancelling ones), and swear by them: you have your peace and quiet – and people almost never try to speak to you if you are wearing them.

2. **Define time spent travelling as a combination of 'contact time' and 'time on your own'.**

Of course business trips are also useful for making contacts. But make sure even at the planning stage that you also have meals and rest periods without contact. This is important for recharging the batteries. When I'm on seminar trips, I eat with the participants at the most once, and meet buyers, business contacts or friends only every second evening. Here the principle you will find in Chapter 6 about networking applies: quality rather than quantity.

Sometimes you will have to defend your 'time alone' by refusing to do something – for example, when colleagues, seminar members or other contacts invite you to come with them to a meal or an event. Refuse in a friendly way, but briefly. Don't explain too much. Try 'No, not today – but I'll see you tomorrow. Have fun tonight!'

3. **Avoid casual conversations on journeys.**

Extroverts like to chat to the people sitting by them while travelling. If you are tired, this can very quickly get on your nerves – and on top of that you can soon feel helpless in the face of the situation. But there is something very simple you can do about this: have a few sentences ready so that you can make it clear in a friendly way if the conversation or the person talking to you is getting to be too much. Here are some examples:

- 'That was a good conversation, thank you' (then look back at your computer or a sheet of paper).

- 'I ought to get on with my work now' (and then do so straight away).

- 'Right, I'm just going to close my eyes again for a bit before we land.'

- 'Thank you for your tips – and now I would like to know how this book ends.'

- 'Let's swap cards, and I'll get in touch with you again about this information.'

Sometimes you will meet interesting people on your travels who could well become networking contacts. You should be sure to exchange business cards on pleasant occasions like these so that you can stay in touch after the trip.

## ✱ Key points in brief

- Introverts are just as capable of working in **teams** as their extrovert colleagues, though they work using different means and emphases. The variety this brings into the group can prove very fruitful.

- Introverts' particular needs – working without interruption, having the occasional rest, communicating in moderation – can fit in with workplace requirements using specific strategies.

- Quiet people have a great deal of executive potential. Their recipes for success can be summed up in four **leadership strategies**: building up self-confidence, paying full attention to the person in front of you, making sure you have a good overview, and working on your personal dialogue and conflict-handling skills.

- It is important for your career to make your own **achievements known**. Any quiet person can bring this off by communicating purposefully. Five principles help with putting this into practice: keep your superiors and yourself informed, build up contacts with colleagues and superiors, show what interests you, take responsibility yourself, and delegate responsibility to others.

- Many quiet people prefer exchanging emails to telephoning as **communication tools**. Telephoning is preferable in certain circumstances and it is also possible to take a great deal of the stress out of it. Distance from the person you are communicating with can make email contact pleasanter, and is to be recommended in certain situations. But emails should not be used to avoid direct contact.

- **Business trips** can use up a lot of energy but can be made more pleasant by a few simple means: by spending time alone occasionally, by ensuring time alone before and after social occasions, and by dealing confidently with people you talk to on journeys.

# Part III

How to make your presence felt and be sure you are listened to

# 6.

# Testing your courage: how to establish and cultivate contacts

We human beings are social creatures. This is why we keep meeting other people all the time – not just because there is something to talk about or to be done, but also because we simply like being in touch with other people. In principle, anyway.

Anne (40) needs this sort of informal contact for her work. She is a flexi-introvert (one of the socially accessible introverts you met in Chapter 1 and she likes handling people. She is in charge of the press and public relations department of a medium-sized company and likes dealing with a whole range of types: with journalists just as much as with colleagues in almost all her firm's departments.

Anne works long hours, with a lot of variety and frequent interruptions: people appear in her doorway, the telephone rings. And so Anne loves to put her feet up with a good book in the evenings and have a rest. But that doesn't always happen: it is taken for granted in her job that she will attend events and also be present at various social occasions in the evenings. And it's also quite clear to Anne how important it is to make and cultivate contacts informally. But she still feels that, after evenings like this, she has talked a lot without achieving much. Only recently – at a major conference in Switzerland – she found it particularly tiresome after a long day full of lectures to get talking to people she didn't know in the evening. She stayed for an hour and a half, and then went wearily back to her hotel room.

## Cultivating contacts and small talk

Anne doesn't get much out of most social occasions and notices that casual small talk can easily leave her exhausted. But it is precisely after the 'compulsory events' that conversation with colleagues and business contacts (and also interesting strangers) makes for contact that is more relaxed than during the working day. Cultivating relationships is central to small talk – even when it seems to turn around food or the new offices. Personal and professional networks are not built up during the official programme of an event. Genuine contacts come from conversations with the people you are sitting next to, during coffee breaks or when having a beer together in the bar, long after the lecture hall is empty.

## Exchanging information unofficially

But the silly thing is that when extroverts are cracking open a bottle of wine after the long keynote speech, arranging to meet each other for breakfast or holding mini conferences in the corridor introverts prefer to use these 'unofficial' time slots to rest after the hubbub or to go jogging on their own. I keep recommending short spells of time off in this book, but they too should be used sparingly. Otherwise they can create a personal disadvantage: opinions are tested against each other on all these informal occasions, decisions considered, alliances formed. It is away from the conference room and your desk that you show how well you fit into the team. And you will also gain access to information that you would not have until later officially. Or not at all.

BUILDING UP RELATIONSHIPS IS A REQUIRED PROFESSIONAL SKILL.

## Building up networks in your own way

The ability to take advantage of social occasions, master small talk and build up networks is just as important for introverts as for extroverts. But there is one essential difference: extroverts like all these activities and the stimulation that comes from them. But introverts often find them stressful and find that informal conversation is not much fun (see above). Every network has to be cultivated, expanded and sometimes repaired as well, so that it can fulfil its function. This requires a certain amount of single-mindedness and the investment of time, energy and possibly also money. But introverts can also make these investments successfully, and enjoy doing so – provided that they run the networks in their own way. In concrete terms, this means that networking for quiet people is different in quality, and also has different goals. Introverts like Anne are not so bothered about stimulation. They are not only perfectly happy to have lunch on their own, but actually relish the time to themselves. And they don't need a large circle of acquaintances either, but are quite content with a few really good contacts. What is important to them is the quality of a relationship: it needs to be long-lasting, and to make personal sense to them.

A CONTACT THAT QUIET PEOPLE VALUE HAS TO BE LONG-LASTING AND MEANINGFUL.
QUALITY IS MORE IMPORTANT THAN QUANTITY.

There is a kind of networking that quiet people find pleasant that accommodates these preferences. It is suitably different from the kind of contact development that extroverts prefer. This chapter deals with this particular kind of introvert networking.

## Cultivating contacts: networking

Networking covers everything concerned with the topic of contacts: we all live in networks of relationships, privately and professionally. We know people – and people know us. We meet in families and circles of friends, in sports clubs and while having a drink with a regular group, in professional associations and Rotary clubs, at receptions and conferences. Networking can happen whenever you are not alone: at a family celebration, a party, your daughter's swimming gala or in the checkout queue when shopping. To cut a long story short, all networking activities are about deliberately establishing and cultivating contacts.

### A place for exchanging information

Networks are not cliques or conspiracy clubs (though there are institutions that are difficult or impossible to access). Basically, they are huge locations where information can be exchanged. We live in a world that offers us a lot, and also requires us to make a lot of decisions. That is why we are happy to listen to people who make it easier for us to decide – for example, when we are looking for a doctor or an accountant, a graphic designer or a good babysitter. This also applies to people responsible for staffing: networking expert Monika Scheddin estimates that 85 per cent of all management job appointments are made via contacts – in other words, they go to known people who have been recommended.

So what we are talking about here is encounters with people that you associate with and stay associated with voluntarily. Sometimes these people are organized and linked by a common interest – for example, in a group representing certain interests or at a sports club. But networks are quite often not regulated formally – for example, a group of neighbours or of friends from college or university who meet up once a year. Both introverts and extroverts benefit from these more or less close connections via networks. They can offer guidance (access to information, professional prospects, support and further training, comparison with colleagues, advice and feedback from competent people of a like mind) or platforms (initiating co-operation and business contacts, making your own performance visible).

## Benefiting from networks

Networks can also take some of the strain, by relieving you of a project that is too far beyond your key skills, for eaxample. Or a group baby-sitting arrangement! And many networks can add to your quality of life by providing shared sport and leisure activities, even if they have some relevance to your job: from playing golf to mountaineering and from group travel or relaxed evenings by the fire to joint cooking activities. There is one thing all joint networking activities have in common: they offer mutual benefit to all active participants.

THE KEY QUESTION: HOW CAN YOU, AS A QUIET PERSON, NETWORK IN SUCH A WAY THAT SUITS YOU AND ENABLES YOU TO USE YOUR STRENGTHS?

There are many clever guides to the subject of networking. I want to ask one question again here: how can you, as a quiet person, network with an eye to your strengths and needs – in other words, in a way that suits you? I'm restricting myself here to strategies that offer an answer to this question. You can work out your own plan at the same time: you will find questions after every strategy that will lead you step by step towards your own personal networking activities.

# Strategy 1: Set yourself clearly defined aims

Your analytical skills (strength 6) will help you when you are planning with a definite end in mind, but so will reducing things to essentials (substance, strength 2) and your ability to concentrate (strength 3).

## ? Two questions for you

1. What aims are you pursuing with your networking activities?

| Private aims | Professional aims |
|---|---|
| hobbies (including sport) | contact with colleagues |
| easing the burden (e.g. support) | sharing information |
| personal development | help, additional training |
| shared experiences | comparison with others |
| new stimuli | new career prospects |

2. So which networks are of interest to you?

   Formulate your answers as precisely as possible.

| Private networks | Professional networks |
|---|---|
| (e.g. societies, initiatives, friends) | (e.g. organisations, clubs, close colleagues) |
| _____ | |
| | _____ |
| _____ | _____ |
| _____ | _____ |
| _____ | _____ |
| _____ | _____ |

   Now try to draw up a ranking table: number the networks you have listed
   in each column separately according to their importance – so the most
   important private and professional networks get a 1, the next a 2, and so on …

When you have filled in this box with your answers, you will know where
it is worth your while to invest your energy and other resources.

## Strategy 2: Define your resources

As a quiet person, you are particularly well aware that the resources that
matter for the networks are not limitless. So it is all the more important
that for this second strategic step you make a conscious decision about
how much time and energy you want to 'spend', and on what.

### ? Two more questions for you

1. Which of the following resources can you, and do you want to, invest in
   your networking activities?

| Private networks | Professional networks |
|---|---|
| Time:_____ | Time:_____ |
| (per day/week/month?) | (per day/week/month?) |

   You need time for things such as attending events, cultivating contacts,
   communication and for (honorary) posts.

**Money:** _____        **Money:**_____

(per day/week/month?)              (per day/week/month?)

You need money for things such as membership fees, travel expenses, board and lodging and also attendance fees.

2. Now allocate things more specifically: what proportion of your time and money do you want to invest in each network? Under 'use' state what exactly you will use each of them for.

At this point you should take into account the priorities you set earlier under strategy 1 (question 2): the more important the network, the more resources you should invest.

| **Private networks** | **Professional networks** |
|---|---|
| Network:_____ Use:_____ | Network:_____ Use:_____ |
| Time:_____ Money:_____ | Time:_____ Money:_____ |
| Network:_____ Use:_____ | Network:_____ Use:_____ |
| Time:_____ Money:_____ | Time:_____ Money:_____ |
| Network:_____ Use:_____ | Network:_____ Use:_____ |
| Time:_____ Money:_____ | Ime:_____ Money:_____ |
| Network:_____ Use:_____ | Network:_____ Use:_____ |
| Time:_____ Money:_____ | Time:_____ Money:_____ |
| Network:_____ Use:_____ | Network:_____ Use:_____ |
| Time:_____ Money:_____ | Time:_____ Money:_____ |
| Network:_____ Use:_____ | Network:_____ Use:_____ |
| Time:_____ Money:_____ | Time:_____ Money:_____ |

## Decide on use of resources

Strong points such as analysis, substance and concentration will get you through the first two strategies in your networking activities without your needing to make an undue effort: you decide on your resources, and also how you would prefer to deploy them. When you put your plans into practice, it is possible that your priorities might shift, or you might use them differently from the way you had planned. Both of these things are OK: the most important thing is to have a master plan that makes sense for you and, above all, that will give you some ideas about definite steps that you could take in your own contact management.

Let us now move on to two strategies that take account of how you like to communicate as a quiet person.

# Strategy 3: Introduce people you know to each other

## Allow others to benefit from each other

Let me repeat that most quiet people prefer talking to one or two people rather than talking in groups. Their strengths include caution (strength 1), which in its restrictive form as fear or anxiety (obstacle 1) can make establishing a contact with completely unknown people feel more like an unpleasant experience. This third strategy takes this tendency into account and is as simple as it is effective: introduce people from your circle of acquaintances to each other if you think that they have something to say and can benefit from each other.

## Make a name for yourself by mediating

Communicate by using social media (see later in this chapter) and in conversation when one of your contacts has published or achieved something interesting: perhaps a book, an interview or an honour such as a prize, for example. This is how to get to know your acquaintances better. Making positive references to other people and actively establishing connections means that you make a positive impression as well: you create benefits for the people concerned and become visible yourself as someone who likes drawing attention to others and creating benefits for them. This is advanced, ingenious networking.

Planning your first six attempts at mediation.

---

## ❓ Another question for you

Which people can you put in touch with each other?

| **Private networks** | **Public networks** |
|---|---|
| Who:_____ | Who:_____ |
| With whom:_____ | With whom:_____ |
| Why:_____ | Why:_____ |
| Who:_____ | Who:_____ |
| With whom:_____ | With whom:_____ |

Why_____    Why_____
Who:_____    Who:_____
With whom:_____    With whom_____
Why_____    Why_____
Who:_____    Who:_____
With whom:_____    With whom_____
Why_____    Why_____
Who:_____    Who:_____
With whom:_____    With whom_____
Why_____    Why_____

# Strategy 4: Ask your acquaintances to introduce you to someone

This strategy complements the previous one and is based on the same principles. It too is extremely simple: you ask people you know already to introduce you to someone you would like to meet. Incidentally, this strategy works very well with high-ranking individuals who are approached by a lot of people: a common acquaintance can work wonders here. You can contribute to things working out well by thinking up a good way into the conversation. You will find suggestions about this in the section 'Contacts: take needs into account' later in this chapter.

## ? Another question for you

Which people would you like to get to know – and who could you ask to introduce you to them?

**Private networks**

Who:_____

Person making introduction:_____

Why:_____

Who:_____

Person making introduction:_____

Why:_____

**Public networks**

Who:_____

Person making introduction:_____

Why:_____

Who:_____

Person making introduction:_____

Why:_____

| Who:_____ | Who:_____ |
| Person making introduction:_____ | Person making introduction:_____ |
| Why:_____ | Why:_____ |
| Who:_____ | Who:_____ |
| Person making introduction:_____ | Person making introduction:_____ |
| Why:_____ | Why:_____ |

## Strategy 5: Be consistent

Good networking thrives above all on one quality: consistency. This means two things, as follows.

### Persevere in being active

Firstly, you should be active in a network for a long time. Only then will you become aware of the real advantages, and your work on relationships will bear fruit. It can easily take one or two years (depending on how frequent the meetings are) in networks that rely on personal rather than digital encounters for you to become established as a member and build up reliably lasting contacts – provided that you actually are active. Non-active members do not establish contacts. So keep at it patiently: your tenacity (strength 8) will help you out here.

### Network accounting

Secondly, consistency means establishing your contacts patiently and then cultivating them. This involves communicating with people you find interesting in a particular network. And this in its turn requires you to keep some sort of account of the events you attend: who did you meet? What did you find interesting? What information about the person you talked to do you want to retain?

A lot of experienced networkers use computers to collect this information: this works on digital networks such as LinkedIn, though you can only list people who are active there with contact data. And there are also a lot of contact management programs and apps that you can use, and some email programs offer contact management options. In short: simply try out what appeals to you.

So, you see, the administrative efforts needed are not limitless. Your important capital for this fifth strategy is your own systematic analytical thinking (strength 6) and the above-mentioned tenacity.

---

**?  More questions for you**

1. Explain how precisely you have recorded the contacts you want to establish and cultivate until now?
2. What do you need to cultivate your contacts even better?
3. How can you get hold of the necessary aids?
4. How long will it take you to deal with the necessary changes?

---

Now we have come to the end of this section you have your own first plan, which will help you to be able to network positively and 'quietly' from now on. Start putting it into practice soon!

# Contacts: quiet people's strong sides

## Quiet contact strategies

Quiet people have particular strengths that make it easy and pleasant to deal with other people. These strengths are a kind of capital in social dealings – and at the same time the best starting point for demonstrating the contact strategies that are particularly appropriate for quiet people. The thing is that we are all good at things we find easy. So let us glance at things that quiet people are usually good at when dealing with others.

## Strength 4: Listening

It helps to keep your ears open

Being able to listen: that is one of the great strengths quiet people have in conversation. Quiet people have to rely less than their extrovert contemporaries on responses and confirmation from the people they are talking to. But introverts like to collect impressions and information – and the best way to do this is to keep your ears open. If someone can listen, it is wonderful for the person they are talking to: attention is being paid, and so there is a space in which they can express themselves without any sense of pressure. What they say is being taken in. Extroverts like to sort their thoughts out while they are speaking (while introverts prefer to use ideas that have been carefully thought through and precisely formulated – perhaps). This attentiveness does just as much good to them as to another introvert who they may be having a conversation with, who can (for once) express himself without feeling under pressure.

## Genuine listening boosts presence

Listening comes in various qualities. It is at its best when the listener's ear is open in two ways at the same time: firstly, the person it belongs to is unprejudiced in the best cases, and curious about what the other person is saying. In other words, he does not allow himself to be constrained by prior assumptions or stereotypes, nor is he bored. Secondly, the listener has free capacity behind his ears – that is to say, he is not trying to put what he wants to say next into words while the other person is talking. This kind of attentiveness shows best when listening with good, deliberate eye contact. But you cannot fake this particular kind of attention while listening in the long run: real listening gives you presence and intensity thanks to your ready ear, and that is much more than a body language strategy. Learn to appreciate the fact that you have this strength: a lot of extroverts have to make a major effort to acquire it.

Anne, who you met at the beginning of this chapter, hadn't really been aware of her listening strength until now. In the meantime she has become very skilful indeed at deliberately including what she has heard in what she says herself. She does this by following up certain points with interest or by actively taking matters alluded to into account. Anne has discovered that doing this makes her conversations much more intensive – and her contacts too!

Here are a few examples to help you to use things you hear to establish contacts.

## From listening to a genuine exchange of views: sample sentences for active listeners

- 'You just mentioned that (you once organized a conference in Leeds with this firm). How (happy were you with it)?'

- 'I will have a complete rethink about (our conference in Leeds) – now that you have (made such a convincing case for Manchester).'

- 'I keep coming back to what you just said: (is it really so important to start on the planning a full year before)?'

## Strength 5: Calm

It is said that calm is a source of power. This applies to small talk as well. Quiet people are easily distressed by, or at least uncomfortable with, restlessness and noisy surroundings, or when dealing with people who are on edge. The other side of this coin is that they are the very people to introduce calm into an encounter – and an ideal atmosphere for a relaxed exchange of views. Calm introverts are able to make space for listening, reflecting and talking by slowing the communication process down.

Seeing calm as something positive

If you are to do this, it is essential that you as a quiet person see calm as a strength: if you actually believe that talking rapidly, a very dynamic approach to raising topics or a lot of gesticulation are the best things to strive for (incidentally all typically extrovert behaviour patterns), then it is difficult to see your own calm behaviour as something especially positive.

I am going to provide you with some evidence to make you believe that a calm approach to small talk is something positive.

Keeping calm is a sign of confidence and composure

By leaving time for talking and persuading, you show that you are giving yourself space and room for manoeuvre. You are not putting yourself under pressure. Status signal experts agree that calm people show confidence, composure and high status overall.

## Seem single-minded

But for making this major impact it is essential that everything you do or say when discussing things with other people seems single-minded and definite. This is a natural way to behave, given real inner calm, and it means that all your movements – whether they involve your eyes, hands or feet – have a beginning and an end and seem motivated. You are speaking in full sentences and give the impression that you know exactly what you want to say.

## Being calm relaxes the person you are talking to

Extroverts find it easier to attract attention when talking about things. But in most cases they are not in the majority. (If you want to experience an overwhelming majority of extroverts, I recommend TV events.) As a rule you will find about 30 to 50 per cent of people tending towards introversion on social occasions. They find talking to other introverts wonderfully relaxing: talking to people who don't make them feel pressurized when exchanging ideas, and are even prepared to wait while they pause for thought or have to search for a word. Don't you find the same yourself? In Western cultures, pauses are probably the most undervalued conversational resource …

## Taking the pressure out of situations

A lot of people find small talk stressful. They feel slightly uncomfortable in social situations with people they don't know. Other introverts in particular, but also a lot of extroverts, are delighted when someone like you is able to conduct a conversation calmly and steadily, and even with some pauses. The calm and pleasant manner typical of introverts can create a sense of relaxation and calm in the exchange of ideas, and take the pressure out of the situation for everybody.

This is why extroverts also benefit from calm conversations: they give them a platform for exposition, talking, performing. It is important when dealing with extroverts for you to make it particularly clear that you are listening: by movements around your eyes and mouth, by nodding, with little phatic noises ('fillers' – as on the telephone) and by carefully aimed questions. Also be very careful to maintain eye contact.

Keeping calm saves energy

This third 'calm bonus' brings you a personal benefit. If it costs you a lot as a quiet person to communicate with other people on social occasions, it is a tangible advantage to economize on your valuable energy.

Focusing energy

Inner calm can help you to do this. You can reduce speed and pressure when talking to other people. You can keep things up for considerably longer than when acting aimlessly, frenziedly or under pressure. And you are also better placed to focus your energy on strength 3, concentration: on people and on situations that you have (perfectly calmly) identified as interesting or valuable.

---

## How to make best use of your inner calm on social occasions

Make sure that you actually are calm before a social occasion: how we come across is due to how we feel – not to the effect we want to make.

**Physical strategies**

- Take deep, slow breaths to prepare yourself and also during the event. Give yourself and the person you are talking to a pause to breathe deeply when you have said something important.

- Use the calm rhythm of your breathing to make your voice sound calm as well. This will show in two areas in particular: firstly, in a suitable rate of speaking – not too fast, but sufficiently dynamic – and, secondly, in a deep pitch within your own vocal range. Speaking in a deep voice makes a relaxed and confident effect.

- Sit or stand up straight, so that you feel a pleasing tension in your spinal column.

- Consciously relax your shoulders, elbows and knees.

- Use your inner calm to maintain comfortable eye contact: look at the other person in a friendly and composed way. Here it will be relaxing for both you and the person you are talking to if you don't fix your eyes on a single point on her or his face, but allow them to move between the eyebrows and the tip of the nose.

## Mental strategy 1: It's your choice!

Keep in mind that you are making a conscious decision and thus a choice: *you* are deciding to be at this event. *You* are deciding who you will talk to, and for how long. *You* will also decide when you are going to leave. No one will be counting how many contacts you make or looking at what you do in the course of the evening.

Thinking like this will make you act confidently – not as someone who has been pushed into it reluctantly. This mental attitude will give you a sense of liberated calm even before the event: you are in charge of things and deciding where to take them. And by doing this you are also signalling to others that you know exactly what you are doing. This will have a positive effect on the way you relate to people and on your self-esteem.

## Mental strategy 2: You (and only you) determine your objectives

Establish definite objectives for yourself and then pursue them during the event. This will give some definition to what you do and ensure that your calmness seems confident and high in status.

But there is one condition: the objectives should seem attractive and achievable to you. So don't burden yourself with anything that is too stressful for you and/or doesn't even seem worth bothering about.

As an illustration, here are the objectives that Anne has formulated for herself to use at typical events in her professional life:

- Get into conversation with three strangers who make a pleasant impression.
- Find an expert on what I am working on at present and ask about two things that are bothering me about it.
- Keep at it for two hours and people-watch as much as I want during that time.
- End a conversation politely if it is getting too stressful.

So you see there really is a lot of strength to be gained from calm. But you have other advantages as a calm person making small talk, and in social contexts generally. Here is the next strength that you could well have in common with other quiet people.

## Strength 6: Analytical thinking

Evaluate conversations thoroughly

Quiet people spend a lot of time checking observations against what is happening in their own minds. This gets them used at an early stage to filtering what they see and hear and then weighing it up – with the pleasing side effect that a lot of quiet people have strong powers of analysis. Or, to put it more precisely, those of them are who are more markedly 'left-brainers' according to the distinction made in Chapter 2. This is important not just in the fields of monitoring and academic matters, but pleasingly for small talk as well: if you can identify the essentials and conversation patterns easily, you will also find it easy to develop a conversation further in terms of the stage reached and the person you are talking to, and to evaluate information purposefully in a number of subject areas.

In principle, every informal conversation that you enter into on social occasions falls into three phases that form a kind of architecture when taken together. Knowing what the individual phases are for your analytical approach will enable you to deal with them appropriately.

Analysing small talk (1): phases and their functions

Small talk does not commit you to anything. It will be clear from the outset whether you and the person you are talking to are interested in going on with the conversation. In the first place, this depends on whether the chemistry is right. If not, it doesn't matter: there are lots of potential people to talk to at social events. Secondly, whether you continue the conversation or not depends on whether you have something to say to each other. Here you can get off to a good start by keeping an eye on essentials.

The following questions will help you to get off to a good start.

---

 **Starter questions**

**What do we have in common in this situation?** – We are both drinking the same red wine. What does the other person think of it?

**What is interesting about the occasion?** – This is my first stag party: my colleague is getting married. How does the person I'm talking to know him?

**What would I like to know?** – This business trip to Singapore is exciting. But what's the best way to get from the conference hotel to the airport tomorrow morning?

Once you've hit on a topic by using this strategy, take the initiative and start up the conversation. The advantage of this is that you do not have to react quickly to the other person's remarks, but can take charge of things yourself, with a topic that suits you.

### Don't start with a cliché

'Well, how are you?' is probably the most usual starting point for people who know each other. If someone starts off with this question, avoid platitudes ('Fine!' 'Not so bad!'). Answer positively and specifically instead – in the best case what you say will lead to a really pleasant exchange. So say something like 'All the better for seeing you!' or simply 'Peter – we've not seen each other for ages!'

### The middle section

In the middle section you need to keep the conversation going so that it becomes pleasant and rewarding for you and the person you are talking to. This doesn't mean that you have to do all the talking. Listen (this is your next strength: see below), or ask open questions with a show of interest – in other words, questions that can't be answered with 'Yes' or 'No' and that can usually be recognized by an introductory word beginning with 'W'.

Sample open questions: What's the best way to …? What's happening next? Where can I find …? Where do I get …?

Well-chosen questions soon bring a conversation to life. And if you also use a simple pattern to filter what your opposite number is saying, you will find it easy to keep the conversation going if you want to.

Ask yourself what you can pick out from your opposite number's remarks to move things on or to change the subject.

You can change the subject by introducing sentences like 'Apropos of X …' or 'As you just mentioned X, …'

You should be sure in the middle section to throw in your own comments and impressions: you are conducting a conversation not an interview.

An informal conversation can be long or short. The most important thing is that you can bring it to an end at any time without giving any particular reason. This comes as a great relief to many quiet people: it gives you some room for manoeuvre if you find that the situation, or your opposite number, is taking too much out of you.

It's easy to end a conversation in a small talk situation. Just say: 'Thank you for the nice chat. I'll see you again later.' Or: 'I hope we can carry on with this conversation soon.' The casual, easy nature of small talk is very much to your advantage in this situation: you can cut off the conversation when you want to – without apologies or reasons. Even something like 'Oh, I've just seen an old friend I'd like to say hello to!' is completely legitimate: everyone knows that social occasions are about keeping up contacts.

If you feel you want to pursue a contact you have made, you could suggest exchanging business cards at this stage. I like using cards, as it means that I can make a lot of notes later (in my hotel room, for example). This takes the load off my memory, and leads into a phase where introverts can be in a strong position: the follow-up.

## The follow-up

A lot of quiet people are particularly good at communicating in writing (see strength 9). This gives them a definite advantage in written follow-ups after networking events. For example, I can offer my opposite number a contact in the LinkedIn social network (see below) or send him a newspaper article on one of the subjects in hand. I can take this opportunity to thank him for the pleasant conversation we had, and where possible refer to a detail in the conversation itself: 'I remember what you said at the Singapore conference. I've actually managed to get the Bordeaux you recommended from my wine merchant. Many thanks again. As promised, I've attached … to this email.'

You'll find more tips for your own follow-ups below.

---

 **Three tips for your follow-up**

1. Write on paper rather than sending an email – emails are acceptable, but letters and cards are getting rare and have the desired effect: people notice them.

2. Write something that brings some benefit. The person concerned should feel he has had a pleasant surprise that he didn't expect, but can make good use of: a link, an article, a tip about a place where he can find something he needs ...

If you decide to send an email, please try to avoid attachments containing a lot of data – these often end up in spam folders. Send a link instead, or if your text isn't too long, copy it into your email.

3. Write as soon as you can. The person concerned will probably remember you clearly for up to four days later.

Analysing small talk (2): The best way to find suitable subjects – suitable for you, as well!

### Introverts need substance

You have just seen how to find topics at the beginning or in the middle of your small talk, and also how you can control a conversation. This is often too little for quiet people like Anne: they like to have much more substance in their conversations with other people, even if the occasion is an informal one and mainly about establishing relationships. They like a social contact to give them some opportunities to think things over – if they are interested in a person, or that person has some special significance for them, or because an exciting opportunity arises for an exchange of ideas about a particular topic.

### From small talk to big talk

But the actual challenge is to be found somewhere quiet people much prefer: in depth. Many introverts particularly like small talk when they manage to turn it into 'big talk' – in other words, into talking about something substantial that interests them and facilitates a different kind of discussion. It is ideal if calm is an element here too, so that there is time and space to talk things through – with pauses between the different phases of the conversation and in a peaceful atmosphere. Then discussing the subject matter with a pleasant opposite number can even mean that the introvert involved actually *derives* energy from the conversation, rather than *investing* it – with pleasant side effects such as delight and a sense of profound satisfaction.

'Big talk' is traditionally associated with the notion of true conversation, which used to be seen as an important social skill. Today, in the age of texting, Facebook postings and tweets, a lot of people have trouble in becoming absorbed in a substantial topic – never mind initiating one. But it is possible to learn how to conduct a conversation worthy of the word. People with an eye for what is essential (those with strength 2) usually do not find this difficult. And if you make an effort to conduct a genuine exchange of ideas, you will soon see what a positive effect this has on your relationship with the person you are talking to.

Choosing topics cleverly

As we have seen, it is simplest in the early phase when talking to an opposite number to choose a subject that you know brings the two of you closer through something you have *experienced together*: your last meeting, your last communication – or simply how glad you are to see him or her again. And something *on the spot* can bring you closer to the person you are talking to: knowing the hostess, the route to or from the airport, the choice of food in the buffet or the programme for the evening.

Tips for choosing a topic

You don't have to be a philosopher to find a way to go on to something more substantial. Rack your brains and draw up a list of topics that meet one condition: you are really interested in them. Here is a list of suggestions that you can expand as much as you like.

---

 **Subjects of some substance**

- Situations that you have been through (possibly together) in which someone or something impressed you: the keynote speech (conference) – the famous speaker, 87 years old, completely captivated the room.

- Things that interest you and that you think might interest your opposite number as well. Example: the building the IT conference is taking place in used to be a chocolate factory. You wonder what common features there might be.

- Things you'd like to find out more about – especially if your opposite number is familiar with them. Network meeting example: ask whether your opposite number's firm has a quota for female employees. What does she think about that?

- Questions that are in your mind because of certain impressions gained from the surroundings you are in: what effect is the background music making?

---

# Contacts: take needs into account

You have taken the first step after that last section: you know what kind of exchange of views works well for you. You can now search single-mindedly for people and situations that will make your life more worth while.

> ## ❓ A question for you
>
> Which strengths help you to get talking to people you don't know?
>
> I find it relatively easy to turn 'small talk' into 'big talk'. (Strength 2) ☐
>
> I am a good listener and can make use of what I hear to keep conversation moving. (Strength 4) ☐
>
> It is easy for me to find inner calm. (Strength 5) ☐
>
> I have a repertoire of topics that have proved useful for getting things under way. (Strength 6) ☐
>
> I quickly pick up what is important for other people. (Strength 10) ☐
>
> I am good at responding to people. (Strength 10) ☐
>
> I have other small talk strengths, namely _____
>
> _____
>
> _____
>
> _____
>
> _____
>
> _____
>
> _____

## It is not always possible to avoid noisy situations

But you also have to accept that you will sometimes have to talk to people under less than ideal conditions. A party with loud music. The tense office Christmas party as an annual duty. Or, pure horror for a lot of introverts, including the author: the getting-to-know-you party in all its many manifestations, which is actually intended for gaining as many contacts as possible, whatever 'gaining' might mean here.

On occasions like this you can limit the amount of energy you expend to a reasonable extent and make sure that you feel as comfortable as possible. That is why it is important to know exactly what your obstacles are. Let's have a closer look at this.

## Obstacle 2: Over-attention to detail

A lot of quiet people find small talk situations difficult because they increase the tendency to give too much attention to details. Introverts who tend to see individual trees rather than the wood with its pathways can easily get lost in 'chaotic' social situations and are also particularly prone to suffering from over-stimulation (obstacle 3).

So it is all the more important to structure any given situation carefully. The following simple strategies will make it easier for you to move around confidently in a group of people and to feel sure of yourself.

Small talk: strategies increasing clarity

1 Think 'quality' not 'quantity'.

Quiet people have a particular way of creating close relationships between themselves and other people of their choice. Here the stress is on 'of their choice'. Instead of forging a lot of contacts with a lot of people, introverts prefer intensive, regular contact with a small number of people. And they then also invest in these relationships. Many introverts find one-to-one conversations more pleasant than exchanging ideas in a group of people. They feel more relaxed with one other person, and the number of ideas coming over stays within reasonable bounds. The given topic is more manageable within these bounds, and it is easier to consider the other person's point of view, simply because there is just one other person involved. Therefore talk to individuals if you can. If you talk to three or four people one after the other at an event, that is a good result if the conversations are pleasant ('deep' rather then 'broad', moving from small talk to real conversation) – and is more likely to lead to a lot of more long-lasting contacts than a typical extrovert's 'broadly' based contact strategy.

2 Position yourself in the room.

At the beginning of the event, look out for various *'getaway points'* you can escape to if necessary. This gives the space a manageable structure and also protects you from obstacle 3: over-stimulation. Find a seat from which you have a good view of the entire room. If you are looking for new people to talk to, it makes sense to place yourself near the door.

3 Find some possible people to talk to.

Look for people who seem friendly (on their own, or in small, open groups). You can also make arrangements with individuals before the event – for example, if you feel you'd like to meet them personally after an exchange of emails, or if you want to talk about something specific.

4 Set yourself personal targets.

Have something definite in mind for the occasion that works for you and for the position you are in at the time: plan to get into conversation with a particular person (e.g. by being introduced – ask someone who knows you both). Or make up your mind that you are only going to stay for as long as you feel comfortable – and then go when you feel like it, or take a break.

## Obstacle 3: Over-stimulation

Too much at once is too much, and thus harmful. This also applies to good things in life: to chocolates, to red wine and also to people. For introverts, 'too much' often means too much to take in. And that is precisely what over-stimulation is: a situation drains your energy because there is too much to take in. That is exhausting and takes the pleasure out of meeting other people. And that makes it stressful. So it is not unusual for a lot of introverts to ration social occasions carefully and to choose them so that they do not wear themselves out. This is also perfectly legitimate – no one is obliged to be with other people all the time. But I am talking here about the situation itself: how do you avoid having to use up too much energy too quickly?

Small talk: anti-over-stimulation strategies

1 Ensure that you feel comfortable on all social occasions. Don't put yourself under pressure, but take breaks from talking to other people. Two things are important here: you should be alone and be able to relax. There are various possibilities: go to the toilet; look at the pictures on the wall; sit down quietly with a good drink and take a relaxed look at the people around you. Take several slow, deep breaths between conversations: this calms you down, provides you with oxygen and has

the effect of a mini-break. And your contacts will also seem much more interesting and immediate if you have 'freshly charged batteries' – that's a good start!

2 Avoid doing several things at the same time. That reduces the number of stimuli your brain has to deal with, and enables you to concentrate better on what you are doing. This will boost the impact you make as well. So focus on the person or people you are talking to or doing something with. Once you have finished this particular exchange of ideas, think about your next target – or help yourself to something from the buffet first.

3 Too much noise really drains quiet people's energy and is a major cause of over-stimulation. I have noticed that I and other quiet people are inclined to see noise as a kind of natural force about which we can do nothing. The extroverts around us don't have so many problems with volume, so it seems to be just 'our' problem. But don't worry: there often is something that can be done if you notice that your surroundings are too noisy at a social event. If there is nothing you can do about the noise level (e.g. a plane landing during a conversation at the airport – or on Carnival Monday in Cologne), you can't use earplugs but you can reduce the stimulation: concentrate very hard on the person you are talking to. This will cut out the background noise and also make it easier to understand what is being said. And there are many other situations in which you definitely can cut down troublesome noise. The extrovert gym receptionist would be very happy to turn down the music that makes your workout into an ordeal and renders it impossible to talk to anyone else. But of course you have to ask her first. Follow these guidelines when you do so: firstly say quite objectively what the problem is, secondly what is causing it, and thirdly what you would like to happen. So you say to your gym receptionist: 'The music in the strength training room is really loud today. We can talk much better when its at a more normal volume. Would you mind turning it down?'

## Obstacle 4: Passivity

If you look round carefully at social events, you'll see introverts everywhere who only seem to be active: they are getting something to drink or looking at the messages on their smartphone. Or going through papers, or looking at their watches. It's just not looking good on the contact front …

Opportunities for trying to make contacts usually seem unstructured. Quiet people are often uncertain what they can and should do to link up with other people in the room. This can easily lead to uncertainty and lack of confidence. So these quiet people do not feel comfortable with themselves. They feel greatly tempted to do nothing at all at first, and to hold back, instead of purposefully trying to do something about making contact. In this way they are making themselves dependent on others: if they don't take the initiative, the quiet ones will be left on their own. But if the others do take the initiative, the passive ones have to respond to whatever opening comes, and can't decide for themselves who they talk to and what about. In the worst case they cannot handle the opening at all, or not quickly enough, and thus they miss the opportunity to make a pleasant contact.

Tips for making contact

So the obvious conclusion is this: it is better to take the initiative when making contact. You'll find it easier to do this if you cut down on the complexity and thus the degree of uncertainty in communication. You can do this by following a simple principle: do something definite that will structure your networking activities and your time. Here are a few interesting approaches drawn from quiet people's experiences.

---

## ! How to take an active approach to social occasions

1. **Take on jobs.** This advice is aimed particularly at people at an early stage in their careers. Help with registration or welcoming guests. Organize the service arrangements. Give lectures or organize work groups. In the professional field this will also show that you are prepared to take on responsibility and make you visible in a positive way.

   An example: I advise young academics I work with in seminars to co-ordinate work groups at conferences or small specialist meetings as early in their careers as possible. In this way they will learn the rules from direct experience, appear as positive figures in their academic community and so find it easier to establish contact with decision-makers.

2. **Get there early.** Take it upon yourself to find out who else is coming to the event. There are different ways of doing this. Look at the conference programme. Check out the name badges that have been laid out – if you get there early, most of them will still be there. Or have a friendly,

interested chat with the organizers and other people at the reception desk: who else are they expecting?

3. **Join queues.** This sounds odd, but it does have an advantage: a place in the queue imposes structure. At the reception desk, the buffet or the bar you have a potential person to talk to behind you and in front of you. There is also a purpose to it, and some waiting time. All this makes the situation pleasantly manageable.

4. **Make use of tables you stand at.** Tables you stand at are ideal for making contacts: they space people out and offer one clear benefit – they are there so that you can put things down. Take your plate or glass and find a table with no one at it, or just one person. There is a good chance that you will soon have company and there might be a nice quiet person waiting for you who finds some security and comfort in the table as well. Just ask politely if there is still space free ...

You now know how you can use your strengths to promote contacts. You are also aware of some traps and temptations that quiet people often have to wrestle with. Finally, we are going to deal with social situations in which the people you are communicating with are not present in person, but in the wide-open spaces of the online networks.

## Contacts in the comfort zone: social media

Digital networks and contact forums – also called 'social media' – are ideal stomping grounds for networking activities: Facebook, LinkedIn, Twitter, Google+, but they also offer partnering services, discussion forums, chatrooms – the range is enormous. All these online platforms have two things in common: they enable you to create indirect contacts, in written form. In this way they fit in with quiet people's strength 9: writing rather than speaking.

Online networking provides an opportunity for essentially reticent introverts to make contact – but not 'really', because you are always at a safe distance in the digital world. Ideas are exchanged with some delay, unlike spoken communication, and you are separated spatially. This too gives a pleasant sense of safety and control: there is plenty of time to respond, which suits introverts, who like to think things over quietly before they say anything. I once read this quotation on Twitter, the platform for mini-blogs: '140 characters is a dose in which people find each other bearable.' I am certain that was not written by an extrovert! But then there are other introverts who see today's digital media more as a necessary evil than a networking opportunity: it is one more activity that needs regular care and attention. A typical sentence heard from this camp (usually combined with eyes raised to heaven) is: 'When am I supposed to find time for that?' Which camp are you in?

---

### ? A question for you

What do digital social networks mean to you?

| | |
|---|---|
| A good complement to real meetings | ❏ |
| Tolerable networking | ❏ |
| A necessary evil | ❏ |
| No opinion/Lack of information | ❏ |

---

Most quiet people, as you now know, prefer to have fewer relationships of higher quality. But a lot of stuff written on the internet either seems superficial or is blatantly gimmicky, or just plain stupid and vulgar. A lot – but not all! There is also a great deal of material on the net that operates in depth and is substantial.

## Tips for using digital networks

One thing is certain: digital media are a part of networking that is unavoidable in our day – and they are likely to be even more important in future. So make the best of it as a quiet person. In this case, the best of it is what suits you. Here are a few tips for using them:

• Make sure that you choose just a few platforms that suit your way of communicating and, above all, what you are aiming to do. Examples: Facebook is a copious hotchpotch teeming with personal and professional contacts. LinkedIn is a purely professional platform in which you can present yourself appropriately. Twitter is a micro-blog in which you communicate with people directly by writing or reading messages with a maximum of 140 characters. Google+ has been competing with all the networks mentioned since mid-2011. There are many other platforms. Choose a maximum of two to start with. Communicate with selected digital sites – and do it regularly!

- Construct your profile in each network so that it fits in with your aims and required messages. Networking is helpful only if you cultivate your contacts and your profile: be clear and consistent in the messages and dialogues you send to or conduct with other people. This will give you the online identity you are looking for.

- At first, don't see your digital media contacts as friendships or professional relationships. But both friendships and professional relationships can develop astonishingly quickly if the exchange of ideas really works. I have decided on XING (a popular professional platform in Germany) and Twitter as platforms that complement each other well. I have also seen that contacts on these platforms have led to more hits on my website and my blog – and to more communication about my work. This does not mean that everyone has to like you and your profile – as in real life, not everything goes right for everyone in the digital world. Both the quantity and the quality of your contacts grow best as they would in nature: slowly and continuously.

- Make sure that you regularly earmark some time for digital networking. This means on the one hand that you should have regular active periods, ideally more than once a week. Post your contributions. Confirm requests for contacts that seem to suit you. Read the messages you receive and reply to them where appropriate. On the other hand, this tip also means that you should not let yourself be distracted by constantly glancing at your Twitter timeline or your Facebook messages while you are doing other things.

- Communicate regularly, and within the public role you opt for. In the best case, what you write in the digital media will establish trust: your readers and contacts will get the impression that they know you a little. So communicate on the basis of what you want to convey: because it is important to you, because it benefits the others, because it highlights certain qualities or abilities. It regularly strikes me that I am not at all surprised when I meet people from the world of XING or Twitter in real life: you find out a great deal about people. As you are used to thinking things through before communicating with them, you are sure to take that into account in your communication.

- Value your digital activities just as highly as other networking activities. People come across very substantial things online every day: new jobs, solutions for their problems, service providers for jobs that are coming up, good advice or requests for commission tenders: the very things you find in face-to-face encounters.

But please remember this as well: real networking starts when, at some time or another, you meet the real person behind the online profile. This meeting cannot be replaced by chat, tweets, Facebook messages or emails. So use the internet to establish the contacts you want and also want to cultivate after a face-to-face meeting. But take the next step after getting to know someone: if a contact seems interesting to you and suggests quality, you should arrange and work for contact in 'real life'. (This is not necessary of course if your Twitter contact is writing from Papua New Guinea ...)

---

## ✳ Key points in brief

Quiet people have everything that is needed for approaching other people on social occasions. This works best and most successfully if you know your own personal preferences and qualities and use them for networking that suits contacts as you understand them.

This **'quiet' networking** is best pursued using five strategies: set definite aims, define resources, introduce acquaintances to each other, get other people to introduce you, and keep your networking active in the long term, and with persistence.

A contact that is of value for quiet people works in the long term and is significant. Quality rather than quantity.

In most cases introverts have three particular **strengths** when dealing with other people: they are excellent listeners, they are calm and they can use their analytical powers to find suitable topics easily and ways of getting themselves over to the person they are talking to.

Quiet people should not forget their particular **needs** on social occasions: they are easily overwhelmed by an undue stream of impressions, they quickly wear themselves out if over-stimulated and they also run the risk of remaining too passive, rather than deliberately looking for contacts and controlling conversations. But there are ways of avoiding these risks: by making sure of an overview, by taking time off and resting occasionally, by carefully planning activities and events.

**Digital networks**, cultivated online, can complement other contacts well, particularly for quiet people who like to express themselves in writing. But they are subject to their own rules and are no substitute for 'real' encounters – they simply complement them.

# 7.
# Conflict between a person and a state of affairs: how to negotiate

Siva is reading for a PhD at a renowned UK university with a university hospital attached. She is conducting research into metabolic disorders in overweight patients. As a biochemist, she is concentrating on certain blood values. To do this she has to work with mice, which she injects with serums and takes blood specimens for analysis. This is hard work, because it is wide-ranging, and demands minute detail in many areas. So far Siva has kept up with the demands it makes: she enjoys her work, and spends a lot of time in the lab in the evenings as well. She has lectured on her first results with great success (and a lot of palpitations) at national conferences. She hopes to finish writing her doctoral thesis within the next ten months. Then she finishes her doctoral procedures until her present job is over. She also supervises master's degrees for two students, which she finds quite time-consuming.

But suddenly the timetable has got even tighter: Siva's own supervisor, a well-known professor, has acquired major funding and expects active help from her with the research. Siva can only handle this new work with additional support. She decides to ask her employer for a research assistant who can take over her routine work in the lab.

## Clarify your own position

This means that Siva is faced with the task of conducting negotiations. She wants to sort something out, and to do that she needs another person to help her: her boss.

## Give and take

Negotiation involves give and take: everyone involved should reach an agreement that they feel able to support and implement – even when they have quite different interests. This means that the supervisor will only agree if he finds the solution useful and open to implementation. In the best case he stands to benefit from it himself, and this makes the decision considerably easier.

People who are negotiating with each other can only agree to a solution if it furthers their own aims. Siva's boss wants her to take on additional research work and supervise master's degree students. For her part, Siva wants to finish her thesis within the agreed time frame. In the best case, the agreement made at the end of the negotiations will lead to a decision that the people involved reach together and also implement at the end of the discussion. In Siva's case, this means: the student assistant post – or another way of easing the burden – has to be arranged.

## Define your starting point

You can cut a very good figure in negotiations as a quiet person. Negotiations are one of the communication techniques in which introvert strengths are particularly helpful. But before we get to these strengths, there are two things you should be aware of: firstly, you will find something out about the basis for negotiations – about determining your own position. Your negotiating position defines your starting point, from which all further strategies are developed. Secondly, you get to know the various stages of negotiation and what is involved at each stage, so that you can make appropriate plans for what you have to do yourself.

YOUR FIRST STEP IN PREPARING TO NEGOTIATE IS TO DETERMINE YOUR OWN POSITION. YOUR THEN PREPARE EVERYTHING ELSE ON THIS BASIS.

 **Three points to help you determine your position**

**Point 1: Determine the current position and what you are aiming for.**

- What have you to offer?
- What do you want the negotiations to achieve?
- How does this aim look to the people you are negotiating with?
- What information do you need about the people you are negotiating with and about the object of the negotiations?

**Point 2: Distinguish between what is important and what is flexible.**

- Establish which among several negotiation areas is most important to you. In what order would you like to discuss the points?
- What do you want to achieve in the best case in each area?
- What would be an outcome that you could just accept?

The answers to the last two questions will gain you valuable room for manoeuvre.

**Point 3: Ensure that everything is clear and consistent**.

If you are negotiating in a team (for your department, for example), then agree on points 1 and 2 among yourselves before the actual negotiations. You are strongest if you all want the same thing.

The second point in particular will be highly beneficial: flexibility. A lot of negotiations fail because unduly rigid positions are taken up.

But often there are many ways of getting close to where you want to be – and for the other party as well.

## Understand the other side

You will find out what the other party wants at the negotiations themselves at the latest. Make sure that you understand where the 'other side' is trying to get: it is only by being clear about all the interests involved that you can work out the best way to reaching a joint decision.

Consider the long-term consequences before and during the negotiations: how will the other side see you (or your firm) in future? What effects could that have? What do you want to feel like when you leave the negotiations?

Siva has been able to determine her own position by using the three points mentioned above. Here is a summary.

 **Negotiations about easing the workload**

These are Siva's three points for clarifying her position.

**Point 1: Determine the current position and what you are aiming for.**

- What Siva has to offer: research performance, commitment, reliability
- Aim: to reduce her lab workload (time-consuming routine work) by using a student assistant
- Aim from the supervisor's point of view: additional expense, but on the other hand also more pressure because of the new research project

and more master's degree students – the work needs to be shared out intelligently.

- Information needed about people involved in the negotiations and what is being negotiated about: in principle, are there sufficient resources available to pay for an assistant? Have there been similar cases in the past? How many hours are actually needed to relieve the workload?

**Point 2: Distinguish between what is important and what is flexible.**

- Matters to be negotiated: just one – relieving the workload!
- Best possible outcome: a student assistant. There is already a well-qualified and pleasant candidate ...
- Outcome that would be just acceptable: no supervision for master's work until the doctorate. This new research project is a good opportunity to take up a position – it should certainly be on the agenda.

**Point 3: Ensure that everything is clear and consistent.**

- No one else involved, strictly speaking.
- To be clarified: what does it imply for the workgroup if a student assistant for a doctoral candidate is appointed? Will it be supported or resisted?

Siva prepares for the discussion on this basis. First of all she clears up the unresolved questions:

- To be precise, she needs about 8 to 10 hours relief per week.
- She finds out via the secretary that it is not clear whether funding is available for the new project. But no one can remember that a doctoral candidate has ever had a student assistant.
- The work group is aware of Siva's heavy workload and is happy that she should have some relief at the present stage. But a colleague who has just been awarded a doctorate is not best pleased. He makes is clear that he sees the solution involving an assistant as an inappropriate bonus. If everyone were to ask ...

A date has now been set. Siva examines the various negotiation phases to help her further planning.

## Negotiation phases

Summary of negotiation phases

A set of negotiations goes through various phases. Here is a summary that also includes preparation before the discussion and follow-up work.

 **Negotiations: sequence of events**

**Before the negotiations: preparation**

Function: clarification

Work out position using the three points explained above. Also check on dates, room, people to be present, the media needed and the distribution of jobs.

**During negotiations: phases**

*Phase 1: getting started*

Function: creating a positive atmosphere

How: small talk, asking questions and listening, positive body language, pleasant

*Phase 2: core negotiations*

Function: finding a common position

How: producing arguments, questions, active listening, aligning positions, finding compromises, making decisions

*Phase 3: finishing off*

Function: agreeing on implementation, ensuring positive relationships

How: sum up, share out jobs, defuse situation if no agreement, friendly goodbyes

**After the negotiations: the follow-up**

Function: implement result(s), analyse negotiations: What was good? What could be improved? How?

How: without involving more people: self-reflection, notes;

involving more people: short meeting and exchange of ideas;

here too make written notes of important points.

The first phase of the negotiations, in other words the preparatory work, looks like this to Siva:

- The three points have been clarified – see above.
- Date: fixed. Venue: boss's office.
- No other people involved.
- Media: two A4 pages, one with a summary of all the jobs and projects Siva is working on at the moment, and one with the CV of the candidate who is being considered for the assistant's post.
- Other preparatory work: none.

Siva has also thought about the second phase – the negotiations themselves. Getting started (1.) will not take much time. Siva knows her boss and is aware that he is friendly and, as an extrovert, likes people, but he is often impatient because of his workload. Thus she knows that she has to get to the point quickly. Siva wants to get to the core negotiations (2.) as soon as possible. As her boss does not like being confined to a single course of action, she decides to say first of all that the time available to her is too tight for new projects (she has her summary handy to reinforce the point visually during the negotiations), and that she is worried about this. She will then wait for his answer and take up what she hears. She hopes that she will convince her supervisor about her optimal solution (the assistant) at this stage, but at least get some relief from her workload for supervising the master's degree work.

During the negotiations (phases 1–3) it's worth establishing a framework and boundaries.

## ! Establishing a framework and boundaries

- Insist that everyone can make all the points they want to. This includes you. This also applies if someone in a superior position interrupts you. Say politely 'If I may just finish the point off briefly ...'
- Bring speakers gently back to the point if they wander.
- Use wording appropriate to the person you are speaking to.
- Maintain friendly eye contact and turn your body towards the person you are talking to. Try not to fold your arms or cross your legs.
- Keep calm even when provoked or if time is running out, both inwardly and outwardly. Breathe deeply and calmly if you feel stressed or angry.

Siva gets what she wants: her supervisor agrees that the additional research project (which is very close to his heart) makes a workload reduction necessary. He agrees to appoint an assistant, but would also like this person to be available for special jobs in the context of the new project. He accepts Siva's suggestion of a good candidate with interest – and also the sheet of paper with the CV on it. The result is that Siva is asked to organize an interview and make contact with management. She is very pleased and tells her boss as she leaves how happy she is about her new prospects.

## Introvert negotiating strengths

Some of their strengths mean that quiet people hold a lot of trump cards in negotiation situations. After you have become familiar with preparing for negotiations and the sequence of events, you will soon be aware of the most important advantages quiet people have in such situations – and hints about how to make the best use of them.

## Strength 4: Listening

Listening makes negotiation more pleasant: anyone who has the space to express his position clearly is likely to be more prepared to consider the other person's point of view. It helps to have the right questions ready at the key point in the negotiations (phase 2), but your ability to listen, giving your opposite number the appropriate space, is important as well. The fact that you are listening will make your opposite number feel he is being taken seriously (as will the way you deal with what you have to say). This means that he will in all probability be co-operative and not make such an effort to make himself heard. Again, this takes the tension out of the situation and makes it less stressful for you.

In concrete terms, good listening also provides you with something that is important for the course of the negotiations: key information about your opposite number's point of view and interests. You can build both of these into your thinking and your search for a result. This is to your advantage when fighting towards a result that is acceptable to both of you.

So Siva takes careful note that, when talking about whether to take on an additional assistant, her boss keeps returning to the research project and the resources that are urgently necessary for it. This means that she can establish during the negotiations whether it would be all right for the assistant to be actively involved in the research project. This again expands her room for manoeuvre: suddenly the boss finds the assistant attractive as well!

The three simple questions below make it easier for you to listen systematically when negotiating.

---

**?** **Three key questions for intelligent listeners**

1. What need can I detect?
2. What feelings can I detect?
3. What possibilities can I see for the rest of the conversation?

---

Don't be afraid to take up what you hear – it will mean that you are showing that you are thinking about what you have heard and are taking what your opposite number is saying into account rather than simply insisting on your own arguments. Don't repeat things word for word, but reflect what you have understood. One example: Siva's supervisor says at phase 3, the concluding phase, of the negotiations: 'Well – I hope there aren't any attitude problems!' Siva senses a degree of frustration and answers by reformulating what she has heard: 'That sounds as though you've already had a hard time?' Her boss then explains a problem with management and the two of them finally discuss how these difficulties can be avoided in the current case.

## Strength 6: Analytical thinking

As a quiet person, your analytical skills make it easy for you to determine your own negotiating position. You can also match it up to your opposite number's wishes. As well as this, you quickly find out what information you still need to create some positive room for manoeuvre. Your analytical skills in negotiation will help you to formulate this next question precisely.

The key analytical question when negotiating:

HOW CAN THIS INFORMATION HELP YOU TO CONDUCT THE REMAINING NEGOTIATIONS?

Listening leads to solutions

Siva had not been able to find out before the negotiations whether the necessary resources for an assistant were available. So she listens very carefully when the conversation turns to financing the research work as well as the institution's routine work. Here she thinks it would not be sensible to ask about funding directly, so she alludes to it obliquely by mentioning that any delay in her work could generate costs and, above all, create a bottleneck in financing her own job to the point of gaining her doctorate. This means that the idea of the available resources has at least been raised. The money for the assistant is there – and a relatively favourable solution in comparison with the alternatives!

## Strength 8: Tenacity

Steer the conversation to where you want it to go

A persistent introvert has one clear advantage in negotiations: he remains patient and respectful while putting his case – but he keeps at it. Patience has meant many a success after much to-ing and fro-ing. Rigidly insisting on a position is persistent, of course – but neither elegant nor particularly likely to succeed. The best thing to do is to exploit your own stamina by using suitable language to steer the conversation towards what you want. You'll do that easily by keeping some sample sentence designs at the back of your mind:

 **How to persist with your issue**

Here are some sentence designs for conducting your negotiations.

- 'Let's come back to X again: (...)'
- "What you are saying reminds me of something you mentioned right at the beginning, and that is ...'
- 'How do you think that can be compatible with (...)?'

These language strategies will keep you on track – and help you to take your opposite number with you. That is a real leadership performance!

## Strength 10: Empathy

Taking your opposite number with you like this is particularly important when negotiating, so your empathy will be very much to your advantage. But there is more to this strength: it means that you not only have an eye on where you want the negotiations to go, but also on your relationship with your opposite number over and above the subject of the negotiations.

Quiet people with empathy want to reach a decision in a spirit of genuine agreement, and not to over-persuade or manipulate their opposite numbers. This sort of approach is ideal for negotiations. Siva did not want to spoil her relationship with her boss even if she hadn't been able to get what she wanted.

Empathy does not depend on status: quiet bosses who have this strength too value it when their employees reach decisions in negotiations on their own initiative and not under pressure.

If the negotiations do not come to the right conclusion, empathy will help to make it a peaceable conclusion. By saying 'Pity – but perhaps I will be able to convince you next time!', the one who has not succeeded this time is not only distancing himself from the immediate situation but also showing sporting spirit and wonderfully serene confidence. There is no risk of conflict and undue self-projection – which is not the case for many extroverts.

Introvert obstacles when negotiating

Just as you can exploit your strengths during negotiation there will be possible obstacles waiting for you that can bring 'quiet' challenges and requirements with them. This section will focus on these possible difficulties – and on the question of how you can best address them.

---

### ❓ The question for you

Which of your personal strengths can you use to be successful in your next set of negotiations?

**These are my strengths ...**          **... and this is how I intend to use them:**

_____          _____

_____          _____

_____          _____

_____          _____

---

Obstacle 6: Being unduly cerebral

Introverts who are strongly analytical are prone to going into negotiations with a false belief. This belief says that the best arguments win. It would be nice if they did! If it was always just about what was best, then our world would be in very good shape. But we are human beings. Human beings have feelings. And arguing against feelings – or simply arguing as though your opposite number does not have feelings – always goes wrong.

Emotional situations in negotiations

Feelings come in all shapes and sizes. Let's go back to Siva's negotiations again. In her case there are three factors in particular that influence her boss's emotional attitude and the negotiating exchanges between the two of them: firstly, Siva and her supervisor work together every day. This has led to a certain closeness. Fortunately, in this case they work together on a basis of mutual trust and fundamental respect for each other, in other words two very positive emotional positions. Secondly, there is a difference in status between Siva and her boss. This too generates emotion: how does the supervisor, her superior, address the fact that Siva is asking for something and aiming for a result? How is it if he does not see things in a way that fits in with the realities of this doctoral candidate? Under what conditions should he accept an employee's suggestions? And how will this look to other people involved, the colleague with a doctorate, for example, who made critical comments?

There is a third factor that is banal but equally important in the emotional sphere: what is the supervisor's state of mind that day? Has he got a headache, or just had a row with his wife? Or is he in an ideal mood, just after his early morning jog? So you can see that feelings add a quite particular extra plane of depth to negotiating. So you should:

> TREAT THE EMOTIONAL PLANE AS A PART OF THE COMMUNICATION PROCESS IN EVERY NEGOTIATION.

To confront the next obstacle you have to overcome some feelings that can represent a temptation to hold on to positions unduly.

Obstacle 8: Locking onto your own position

Anyone who has to negotiate must be prepared to be flexible. The reason for this lies in the very nature of negotiation: it is about matching your own and your opposite number's interests to each other. To do this you have to move towards each other in the course of the negotiations. This movement comes into being if you weigh criteria for making decisions, alternatives and approaches to solutions, or develop them further. New aspects are often introduced that are significant and need sufficient space in the negotiations.

Locking on to your own position can hinder you here. Many introverts value a position that can be calculated and peace and quiet in which to think it over. It is easy to lose sight of all these factors amidst the rapid to-ing and fro-ing of a negotiation. This can undermine both confidence and harmony: it is like treating a piece of music in four/four time as if it were a waltz in three/four time. But you can take countermeasures: you can use your analytical strengths (and also your fondness for writing things down!) to ensure that you have room for manoeuvre in your negotiations. The key step is to introduce structure to new and complex pieces of information.

---

 **Remain flexible by analysing**

Help for conducting your negotiations

Make notes during the negotiations so that you are fully in the picture. You can use your headings to shift emphasis or you can postpone dealing with some points in agreement with your opposite number and capture them finally by writing them down.

Notes almost never slow down a discussion – on the contrary: when you write something down, you show your opposite number that you are taking what he says seriously.

---

Obstacle 10: Avoiding conflict

There will always be negotiators who consciously or unconsciously apply pressure in order to strengthen their position. They insist on quick decisions, speak faster and faster, talk more loudly or signal impatience through their body language, by drumming their fingers, for example, or leaning forwards. Extroverts who are easily wound up during negotiations simply because of their temperament are particularly likely to behave like this. But speeding up can also be used deliberately as an instrument of power that your opposite number exploits to put you under pressure in order to push you into making a decision. A lot of quiet people feel in situations like this that their opposite number is deliberately introducing the potential for conflict into the negotiations – in other words, very unpleasant. The consequence: you allow the pressure communicated to make you feel under stress, and this can easily weaken your own negotiating position.

If you are negotiating with someone who puts you under pressure, the first step should be to distance yourself inwardly. Pay close attention to what is happening, observe the situation and your opposite number, as if you were watching a film. This will make it difficult for you to react instinctively by retreating, or by defending yourself aggressively.

## The first step: make yourself aware that your opposite number wants to put pressure on you

Keep in mind that it is you who decides how the negotiations will run and what will come out of them. No one is compelling you to accept a raised tempo or time pressure from your opposite number. So slow down instead: take a deep breath, and stay at your own pace and with your own strategy.

## The second step: take a deep breath – and keep to your own pace

Here you can use both language and body language: sum up briefly what is important for your opposite number – but without stating what he is asking for ('I understand that the most important thing for you is to stick to the budget'). This makes it clear that you are keeping an eye on the other person's interests – without giving way to him. When you speak, stick to your usual speed and volume. Maintain steady eye contact: be attentive, but without staring. Move your eyes in the 'professional triangle' on your opposite number's face between the eyebrows and the tip of the nose.

Saying nothing is also a powerful negotiating strategy. A person who says nothing rather than rushing to keep speaking after making an offer radiates confidence. You can also keep silent when your opposite number makes you an offer: no one is compelling you to change your position immediately. So think quietly about the offer. It could even be that your opposite number will correct himself spontaneously … If the pressure your negotiating partner is exerting in this situation gets too stressful for you, and if you think it is possible, you can also suggest a break: postpone the rest of the conversation until later.

## The third step (optional): suggest a break!

Sometimes it is not possible to postpone negotiations – for example, if your opposite number doesn't have a lot of time, or is not usually available on the spot. This is the time to persevere and keep going! Use your listening, analytical thinking and tenacity skills. Then stick to the first two steps, which taught you to live with your fear of conflict. The best of luck with it all!

---

## ❓ A question for you

How will you deal with your needs and obstacles in future?

**My obstacles ...**                    **...... and how I intend to deal with them:**

_____          _____

_____          _____

_____          _____

_____          _____

_____          _____

---

## ✳ Key points in brief

- When you are negotiating, the key thing is to work together towards a position that all concerned can live with.

- The most important points when preparing negotiations are **clarifying your own position** and **planning the phases** of the conversation itself. Both parties feel secure if the discussion does not keep going 'all round the houses'.

- The following **strengths** are particularly helpful for quiet people who are negotiating: listening, analytical thinking, tenacity and empathy.

- Then again, particular **obstacles** in negotiations are too much detail, fixation and avoiding conflict. But anyone who is aware of his personal 'pressure points' can learn to keep them so under control that they do not create any disadvantages or cause undue stress. This applies particularly to avoiding conflict.

# 8.

# In the spotlight: how to speak in public

Manuel is a recently appointed department head in a middle-sized
company in the metal industry. He has already worked for several years
in the management team he is now to direct. He is familiar with the
financial situation, and also knows a lot of the employees well. Manuel
is confidently at the top of his profession. But so far he has only had to
communicate within manageable contexts: in his management position
up to this point he had to work in meetings with ten (or rarely up to a
maximum of 15) people and, as a quiet person, he always preferred small
groups to large ones. Presenting budgets and annual accounts was never
his favourite job, but he knows his colleagues and has also got used to
these situations.

But Manuel's promotion has faced him with new challenges. Only today
he has found out that Stuart, one of his colleagues in his department's
middle management team, is retiring next month. One of Manuel's jobs
as head of department is to make a farewell speech. The very thought of
a speech like this brings him out in a sweat. He knows the man who is
retiring, and likes him too. But speaking to 120 people and on this subject,
which is well outside his professional routine, is a task that he would very
much prefer to avoid.

## Appearing in public – a development project

Like Manuel, quiet people are often unhappy about appearing in
public. There is too much about the situation that is not to their liking:
communicating with a relatively large number of people, the conspicuous
position 'in the spotlight', speaking for a long time without the possibility
of pulling out – all this can become something of a burden.

### Public speaking can be learned

And now for the good news: most introverts can still bring it off. A
successful public appearance does not depend on things like a talent
for speaking and innate charisma. Both may be helpful, but a successful

appearance can also be engineered by other means. Lecturing and presentation can be learned very easily. Even Barack Obama went down the systematic training for speech-making route. Before he had worked steadily towards becoming the epitome of the charismatic, rhetorically polished speechmaker he was dismissed as 'stiff and professorial', 'soporific' (*Time* magazine, 8.5.2008) or as 'stiff and monotonous' (Ted McClelland, retrospective in the *Chicago* magazine, June 2007).

But then, in July 2004, Obama caused a furore all over America with his speech at the Democratic Party Congress in Boston – by speaking 2,297 words in 17 minutes. But he hadn't transformed himself into a talented speaker overnight: he had been working on developing his personal speech-making style for several years, and specifically on presenting himself as the great political hope. A gradual, persistent development process had made him a successful presence – and this contemporary example of an introverted leadership personality shows that this kind of development process can take an individual a long way.

## Routine creates confidence

Even if you don't want to become President, Prime Minister or Chancellor, you can grow personally and gain professionally by learning to speak in public. The initial phase is the most challenging, when you are still relatively inexperienced. But the more often you take on the risk of facing an audience and the more regularly you use the strategies recommended here, the more secure and confident you will become when speaking in public.

## When does a lecture count as successful?

Imagine thinking after a lecture: yes, it was worth it. It went well. In what circumstances would you say something like that? To put it differently: what exactly makes an appearance successful?

So that you can have a clear idea of what you can achieve in the best case scenario, you will find a summary here containing three essential criteria for success. Please bear in mind that this summary is not there to raise the bar and make you even more stressed. On the contrary, it is intended to give you a guide to turn the vague concept of a 'good speech', into concrete qualities. This is a promise: you can achieve everything you read in the list below by using a very small number of strategies. As Barack Obama found out, the essential thing is practice!

## The three major success criteria

Your lecture counts as successful when you present yourself to the audience in a way that suits you personally

The first criterion relates to your *role as a speaker*. Every audience likes to hear authentic people speaking. But if someone is just playing a part and so pretending to be someone he isn't, he's subjecting himself and other people to strain – to say nothing of the fact that playing a part like this requires years of training as an actor. But you shouldn't try acting – and nor do you need to. Be faithful to yourself instead! That will save a great deal of energy, and is much more effective. So if you tend to be objective and restrained in your movements, keep it like that for an audience as well. You don't have to put on a show to interest other people in your subject and to convince them about your concerns. Aim at other positive effects instead, such as making people believe in what you are saying and conveying that the matter is in good hands with the benefit of your expertise. Or give them the impression that the matter means a great deal to you. You can create this sort of effect by appearing calm, thorough and well informed. Pursue a calm approach if humour is not your thing. Stick to restrained gestures, rather than bold ones if you are more comfortable with that approach. In brief: find your own, personal style. A hint of a smile in the right place can have much more of an effect than a great roar of artificial laughter that does not reflect your real self.

---

## ❓ A question for you (for your next speech)

What should be your chief characteristics as a speaker?

Here are a few suggestions:

| | | |
|---|---|---|
| relaxed | objective | conversational |
| humorous | warm-hearted | simple (even when dealing with difficult matters) |
| optimistic | reflective | |
| motivating | lucid | powerful voice |
| encouraging | honest | vigorous movements |
| serious | determined | lively intonation |
| substantial | clear | calm gestures |

Additional qualities:_____

_____

If you are not sure where your strengths lie, consult the people who are closest to you. How do they see you? One thing is important: if you want to make a confident impression on your audience, you'll achieve this best and most simply by exploiting your strengths and building your performance on them. And, as this book has already shown you, you should also note when making a public appearance that your obstacles lie in the shadow of your strengths, and you should be aware of these obstacles, be familiar with your own pressure points and needs, and not allow yourself to be surprised by them.

Manuel is a head of department, and his strengths lie in the fact that he speaks calmly and at the right volume, and can address his audience as if it were a personal conversation. He can also see that he can exploit this personal note particularly well on this occasion: a farewell speech that is also his first appearance in front of the whole team he wants to forge good links with as their boss.

Your lecture will be a success if you convey a clear message

The second criterion is about the *content of your lecture*. What exactly is the key point your lecture is making? If your listeners take just one sentence from the points you are making as a key message, what should this sentence be? No speaker should ever take the stage without a key message – it does not matter whether it is about paying tribute to an individual, making a sales pitch or arriving at a scientific hypothesis.

Manuel has already formulated his key message. It is this: 'We appreciate you, Stuart – and, like you, we are excited about this new phase in your life.' He takes this as a basis for collecting particular information about Stuart that he can use to illustrate this point: what have he and Manuel done together? How did the department see him? What makes him distinctive as a colleague? Manuel wants to use all this information to construct his key point and to lead up to it.

As a rule, quiet people find this second success criterion relating to content the easiest. And this does not just apply to those who are particularly good at analytical thinking – strength 6: quiet people are generally inclined to think very carefully about what they want to say before actually saying it. Discipline is needed to reduce one's own lecture to a single statement. But it is worth the effort: once you have established what is the key point in your lecture you will find it easy to systematically construct and explore all the other points you are making. This also helps you to find your way around the material – and helps the audience as well!

> ## ? Questions for you (for your next speech)
>
> What is your key point, in a single sentence?
>
> _____
>
> What material do you need to construct your key message and to lead up to it?
>
> _____
>
> _____
>
> What material do you need to present your key message in a lively and interesting fashion?
>
> _____
>
> _____
>
> _____

Your lecture will succeed if you tune in to your audience and their needs

*Positive contact with your audience is* the third major success criterion. Your lecture can only be really successful if you manage to get your points over to the audience. In concrete terms, this means that your audience *can* follow you (because you provide them with enough signposts) and also *want* to follow you (because what you are saying is interesting). This criterion makes your role as a speaker easier: it relieves you of the burden that you have to make the most positive impression personally while you are at the same time standing in the merciless glare of the harsh spotlight. Instead, the focus is on what the audience needs, and thus on putting your points over and addressing other people – and with all this remains the question of what your audience needs. Or more precisely: how to proceed and what is the best way to make the content interesting for the people who will be sitting listening to you?

A meaningful answer can be found by asking further questions that will help you when you are preparing your lecture: what information does your public need? What do they already know about the subject? What is the best kind of language to use? What sort of mood will the people you are speaking to be in, and what expectations will they have of you? Do you want to surprise your audience, or try to meet what you assume will be their expectations?

This criterion shows Manuel that his audience will be mainly interested in *him*. How will the new head of department behave in this new role? How will he treat his fellow employees? He decides that he will say goodbye to Stuart in such a way that his fellow employees will sense that the person standing in front of them is humane, and respects them. And besides this, they will see he can think clearly.

---

## ? Some questions for you (for your next speech)

What sort of people are likely to make up the audience?

_____

What are the important qualities needed for your speech?

_____

How does your audience rate you and your role?

_____

Is your audience made up of several groups with differing attitudes? What are they?

_____

How well informed is the audience about your subject?

_____

What might the audience think about the subject?

_____

What common denominator can you find for your audience (and possibly use as a starting point for your speech)? (Examples: background, training, interests, affiliations, opinions ...)

_____

_____

How do you intend to vary your subject matter on the basis of these questions?

_____

_____

_____

## Triangle of success criteria

If you follow these three success criteria you are already well on the way to a successful speech. The diagram below shows you the links between them:

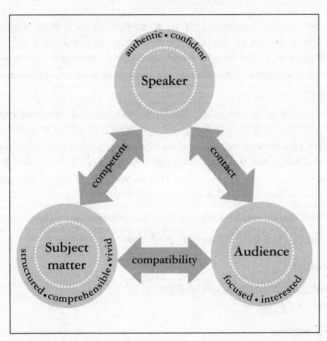

The next step takes us on to the preparation phase. Invest time here and you will both gain confidence and promote a responsive attitude. This is a particularly pleasant stage for quiet people: a speech can be prepared in peace and quiet, alone, without any audience at all …

# Opportunity and protection: the preparation phase!

## Advantages of planning

Think before you speak: this advice probably came initially from a quiet person. Ideally you will have plenty of time to do this. But usually time will be tight – and then it is all the more important to work purposefully and with concentration (strength 3) when you are preparing what you are going to say. This planning approach gives you two advantages straight away. Firstly, what you say in public has been thought through and well structured. Secondly, you feel much more secure as you are on firm ground in terms of what you intend to say.

Always base your preparation on the strategies from the previous section: answer the questions in terms of the three success criteria, i.e. relating to you as a person, to the subject matter and to the audience. This is your first set of guidelines. This section will show you how to structure your subject matter.

Any speech – it does not matter whether it is a toast, a company report or Manuel's farewell speech for Stuart – falls into three parts. It has an introduction, a central section and a conclusion. This is not just a matter of labels: each of the three sections has a particular job to do and it is important that you have this at the back of your mind when arranging your material. You will find a short summary below.

---

 **Sections of a speech, and their purposes**

**Introduction**

- Arouse interest in the subject matter.
- Establish a position.

**Central section**

- Present the subject matter lucidly and in an interesting fashion.

**Conclusion**

- Define the key point and where it is leading clearly.
- Make it clear what the audience are supposed to think, do, support.
- Reach a positive conclusion.

---

The structure sheet below addresses these different requirements. I often use it in my seminars. It will help you to structure any speech you may be making in a very short period of time. Of course you need to know what you want to talk about – but that is not usually a problem for quiet people. Use the sheet when you are preparing the speech so that you can position the appropriate subject matter in the right place.

As a public speech is not a conversation, you are very unlikely to encounter problems with the speed at which you communicate if you prepare thoroughly; this is because you are acting in a considered fashion, and do not have to act and improvise spontaneously.

# Play to your strengths when lecturing

Most quiet people see speaking in public as extrovert territory – as a platform that extroverts love and that also seems to be reserved for extrovert successes. This can be very discouraging. But quiet people have some plus points in their favour, and they can use these to help them deliver excellent speeches and lectures.

## Typical introvert strengths

As in the last two chapters, you will also find typical strengths here that I have often found in introverts – in this case, in introverts delivering lectures. I want to use these examples to demonstrate something that quiet people often overlook: the fact that they can exploit their own advantages to score valuable points with an audience.

## Strength 2: Substance

People of substance know what they are talking about. This of course becomes even more evident in a speech given to an audience: Manuel would never dream of appearing in public to say trivial things or to express ideas that he has not thought through.

## Preparing a speech: structure sheet

**Title:**

Key point:

### INTRODUCTION

'zoom in':

lead into the subject from something familiar, or something surprising

summary of contents:

### CENTRAL SECTION: DIVIDE INTO THREE SECTIONS/ASPECTS

**Aspect 1:**

implication/advantage

**Aspect 2:**

implication/advantage

**Aspect 3:**

implication/advantage

### CONCLUSION

summary/repetition of the key points

'zoom out': placing what has been said in a wider context

Here is a summary showing the most important and best consequences of using material that is rich in substance when lecturing:

! **Advantages of lectures with substance**

1. They do not include any boring platitudes or empty clichés ('I am pleased that so many of you have turned up …' 'Before I finish, I would just like to …'

2. Subject matter has been thought through and examined carefully.

3. No conspicuous self-promotion or feeble jokes.

4. Information about the lecturer him- or herself is well-chosen and fits in with the subject matter.

5. The importance of the subject matter is clearly demonstrated.

To sum up: these advantages mean that the lecturer (without putting themselves in the limelight) concentrates on the subject matter, gets to the heart of it and takes account of the audience's time and attention span. Substance does not make an impact only in terms of the subject matter. It also gives the audience the impression that the speaker in front of them is telling them something about him- or herself that relates to the subject matter. So ask yourself: what is important, relevant or interesting for you personally about the subject of the lecture? How much of this can you put over in the lecture?

WHAT ARE YOUR PERSONAL LINKS WITH YOUR SUBJECT MATTER?
HOW MUCH OF THIS CAN YOU FIT INTO THE LECTURE?

When asked this question, Manuel remembers a trip to a further education institution that he and Stuart took together. This gave him an opportunity to see a surprisingly different side of his colleague: Stuart told him (reticently at first, and then with increasing enthusiasm) about the first exhibition he had just been offered as an amateur sculptor. Nobody at work knew about this – but now Manuel had the new retiree's permission to talk about it. What wonderful material: now Stuart can concentrate on something that is important, valuable and of solid significance to him. And Manuel can tell the audience how impressed he was when he saw the sculptures …

## Strength 3: Concentration

Even though the subject matter has been fully addressed as far as Manuel is able, he is now worried before he takes the stage that his calm approach and conversational style could be unsuitable for many listeners and could seem out of place and boring in this arena. But as concentration is one of his strengths he does not need to worry about this too much. Manuel can score points by using increased intensity where an extrovert would speak energetically, with sweeping gestures and vibrant delivery. That is to say, he can pay full attention to the situation, the content and the audience, and put all his energy into the lecture. The crucial thing is that Manuel is concentrating his energy where it helps the lecture: by taking *this* opportunity to present *this* subject matter to *this* audience.

Of course concentrating on oneself can be counterproductive when lecturing and unsettle the lecturer. And focusing intensively on yourself is not really necessary: body language and voice tend largely to adapt themselves to the speaker's mood and to what is happening in his head. That is why they can make such an impact: they often give away far more than the person concerned actually wants!

### Keep to a few, clearly defined gestures

Large gestures are not important. It is much more important for movements to be clearly defined or, in other words, for them to have a beginning and an end. The same is true of intonation: you do not need to overdo your intonation – but be careful to articulate every sentence right to the end (in other words, don't let it fade away), and introduce deliberate pauses at important points. Also make sure that a statement sounds like a statement and not like a question. Making a statement sound like a question ('That is what I wanted to say?') is something I often hear from quiet people; it means that they are unintentionally but quite literally making their intonation 'question' their assertions and ideas, and thus robbing them of the forcefulness that the speaker's concentration strengths have made possible.

To sum up, it can be said that concentration enables you to do what you do calmly, powerfully and with dedication. Use the powerful impact you make when you take the stage!

## Strength 10: Empathy

### Take your listeners' points of view into account

You must already sense that anyone who stands up in front of an audience cannot put him- or herself into the position of each individual in that audience. Even so, empathy as a strength is a particular advantage for a quiet lecturer. An empathetic speaker is in a position to think himself into his listeners' points of view, to find out what those listeners need, and to address these matters first. Unsurprisingly, it is the classic, highly extrovert limelight-hogger who all too often sweeps the audience's needs aside – and fails to take heed of the third success criterion: that of paying due attention to the listeners' needs.

But what does empathy mean in a lecture situation? Let's go back to Manuel and his farewell to Stuart. As Manuel is able to think empathetically, he will do the following things in his speech:

- take into account what his fellow employees think of Stuart: they will miss him, and Manuel will stress this in concrete terms
- be able to assess what the audience will find particularly interesting: in this case it is he himself in his new role
- ensure that the audience will find a way of tuning in to him as a speaker: this will include his shared experience with Stuart as an amateur sculptor
- include the audience in the event: at the end of his speech he will ask Stuart's three closest colleagues to come forward and get them to hand over the department's present, adding a few words of their own.

Speak without notes

And Manuel will definitely follow the advice his coach has given him: he will speak without notes and only have a few headings in front of him so that he will not be tempted to read from his manuscript and thus avoid contact (obstacle 9). Manuel will also be sure to maintain good eye contact, so that he can assess his audience's reactions and take them into account where appropriate: for a good speaker, every instance of public speaking is a dialogue.

---

## ? A question for you

Which of your personal strengths can you exploit particularly when lecturing? Write brief notes to show how you can use these strengths most effectively.

Strength 1: Caution

Strength 2: Substance

Strength 3: Concentration

Strength 4: Listening

Strength 5: Calm

Strength 6: Analytical thinking

Strength 7: Independence

Strength 8: Tenacity

Strength 9: Writing (rather than speaking)

Strength 10: Empathy

Additional strength:_____

Additional strength:_____

Useful in the following ways:

_____

_____

_____

_____

_____

_____

_____

_____

_____

_____

_____

# Getting over difficulties when lecturing

## Typical obstacles for introverts when lecturing

So far, so good: so quiet people have strengths that help them in public speaking. Then why do so many introverts particularly dislike speaking in public – and why are so many of them ineffective as speakers? The fact that quiet people prefer to speak to a small number of people, or to individuals, is not an adequate reason, as the converse shows: a stimulating lecturer who can fill a hall does not inevitably have problems when talking to individuals.

The answer to these critical questions is to be found in the particular obstacles faced by quiet people. Let us look at a few typical difficulties.

## Obstacle 1: Fear

Fear can take on a number of shapes in the public-speaking sphere. One of them is *stage fright,* the sense of unease that grips the body before and also during an appearance. Three-quarters of all people are said to be afraid before appearing in public. So the figures alone show that stage fright cannot be the domain of quiet people alone. It also features regardless of how experienced or competent the person suffering from stage fright is: even experienced actors, the most intelligent professors and highly talented musicians have stage fright before their appearances. It is a physical response in the first place. Let us take a closer look – the more you know about stage fright, the less of an ordeal it need be – and you will be able to handle it much better.

Stage fright is a moderate form of fear, or anxiety, before appearing in public. It has a large number of advantages: even a small dose of adrenalin makes people wide awake and alert in front of an audience. It is biologically impossible to be tired and bored if the body is functioning as described above.

> **!** **Stage fright: what causes it and how it affects the body**
>
> - Stage fright is a stress reaction. The body is intended to be able to react quickly in order to be able to master a situation that is seen to be dangerous. It does not matter whether this danger comes from a vicious dog or a public appearance: roughly the same thing happens physiologically.
>
> - This reaction is triggered by the sympathetic nervous system, the part of the vegetative nervous system that is responsible for boosting the organism's performance, such as if there is a sudden sense of stress or when a person is attacked or has to escape.
>
> - The sympathetic nervous system triggers a burst of the hormone adrenalin in the adrenalin medulla. Cortisol is generated as a second stress hormone.

- The two hormones confine the body to a limited number of responses to help it handle the danger (at least in the case of the dog attack). These reactions are attack, escape or paralysis.
- Stress hormones also have differing effects from person to person. Possible effects among others are higher heart rate, rapid breathing, change in the blood flow (linked with going red or pale), spasms or trembling in individual parts of the body, problems in the digestive tract (nausea, flatulence and belching, diarrhoea, a need to urinate), or also problems in the nervous system (increased perspiration rate, fluttering eyes, headaches or dizziness).

## Overcoming fear of appearing in public

But as is the case with so many substances, it is not the dose that matters with adrenalin either. It is only bad when stage fright mutates into genuine *fear of performing in public* – the second form of fear after stage fright that makes public speaking seriously difficult. The fact is that fear of making a public appearance creates an actual block: you feel that you are a helpless victim of the situation. You can no longer say what you want, and you cannot perform to the best of your ability. Poor breathing (caused by stress) and the concentration of blood in your extremities (but not in the brain) and the raised mental stress level can lead to concentration problems and in the worst case to blackouts. Contact with the public becomes more difficult. And seeming confident and competent, with a real fear of appearing in public threatening you, is a real challenge.

The obvious question is this: how can this anxiety – both stage fright and real terror about appearing in public – and its negative symptoms be overcome? Willpower and self-discipline are not the best way, as a glance at the physical consequences caused by the stress hormones will show: symptoms like headache, blushing and nausea cannot simply be willed away

### Anxiety resistance strategy number 1: Speak in public regularly

But there is something you can do, and you can do it on three levels: the first is *habit*. Make sure you practise regularly. If the lecture is a particularly important one, you could rehearse with an audience of friends or trusted colleagues. If you deliberately expose yourself to lecturing situations on a regular basis, the anxiety centre in your brain will repeatedly register that you can handle public speaking without serious consequences. This will make the anxiety less intense, and the anxiety symptoms will be alleviated as well – something that used to be seen as a dangerous unknown gradually becomes a habit – a phenomenon known as desensitization. Experience makes you more relaxed and more secure. The inner resistance you feel when speaking in public does not go away completely, but it weakens with time. The anxiety loses its strength.

A good and at the same time unbeatable way of speaking in public regularly is to join a toastmasters' club. These clubs have set themselves the aim of making their members into better speakers and leaders. The method used is peer coaching – anyone making a speech is assessed by another member. You will also learn to be an assessor yourself, to speak off the cuff, how to chair a meeting – in brief, speaking in front of other people in a variety of situations. There are toastmasters' clubs all over the world; you will find the appropriate link in the list of useful websites at the end of the book.

One reservation should be mentioned here: if you suffer from a particularly severe form of anxiety about speaking in public, it is best for you to be helped through the desensitization process by someone with appropriate psychological training.

Anxiety resistance strategy number 2: Use mental strategies

Secondly, you can reduce your anxiety about speaking by applying your conscious thinking skills. You will remember that consciousness can influence physical processes.

### THE RIGHT MINDSET FOR HANDLING ANXIETY: I AM WELL PREPARED!

First of all, make sure you are well prepared: when you tell yourself confidently in the preliminary stages that you are well prepared, this mindset will get rid of a lot of your anxiety from the outset. But of course you must actually be well prepared. This takes a load off your short-term memory, which functions to a rather more limited extent when quiet people are under stress. You will also have more room for improvisation if something unexpected should happen.

### ANOTHER MINDSET FOR HANDLING ANXIETY: THE SUBJECT MATTER IS WORTH THE RISK.

This mindset appeals to your 'higher self'. It helps you to look away from yourself and aim at a higher goal. The subject matter is so important that it is worth all the effort and personal discomfort associated with appearing in public. Interestingly, this strategy offers particular relief to introverts: the cerebral cortex soothes the anxiety centre in your brain. Do try it: it works.

Anxiety resistance strategy number 3: Look after your body

Finally, we should mention something that many of my quiet clients allude to as the ultimate catastrophe: your mind going blank This is where you completely lose the thread – i.e. access to what you want to say. But you do not lose what *you have already said*, so this becomes a good reference point: repeat it, or sum up the key subject matter.

But before you do this, engage in a second activity at the same time: breathe. Or more precisely: breathe in deeply and slowly. There is something very concrete behind this advice. Your mind going blank occurs mainly because of a lack of oxygen and blood supply to the brain. This lack arises because of the adrenalin-induced stress reaction described above. Adrenalin makes you hyperventilate – your breathing becomes rapid and shallow. This means that air is only reaching the upper chest area, unless you do something about this. This and the stress hormone cocktail that has been poured out make a serious impact: no oxygen – and you lose the thread.

So the most important thing for you to do if your mind does go blank is to practise deep breathing again. If you breathe purposefully and slowly into your stomach (or more precisely, into the area just below your ribs), this has two further advantages: firstly, it makes your voice stronger and, secondly, you will be calmer and more relaxed – and this quite literally: tensions are released, and your thoughts flow more regularly. All the meditation techniques in the world use breathing as a centring device.

It is best of all to breathe deeply and slowly before you appear to give your lecture. Find a quiet corner, even if it is the washroom. Breathe deeply and calmly. In this way you will generate energy – and you will appear before your audience with more inner calm (strength 5), giving an impression of confidence.

Body and mind influence each other. You can use mental messages to bring about physical change (relaxation, for example, as in anti-anxiety strategy 2). The converse is also true: breathing can calm your mind. Similarly, you can use your body to moderate your fear by 'acting as if you are'. Strike a pose that suggests a confident speaker. Put your feet together on the floor, distribute your weight evenly and stand up straight. Stretch your spine and hold your head up. A self-confident pose works wonders on your brain. It 'believes' in this confidence because the body is generating it. Try it out, even if it seems peculiar. Remember that there is a wonderful side effect: your audience will see you as a confident person as well – because you look like one.

It doesn't really matter if you go red for a while. People who blush and betray some embarrassment in that way seem appealing, as psychologist Dacher Keltner has shown. This is because the person blushing is revealing that he does care about his fellow human beings – communication really matters to him.

## Obstacle 2: Too much detail

Too much detail in a lecture is often related to fear (obstacle 1). The lecturer tries to seek safety in minor points that he knows well and considers to be reliable. So Manuel, when saying goodbye to his colleague, is tempted simply to stick to the details of his career and deal with these as thoroughly as possible. That would be objectively correct and would bear examination, but it would bore the audience to tears and would definitely be very quickly forgotten.

The effects of giving too much detail occur particularly frequently in scientific and other specialized lectures. Some of my clients and seminar members like to build as many experimental results and details as possible into their lectures (and slides). This certainly supports their results, but they can easily lose their audience by doing it, by making them unable to follow the thread. But what use is even the best thread if it is securely in the speaker's mind but does not help the audience to follow? The three tips below will enable you to strike a good balance between the importance of being precise and keeping an eye on what really matters.

> **!  Precision and the full topic: here's how to convey both**
>
> 1. Keep to your structure when lecturing.
>    This is quite a simple point: no digressions!
> 2. Keep your key point in mind.
>    Ask yourself when reviewing all subject matter, examples, details and stories: does this information help to put my key points across? The following approaches are permissible: leading up to the key point, illustrating the key point and conclusions drawn from the key point. (See the second success criterion earlier in this chapter.)

3. Take more material with you than you want to put over.

    Scientists and professional administrators in particular often wonder whether they have included enough figures, data and facts in their lecture. Don't be afraid to take plenty of this information with you, in dedicated summaries or an additional slide. If someone in the audience wants more detailed information after the lecture, you will be forearmed – without overloading the lecture itself for your listeners.

## Obstacle 5: Escape

Not facing up to deadlines

When quiet people are stressed, a lot of them are tempted to escape from it all. They try to ignore the deadline before a public appearance and thus postpone the preparation work until it cannot be avoided any more. This means that pressure of time is added to the stress of giving the lecture: not a good situation.

Break the preparation work down into stages

The countermeasure is easy. As soon as the lecture date is fixed, plan the preparation work by dividing it up into small stages and setting a date for each of them. Small stages seem less threatening and are easier to manage, and they make for successful results and also help you to feel more secure. Simply make use of the aids suggested in the section 'Opportunity and protection: the preparation phase!' above to help you prepare your speech stage by stage. In the actual lecture situation the desire to escape can be expressed by the quiet person withdrawing completely into his text and thus neglecting contact with the audience and its needs.

This temptation becomes well-nigh irresistible if you have an absolutely fully formulated script in front of you: genuine eye contact is as good as impossible, and so are a lively delivery and expressions that follow the simple structures of spoken language (and not written language, which can easily take over on paper if you are not a professional speechwriter).

Just note headings

You can prevent this kind of escape with a strategy that forces you to reduce your material: just write down headings, not a fully written text. The aim is not perfection here. Spoken language always includes little mistakes in the choice of words, pronunciation or sentence construction. But we are not looking for polished formulations, we are looking for contact. The little mistakes that slip into our spoken language will be corrected almost automatically in the listeners' minds. But if you do not establish any contact, there will not be much in those minds that is anything to do with your lecture. There will be nothing there but shopping lists or holiday plans ...

Have you identified what your personal obstacles are when speaking to an audience? Have you had a chance to make a personal inventory: where do your risks lie – and what can you specifically do to tackle them?

---

## ? A question for you

Which of the typical introvert obstacles might cause you a problem in a lecture situation? Write headings against them to identify what risks you can see and what you can do about them.

**Obstacle 1: Fear**

Risk:_____        What I could do about it:_____
_____        _____

**Obstacle 2: Too much detail**

Risk:_____        What I could do about it:_____
_____        _____

**Obstacle 3: Over-stimulation**

Risk:_____        What I could do about it:_____

_____        _____

**Obstacle 4: Passivity**

Risk:_____        What I could do about it:_____

_____        _____

**Obstacle 5: Escape/lethargy**

Risk:_____        What I could do about it:_____

_____        _____

**Obstacle 6: Being unduly cerebral**

Risk:_____        What I could do about it:_____

_____        _____

**Obstacle 7: Self-deception**

Risk:_____        What I could do about it:_____

_____        _____

**Obstacle 8: Fixation**

Risk:_____        What I could do about it:_____

_____        _____

**Obstacle 9: Avoiding contact**

Risk:_____        What I could do about it:_____

_____        _____

**Obstacle 10: Avoiding conflict**

Risk:_____        What I could do about it:_____

_____        _____

Manuel's farewell speech is a success. His colleagues and employees get to know him as a management personality who cares and thinks about people. And Stuart, who is the main figure in the speech, is moved and proud, as the applause, which is for him too, thunders out.

And talking of applause: never run away from it. Applause is the audience saying 'Thank you' to you – so stay on your feet and accept it!

## ✳ Key points in brief

- Quiet people find public speaking particularly difficult. But you can learn how to lecture – and the more it becomes routine, the easier it will be.
- A lecture is successful if the speaker's personality shows through, if he can convey his message clearly and if he is in a position to tune himself and his subject matter into this audience.

- Good preparation, based on the success criteria and a clear structure, takes a lot of the stress out of a public appearance.

- A genuinely 'quiet' lecturing style is built on personal strengths and avoids the risks associated with the individual obstacles. The first stage is to identify these personal strengths and obstacles.

- Typical strengths shown by quiet people when appearing in public are substance, concentration and empathy.

- Frequently encountered obstacles are anxiety, too much detail and a wish to escape.

# 9.
# Rules of the pack: how to speak up in meetings

Paul's computer is his favourite and most important working tool. He is an IT management consultant, and thrives on his ability to master the pitfalls lurking in system changes and new software packages. Until now he had always had a senior consultant with him at client meetings, and was almost always in touch with the IT experts at the firm he was dealing with. But this week his senior consultant is ill. He has asked Paul to lead a meeting with an important client – it is not possible to postpone this meeting, because it is about an urgent redistribution of project roles in the company, and it has been difficult to get all the people involved round a table – including the managing director, the staff responsible for the budget and several managers and employees from the IT department.

Paul is dreading this meeting. How is he supposed to get a roomful of people who won't stop talking to agree on a decision? He would prefer to bury himself in the IT department and do what he is best at: planning the technical workflow, and passing the arrangements on to others. Diane from the said IT department at the client firm is equally terrified. She will be at this meeting as one of the people involved in the project. Diane knows that for her area of responsibility she needs a budget increase and at least one other person to make the new arrangements work. But how can she bring this off at the planned plenary meeting. And to make it worse, her senior boss will be there too …

## Meetings can be unduly stimulating

Meetings and group discussions are often very stressful for quiet people like Paul and Diane – especially when there are a lot of the kind of participants who like to talk a lot in situations like this. Introverts tend to react like this: they feel over-stimulated (obstacle 3), withdraw into themselves and decide that most of what is being said is hot air. A lot of quiet people feel that little notice is taken of them at these big meetings: a female client once said to me: 'I often feel completely invisible at discussions like this, but I thought it was the limit last week when I plucked up courage and suggested something that really mattered to me. Nobody picked up what I said – but when a colleague said almost the same thing a little later, everybody suddenly thought it was a great idea. I thought I must be in the wrong film!'

## Achievement remains invisible

Discussions that don't produce the desired result are only one of the disadvantages that introverts experience. Introverts who keep quiet in groups can't put their own achievements and ideas over adequately. Sometimes it gets even worse and suggestions made by the above-mentioned female client, for example, are 'pinched' by someone else and meet with a highly successful response. And, in addition, the impression that superiors can get is that the quiet person who is so reticent in discussions is not a good team player. All this can represent a genuine risk in career terms.

So how can you as a quiet person attract attention and make your presence felt in this hothouse atmosphere? And how can you bring all this off with a reasonable expenditure of energy? This chapter will deal with these questions.

# Plenary sessions: Six rules and six implications for introverts

In this section, we are going to look at the rules that govern discussions of all kinds. The more you know about these rules, the better you will be able to negotiate to achieve what matters in meetings – being visible, confident and convincing. And what is said about each of the rules is possibly even more important: you will find typical introvert strengths for meetings (and how you can use them), and equally typical obstacles for introverts (and how you can limit their consequences).

## Rule 1 for meetings: Only people who say something are visible

If you want to give an impression of a competent and constructive approach at meetings, you have to make a contribution. This does not mean that you should be talking all the time – but be sure to say something at every meeting. I know softly spoken introverts that everyone listens to when they speak because of the quality of what they have to say.

Here strength 2, substance, will help you (alongside other things we are going to talk about). The fact is that what introverts say in public usually makes an impact because they have thought carefully in advance about what they are going to say. Introverts do not usually incline towards empty beating about the bush and status-seeking because they are more concerned about the matter in hand than themselves. The group benefits from this when it needs to form an opinion or make a decision (or to let other people need to get a word in). Substance, along with other strengths, makes introvert contributions at this level particularly valuable. Take advantage of this!

Obstacle 1, fear, can inhibit achieving the desired visibility. Saying something at a meeting is also a public appearance, and this was addressed in Chapter 8. That is why it is true both here and there: fear is an obstacle. To cope with fear, please follow the tips given earlier.

Meetings at which new ideas are to be developed are a particularly difficult obstacle. The greatest threats are over-stimulation and passivity (obstacles 3 and 4). If you want to participate actively in a brainstorming session, make use of strength 9, writing (ideally from the preparatory stage onwards). Take a piece of paper and create your own written brainstorm. You'll soon see that you'll find it easier then to make a contribution to those fast-moving meetings!

## Rule 2 for meetings: Attention spans tend to be short

### Get your key point over

Speaking is one thing. But ultimately you can only be successful if the others actually listen to you. Here the trickiest point in terms of *subject matter* for quiet people is an inclination towards over-attention to detail (obstacle 2): introverts tend to get lost in a mass of detail and transform a clear thread into an inextricable tangle of details.

So be sure that you don't get entangled in this kind of detail when making your contributions. This will soon make extroverts in particular lose patience, and lead to a loss of attention. If you answer a question in too much detail, you can easily frustrate the meeting, and lose everyone's attention. So, before you make a contribution, think as you would before a speech: what is my key point? And pay attention to the way you say it: use short, simply structured sentences.

### Make your contribution heard

Attention also depends on a good *voice level*: even the most exciting subject matter will send your audience to sleep if you present it in the voice of a funeral orator. A soft, weak voice, a lack of pauses and unduly rapid delivery also rob contributions of their effect – no matter how rich the subject matter is when viewed objectively. Pay attention to stress in your delivery: each sentence has key words in terms of subject matter, and you should emphasize them appropriately. Also drop your tone at the end of a sentence. This defines sentences as units of meaning and gives them emphasis. Speak loudly enough for everyone to hear you – and get a friendly colleague to comment on your speed of delivery when you are making a contribution: you shouldn't speak in an agitated fashion, or so slowly that it puts the audience to sleep.

### Eye contact with the audience

Another body language resource for gaining attention is *eye contact*. Try to make eye contact particularly with the decision-makers in the room: these are the people you have to win over and convince. Introverts usually feel secure and much more comfortable when talking to individuals rather than lecturing to groups. Take advantage of this fact: look at your colleagues individually when you are making a contribution at a meeting – as though you were speaking to just this one person for a moment. Eye contact with individuals not only makes you feel more secure, it also makes you more forceful, more present, and thus more convincing. You will be the focus of attention – and it will be much less likely for a colleague to sell your idea as his own at a later date!

## Rule 3 for meetings: No decision without clarification of status

### Speaking time depends on status

It is as frustrating as it is true for people who are less status conscious (in other words for many introverts, particularly female ones) that it is not possible to have a meaningful discussion until the participants have clarified their ranking order among themselves. Marion Knaths' book *Spiele mit der Macht* (*Power Games*) shows how this clarification comes about when a group gets together for the first time. And she states quite calmly: ranking order is more important that subject matter! The time allotted for speaking also depends on status. If you rank higher, you can talk for longer, and also deviate from the topic. If your status is lower, you have to be brief, you are likely to be interrupted and your contributions will not have such a substantial response.

Make sure you have sufficient time in which to speak

Quiet people who incline towards avoiding contact (obstacle 9) also like to avoid people who get on their nerves. It is highly likely that the very colleagues who tend to wrangle about status will fit into this category very well. You must resist them, but on your own terms. So make sure you have sufficient speaking time – at least as much as colleagues in a comparable position. But if you prefer to speak briefly, rather than at length, then speak more frequently to compensate for this. And, while you are speaking, note that the highest-ranking person is the most important, that is who you have to convince. This person can be recognized by the fact that everyone else keeps looking at her or him to check how they are listening and responding to the various contributions. You will probably not be interrupted if the highest-ranking person is listening to you.

Self-confident posture

Be self-confident in your posture as well, and turn towards others. That means occupy the space confidently without becoming casual. Use the whole area of your chair to sit on, but don't loll or stick your elbows out. Sit up straight, and look open. Avoid submissive gestures like holding your head on one side or looking away in unpleasant situations. Make sure that your movements are defined, in other words have a beginning and an end: no rocking, no fiddling about with things. The same applies to your voice: the tone can be quiet (strength 5) so long as it is determined and your statement should be delivered with sufficient energy right to the end of the sentence. Take care to breathe deeply (see Chapter 8). Don't let your voice or movements become agitated. Agitation reduces your status. Overall, the messages that you send should convey one thing: you know (polite, friendly and co-operative as you are) exactly what you are doing.

If you are not at all inclined to struggle for a chance to speak at the plenary session, you can use the tips given under rule 5 for meetings and help to prepare the decisions strategically in advance. '*Éminences grises*' (decision-makers who operate behind the scenes) occupy status positions as well …

## Rule 4 for meetings: It is fair – sometimes!

When objective interests are abandoned

In the best of all possible worlds, everyone plays according to the rules – even in meetings! But as I'm sure you know yourself, real life works differently. Of course there is such a thing as fairness and open-minded exchanges of views. But not always. A lot of people who attend meetings find that it is worth going against the rules and interrupting or even attacking if such approaches are not subject to sanctions and increase the chances of making personal progress (visibility, competing for status). Unfair behaviour is particularly stressful for quiet people, and can also cost them in terms of status and effectiveness if they do not handle such situations with supreme confidence – above all when avoiding conflict (obstacle 10), which is one of their personal pressure points.

Here is an 'emergency plan' for you, so that you can act quickly if the need arises: the five most frequent rule infringements in discussions and the most potentially successful ways of dealing with them.

 **Tips for rule infringements**

| Rule infringements | What to do |
|---|---|
| 1. A participant interrupts you while you are speaking. | 1. The best strategy if you are interrupted by people who rank equally with or below you is to stick to your guns (strength 8: tenacity) – and keep talking! Slip the following sentence in, loudly and clearly: 'Let me just bring this to a conclusion ...' |
| | 2. If the person interrupting outranks you, it can be best to let the interruption (by your boss, for example) go through, and keep up with the discussion while he or she is talking through eye contact or nodding. And, if it is possible, respond to the statement directly. |

| | |
|---|---|
| 2. A colleague comments on your statement: 'What Jill is trying to say is ...' | 1. This is clearly a fight for status: the colleague is trying to make it clear that he has the right to interpret what Jill has said.<br><br>2. If you are Jill: never fail to comment on interruptions like this. Suggested formulation: 'Thank you for your support, Rob. What is particularly important here is ...' |
| 3. A colleague tries to put your idea on ice by creating a delay: a working party should examine it more closely, the budget planning decision should be waited for, more information needs to be gathered first ... | 1. The risk lies in the fact that your idea will lose momentum as a result of the delay and 'fade out' – while the colleague can seem to be acting supportively.<br><br>2. Agree with your colleague at the plenary session that there is a lot to think about in relation to this innovation. Then add that you and your team have actually already done this preparatory thinking. Something like this: 'That's right – we need to look carefully at several factors before we outsource this part of the project. And we have done precisely this in the last few weeks. The results are entirely positive. Today we have to come to a decision – we can only complete the project on time if we outsource at the appropriate moment. Otherwise it will get very expensive! Are there any questions about our research?' |
| 4. A colleague stabs you in the back and argues against a previous agreement. | 1. You have no chance of arguing against him at the plenary session if it was an informal agreement. But talk to the colleague straight after the meeting and find out what made him change his stance (or even just the strategy).<br><br>2. But if it is something that has been agreed officially, you should make that clear: 'I am surprised to hear you say that – at the last departmental meeting we agreed that ... How does this all fit together?' |

| 5. A colleague attacks you unfairly at the plenary session: 'But these figures are nonsense!' | 1. Take a deep breath: this too is obviously a power game that your attacker hopes to win. |
| | 2. The ideal answer needs facts: 'Which actual figures are you referring to?' |
| | 3. If you cannot think of a suitable answer, make it clear at the plenary session that you are not going to let this go. You could say: 'I have another matter to attend to immediately elsewhere.' |

## Rule 5 for meetings: Allies help to secure the result

### Important things happen before the meeting

Several people and work areas are usually involved in meetings. If there is one thing I have learned in committee work, it is this: if a difficult decision is in the offing, in most cases it is actually agreed *before* the meeting. In other words, the people who will be affected by the decision form alliances, primarily with other opinion makers, but also with other participants. By doing this they will have neatly ensured that their candidate will have a majority at the forthcoming election, agreed in advance how resources will be distributed or steered resolutions in a particular direction.

### Talk to decision-makers beforehand

Let's take Paul, our opening example. I advised him to talk before the meeting individually to the people who will be responsible for decisions about redistributing the project jobs. The aim is to filter out the various interests and to prepare a decision that everyone could live with, and possibly find advantageous. Paul is a quiet person, and so he prefers individual conversations to group situations anyway, so he did not find this a difficult job. He was careful and went about things with appropriate caution (strength 1). He was also able to listen well (strength 4) to the individuals involved and to put himself in their place, so that he was not just thinking of his own interests and nothing else (strength 10). Paul successfully reached a good compromise on this basis, and he had also hinted about it to the managing director before the meeting. So the MD felt well informed and knew where he was – an important detail in the status game!

The advantages of forging alliances are obvious: the meeting becomes predictable at the most important points, and you are in touch with information and opinion-makers in a way that you would only have been for a short time if at all. And, last but not least, you can reduce the possibility of a participant stabbing you in the back at the plenary session. So you have gained two major advantages for the meeting: certainty and predictability.

## Rule 6 for meetings: What has been decided and putting it into practice are two different things

When there are hitches about putting things into practice

My second insight gained from all the board and managerial meetings I have attended is that what was discussed and passed is put into practice. Sometimes. But what is decided immediately after the meeting is what the actual value of this is – and what happens next?

This is not always the same. After elections, there is rarely much that can be done about the person elected. But proposals that leave the meeting room as decisions made are much less stable. There are many reasons for this, extending from indifference and negligence to clever sabotage or contradictory decisions by superiors who were not at the meeting and then change things around if a result does not suit them.

Quiet people inclined towards avoiding contact and conflict (obstacles 9 and 10) often give in to the temptation to take refuge in hope and take it as a given that resolutions will be implemented – and can then get some nasty surprises. So one question is particularly important here: what can you do to make it more probable that decisions that are important to you really are implemented?

Record resolutions in writing

Tenacity (strength 8) is your major asset here. If something really matters to you, you should stick at it and keep talking to your colleagues who are responsible for implementing it. Is everything working out as planned? Are there any stumbling blocks? And to make a resolution more stable you can also make sure that it is written down: written matter is more stable and easier to check, and so this helps if people start saying things like 'We *never* put it like that!' Various media are available: copies from an interactive whiteboard, an email to all participants or good old-fashioned minutes. What's important is the content. It should always contain the answer to that famous three-part question: who is doing what by when?

It is not always possible to prevent later intervention and decision altering by superiors. But you can fend it off to some extent by a carefully targeted information policy – see rule 5 for meetings.

**? Three questions for you**

What do you find particularly difficult in meetings?

_____

_____

_____

What are the consequences of this?

_____

_____

_____

What do you want to do differently in future?

_____

_____

_____

# Leading a discussion: meetings for advanced students

Paul has been assigned to leading a meeting. This section is about dealing with this kind of task successfully – with the calm strengths of a quiet management figure.

## Planning time

If it is within your power to fix times and dates, be sure that they are convenient: not too early, not too late, not too many meetings on one day.

Leave sufficient time for consultation between the different meetings, and for the initial implementation of decisions made.

## Planning content

The better you prepare for a meeting, the more effectively it will proceed. Here is a checklist that you can simply work through when planning meetings.

> **?  Checklist for preparing a discussion**
>
> 1. Time: when is the discussion to take place? How long should it last?
> 2. Place: where will the discussion be held?
> 3. What are the aims of the discussion?
> 4. What will be on the agenda?
> 5. In what order should these points be dealt with?
> 6. How much time should be allowed for each point?
> 7. Which subjects should be omitted if time is tight?
> 8. Who will be asked to the meeting? Who will be involved in a particular point in the agenda? (List of participants)
> 9. Who is responsible for/leading on which points on the agenda?
> 10. Who are you expecting documents from about this meeting? When should you ask for them – and by when should they be delivered?
> 11. How should the results be recorded? By whom?
> 12. Which media are needed?
> 13. Who is issuing invitations to the meeting, and what information will they provide (agenda)?
> 14. Who will put the documents together and check that they are all there? Who will arrange to dispatch them in advance (if necessary)?
> 15. Who will deal with the general preparation (room reservation, seating plan, media, name badges, snacks, drinks)?

## Implementation

The actual discussion is the greatest obstacle. But you can approach it analytically (strength 6) and work through the following phases in order to chair the meeting.

---

**!** **Discussion phases**

1. Introductory phase: welcome the participants, present the agenda, ensure that people know what is going on (length of the meeting, weighting of the subject matter, special participants ...).

2. Three-phase sequence: (N.B.: these phases apply to each point on the agenda separately)
   - information phase: introduction to the subject by you or others
   - working phase: treatment of subjects – exchange of questions, information and arguments
   - outcome phase: summary, co-ordination, planning for further action, distribution of jobs and responsibilities (who is doing what by when?) *or:* postponing decisions and planning for further action.

3. Final phase: thanks to all present, pick out positive outcomes. Then possibly a discussion of subsequent date(s) and short goodbye.

---

Probably the most difficult obstacle is controlling the process. If there are controversies, deviations and distractions, it is very difficult to find a way back to the direction the meeting should be taking. In a case like this, Paul decides to take a deep breath, keep very calm (strength 5) and lead the meeting back to the appropriate point on the agenda with quiet tenacity – pointing out what time it is, if that is appropriate.

Balance

Pay particular attention to the introverts at the meeting. These can take longer before they say anything, and they often speak more softly than extrovert participants. Ensure that the quiet people get their say – and this is not just for the sake of being fair: you are now aware that introverts are thoughtful and careful, in other words inclined towards security. This can mean that they will introduce important factors into the discussion that their extrovert colleagues do not have an eye on. You are a quiet discussion leader, so you are in an ideal position to make sure that introverts have a say and that their contributions are given due consideration.

Brainstorming as a special case

Brainstorming is used in meetings to bring out as many ideas as possible: for example, how a problem can be solved or a vision developed.

Ideas are thrown about in any order, collected together and not rated or discussed until the next phase. Brainstorming is a wonderful form of communication for extroverts. Racing to come up with ideas spontaneously in a social context – what fun for people who develop their ideas as they speak!

But it doesn't look quite the same to introverts. They prefer to think calmly before they share their thoughts – and to do this alone. Things have usually moved on to the next stage before quiet participants have developed ideas they think are viable in principle: the extroverts are comparing and rating the ideas that have poured out so far. So the introverts' ideas are lost – and with them about 50 per cent of the group's potential. Susan Cain's book refers to recent studies saying that large groups are usually less productive than smaller ones – or than individuals who develop new ideas in complete isolation (Cain 2011). The great exception to this sober summary is online brainstorming under clear direction.

### Brainstorming online or on paper

This means, in principle, that you can substitute other ways of producing ideas on a smaller scale without any difficulty, without detracting from the outcome. Or you can carry out the brainstorming online. But if thinking things over at a plenary session is traditional in your company or organisation, there is an easy way of making a brainstorming session accessible and as profitable as possible: simply ask all the members of the group to take a few minutes to *write down* their first thoughts (strength 9). This approach creates a situation for introverts in which they can think alone and express themselves in their preferred medium. The ideas will not be discussed until the next stage, when they will be shown to everyone on an interactive whiteboard, flip chart or pin-board.

## Dealing with difficult situations and participants in discussions

The summaries in the previous sections will give you a sense of security when leading discussions. But you can find yourself in situations that are stressful for everyone, not just quiet leaders. So it will be all the better if you are prepared for disturbances and difficulties. The following summaries contain the most important stress factors that can crop up at meetings – along with the appropriate strategies to help you, as a (quiet) discussion leader, to deal with difficult people and situations.

## ! Difficult situations in discussions

1. **Nothing doing:** Nobody says anything.

   *Strategies*: Make sure that everyone know where they are: sum up briefly what has been achieved so far. Identify any questions that are still unresolved. Ask your own questions to move people in the right direction.

2. **Differences of opinion** between at least two participants.

   *Strategies*: If the clash is about something concrete, identify the different points of view in neutral terms. Get a sense of opinion from the plenary session if you think this is appropriate. If things get too emotional, and the waves of excitement are breaking sufficiently high, calm the meeting down by taking a short break so that the parties to the dispute can resolve the situation without an audience – and the plenary session will be able to get back to work.

3. **Reproaches:** Participants criticize your approach.

   An example from Paul's meeting: 'But you'd said that you would get the budget plan for the project to us before this meeting!'

   *Strategies*: If the criticism is justified, use your empathy (strength 10) to understand the other person's point of view. Then say what you intend to do about it, in concrete terms.

   Example answer for Paul: 'We have not got all the data yet. I can see that you need the figures for planning purposes. I have already arranged for the data to be available tomorrow ...'

   If the criticism is not justified, act as for 4 or 5.

4. **Provocation:** Here it is not about the matter in hand – someone is trying to break your composure and test you. It could be motivated by status, for example, by boundary issues or by dislike.

   An example from Paul's meeting. A head of department says: 'All this project work on your list simply doesn't exist.'

   *Strategies*: Avoid a fighting match at the plenary session. That would be stressful and the outcome would be uncertain. Instead, take the exchange back to the matter in hand. To do this, make a bridging statement that leads away from the person trying to provoke you and back to the subject. A possible answer for Paul: 'It looks like a lot. And it really is a lot – it's working on four project sections at the same time that makes the list such a long one.'

5. **An attack** by one participant against another, or against you. A decisive tone of voice, a strong judgement and little content in terms of the subject matter are typical of an attack. An example from Paul's meeting: 'That doesn't work either.'

*Strategies*: Take a deep breath – your relaxed approach is worth its weight in gold in a situation like this. Even more than in the provocation example, the attacker wants to show that he is stronger and you are weaker, so it is a matter of status. If you remain calm and confident, the attacker's plan will not add up. Also, challenge the attacker to get back to the subject.

Here are a few examples that could help Paul:

- 'I see that you are sceptical. What has brought you to this view?'
- 'I see that you are sceptical. What do you suggest?'
- 'What do you mean by that?' To gain time, and as an emergency solution, this last suggestion (if nothing else occurs to you) is a wonderful catch-all for all cases.

Let's look round the group of participants: how do you deal with difficult characters and their behaviour?

## ! Difficult participants in discussions

1. **The person who talks too much:** needs attention, and can make others deviate from the point as well.

*Strategies*: People who talk too much can easily cause frustration at a plenary session, and in extreme cases the thread can be lost. It is your job to stop them and skilfully shift their contributions back to the subject of the meeting.

Be sure to avoid conversational aids like nods or smiles. Wait until the person talking has to take a breath. Raise a hand and say: 'Let me sum that up briefly' or 'Just one comment on that.' Then do just what the sentence suggests.

Then act: remind the meeting of the subject in hand ('What do you think about that?'), or illustrate a point visually. You can also ask the person talking too much to sum up: 'What do you feel is the most important thing in this case?'

2. **The dominant person:** often a high-ranking individual, self-confident, inclined to break rules and to intervene. Advantages for dominant people are their air of legitimacy (if they are from the management team and thus can involve themselves in decision-making), and they often make good contributions in terms of the subject matter.

*Strategies*: The best thing to do is to approach the dominant person before the meeting and talk about it. If that is not possible, speak to him or her in a break. Acknowledge what the dominant person says at the meeting, but also encourage others to make contributions: 'Many thanks for that idea. What do the others think about it?'

3. **The aggressive person:** attacks as a matter of principle, wants to make an impact on others – and likes using sarcasm, debaters' highly emotionally charged contributions. Aggressive people drain a great deal of energy out of quiet people.

*Strategies*: Take a deep breath, keep both feet on the ground, try to distance yourself inwardly and reply quietly, in the literal sense: at a low volume. This de-escalates the situation.

As well as this – as explained above under provocation and attack – get back to the subject in hand. Talk to the aggressive person one-to-one after the meeting or in a break, working on a personal level. This can prevent revenge-taking. Example: 'I noticed that the subject is very important to you – have we covered all the key facts, do you think?'

4. **The bad-tempered person:** attacks impulsively or starts shouting, i.e. is led astray by anger from time to time. This kind of person also makes quiet people stressed or lacking in energy.

*Strategies*: Behave in the same way as you would with an aggressive person. Also, anger and its consequences represent an additional obstacle in the case of the bad-tempered person: it simply isn't possible to get back to the point while there is anger in the room. And often people who are displaying anger can't hear anything else: they have simply been completely taken over by their feelings.

Your aim is to address the obvious thing, the anger, on the one hand. On the other hand, you want to get on with the subject in hand. So, first of all, move into the realm of emotion – but in order to de-escalate. In other words, as when dealing with the aggressive person, speak quietly and remain as relaxed as possible. But keep your own feelings under control. Use a short sentence to take things back to the point: 'I am surprised – what do you find disturbing about this suggestion?' or: 'You are not at all pleased about the way the meeting is going. What do you suggest?'

5. **The pessimist:** likes to respond sceptically or negatively, and is often driven by fear (obstacle 1). This can have its advantages at a meeting: if potential problems are aired when a decision is due to be made, it is possible to avoid errors and save a great deal of time and money. But, on the other hand, if negative arguments crop up, there is a risk that people will become discouraged and frustrated – the latter particularly if the conversation is dealing with specific details or peripheral matters that not everyone can follow.

*Strategies*: Listen objectively to what the pessimist finds dubious. Decide quickly (analytical thinking, strength 6) whether these doubts are justified – and, if they are, build them into the rest of the discussion. Also, let the other participants make their own points. If you think the doubts are exaggerated, play an active part yourself: ask the pessimist what he or she suggests in order to avoid a problem he or she has identified or how to reduce a risk that has been mentioned. In this way you will draw attention away from the difficulty and towards resolving it. That is an obstacle for pessimists, so they will ration their contributions more carefully under your chairmanship. Or you can put the doubts to the full meeting and hope that they will be neutralized. Like this, for example: 'What do the other experts here think about this risk?' One problem that should be taken seriously is fear of the new, and pessimists are particularly prone to this. It can be infectious – for example, if they use terms like 'successful complaints in comparable cases' or 'unforeseeable security risks'. Even if the arguments are weak, provocative words of this kind can induce resistance in the other participants on the emotional plane, and can even cause a very good idea to fail. Never repeat these provocative words in your answers, to avoid making people even angrier. Example (when the first pessimistic comment is made): 'You are quite right – it is important to look carefully when dealing with legal paid careful attention to our statements. The concept is watertight.'

6. **The person who interrupts:** doesn't let other people finish speaking, shouts out in the plenary session or embarks upon private dialogues with other participants. All this can really disturb the meeting – and even become infectious – so that, in the worst case, the person interrupting can encourage others to behave similarly.

*Strategies*: Acknowledge the interruption with signals that are clear but not unduly emphatic. In private conversations, pause in what you are saying and look at the person speaking in a friendly and relaxed way. Usually that will deal with the matter, and the situation will calm down. If people shout

out while you or somebody else are speaking, you have to take sterner measures so that all the group has an equal right to speak and a basic assurance is given that anyone who is speaking has a right to finish what they are saying. One of your duties as chair is to establish this certainty.

Example of a comment after someone shouts out: 'Your contribution has the same right to be heard as those of the other participants. Susan hasn't finished yet. Shall I put you down as wishing to speak?'

---

## ? Two questions for you

What disturbance or what kind of participant would be your personal nightmare at a meeting you are chairing?

_____

_____

_____

_____

_____

_____

_____

How do you intend to act in future if this arises?

_____

_____

_____

_____

_____

_____

_____

## ✳ Key points in brief

- It is particularly important for quiet people to know the unwritten rules governing the way meetings run. They can be used as a basis for developing successful participation strategies.

- Leading a discussion can easily be managed as well. What is required are thorough planning and knowledge of the various phases of a meeting, so that the most attention can be paid to the parts of the meeting that cannot be planned.

- Above all, this involves dealing with disturbances and challenging participants. Both of these can be prepared for and managed successfully.

# Licence to be quiet: the prospects for a fulfilling life as an introvert

I hope that the preceding chapters will have given you some ideas about how you can understand introverts better, and how to live and communicate better as a quiet person. What will you do differently in future when communicating? You are welcome to write to me (strength 9!) about your experiences as an introvert and about quiet intentions after reading the book.

Finally, here is one more thing for you: I have summed up the most important and the most valuable material – in other words, the essence of my long working involvement with quiet people – in seven points here. You have guessed, it is all about substance, strength 2 …

## Introversion – a life full of intensity

### 1. Live out the coolness of being quiet – this would be too much for most people

Find your comfort zone on the introvert–extrovert continuum – and make this the place where you usually are. When dealing with other people, find the amount of stimulation that makes you feel good because it is somewhere between boredom and over-stimulation. You will feel best in this place – and your energy management will benefit as well. See your introversion as a privilege – and as a ticket to a particularly intensive life.

### 2. Behave like an extrovert if it is worth while

Leave your introvert comfort zone only for a short time: if it is really worth while, and above all only when you are feeling good and have recovered. Go over to the 'other side' and 'be an extrovert' – as if you were playing a part: when giving a lecture, when having a drink with colleagues or at a conference or in a meeting. But, as I have said, do it for a short time only and in favourable circumstances – not when you are stressed.

## 3. Find strength in calm

Discover ways of withdrawing and resting for all private and professional spheres. Make use of these opportunities as a matter of course: they do you good, and are ways of filling up your energy tank from time to time. Use the inner calm that you gain from this strategy for yourself and other people.

## 4. Find out what your personal strengths and needs are – and live accordingly

Intensity is better than volume. Profound content is better than well-formulated sentences. Working on your own is good for creativity and concentration. Actually it is quite simple: analyse the context of your life from the point of view of an introvert. Develop a sense of your strengths and needs. Use this as a basis for your strategies. Live accordingly.

## 5. Be a quiet ambassador

As you know what introverts can do and need, you can encourage other introverts you come across. Communicate what is important to you in your own language and using your preferred media. Support young introverts. Be confident with extroverts. Our society can benefit from quiet, considered voices. Let yours be heard.

## 6. Win other people over with quiet strength

As an introvert you use different means from those of extroverts to win other people over and convince them. Use your caution (strength 1), your concentration (strength 5) and your empathy (strength 10) to achieve what you want.

You will gain in two ways from using your quiet strength: you are working towards your goal and you are building up positive relationships with the people around you – and by doing that, you will win them to you as well – by remaining authentic and respectful.

## 7. Learn from and with extroverts

Chapter 4 showed you how introverts can benefit from their extrovert partners. Philosophy has generalized this principle of beneficial contrasts by looking at nature, particularly vividly in the Yin and Yang of Taoism. Contrasts can generate positive tension. In terms of our subject, this means that the world needs explorers and preservers of the status quo, long-distance runners and sprinters, thinkers and impulsive people, people oriented towards service and security.

As well as this, the richness of our life lies to a large extent in our flexibility and the scope for action that this opens up. Both introverts and extroverts are flexible, and this flexibility offers a large range of possibilities for broadening our horizons. You can look at extroverts in order to expand your own quiet ways of looking at things and behaving by adding in the extrovert perspective, even if you do not necessarily act accordingly (as under 2.). Simply look at the extroverts around you: family members, bosses and colleagues.

What, you may ask, can you learn from extroverts? I have got many stimuli from the extroverts around me: I use them to work out how to survive conflict, how to act spontaneously despite a full diary, to make other people enthusiastic or to take a rewarding risk. Extroverts also teach me to enjoy myself more in company, to see things a little more sportingly and to be more open to new things – even if they happen spontaneously.

But extroverts can learn from introverts as well. Quiet people can show them how to keep quiet and concentrate on what other people are saying and to think before they act. Your inclination towards substance enables you to show extroverts how to think more profoundly. A lot of extroverts feel particularly comfortable with introverts because they feel accepted – a consequence of empathy.

Quiet people invite us to be stable and thorough. This doesn't sound very sexy, perhaps, but it can have a major effect on the survival of the species – wherever security, ethical principles, tenacity, conscientiousness and analysis rank higher than extroverts' strengths such as readiness to take risks and searching for stimulation and rewards. So it would be comforting for me to think that all the final decisions in certain spheres were in the hands of quiet people – for example, in nuclear energy, on the money markets, in the food industry and in aircraft cockpits. In every other sphere, too, it is true to say: the world needs you!

Go out and make an impact – quietly and intensively!

# For further reading and on-screen research

**www.hsperson.com**

Elaine Aron is a psychologist and expert on high sensitivity. Her website contains a test that you can use to find out whether you are a highly sensitive person. Having this quality is nothing to do with being an introvert or an extrovert.

**www.theatlantic.com**

Available online here: Jonathan Rauch's article 'Caring for your Introvert' (March 2003), which created a stir when it was first published; also a sequel with readers' comments ('The Introversy Continues', April 2006) and an interview with Rauch ('Introverts of the World, Unite!', February 2006).

**www.theintrovertedleaderblog.com**

Jennifer Kahnweiler's blog on introverts in the world of work.

**www.thepowerofintroverts.com**

Susan Cain's website with blog and a great deal of information about successful life as an introvert.

**www.time.com**

Weisskopf, Michael: Obama: How He Learned to Win. In: *Time* magazine online, 8 May 2008: http://content.time.com/time/magazine/article/0,9171,1738494,00.html

**www.toastmasters.org**

Toastmasters International – one of the best ways of learning cheaply and effectively how to speak in public and about management communication. The website will show you local clubs in your area, among other things, and also clubs you can visit when travelling on business or on holiday.

# Thank you!

Ute Flockenhaus got this book off to a wonderful start when I approached her in a starry-eyed way about my idea. She simply said: 'I'll have the title protected.' I shall never forget that …

Frederike Mannsperger's intelligence, flexibility and feeling for language made her the perfect editor.

Dr Fleur Wöss showed me the power of introvert speakers by acting it out for me.

Dr Christiane Buchholz, Christine Herwig, Dr Eva Kalbheim, the late Dr Ursula Kleinhenz, Dr Isabell Lisberg-Haag, Dr Michael Meinhard, Prof. Maria Parr, Tom Peters and Andreas Stickler shared their experiences and ideas in a large number of conversations, and supported me with their friendship.

Lars Schäfer made sure that I kept my feet on the ground, did not lose my sense of humour and finally came up with a manuscript (even without the 79 additional ideas).

John Kluempers PhD and Mr Son are the most important extrovert and the most important introvert in my life. They show me every day what else is really important – and while I was writing the script they provided some very enjoyable evenings with various seasons of *The Big Bang Theory*.

# Index

DESMER (*remembering* CAPULAT). You're a scan-monger, Hugo. You forget I'm your aunt, and India's t. I won't listen to you. I'm an elderly woman, and l r listen to anyone. Capulat, go and look for my dkerchief.

PULAT *exits*.

, between ourselves, do you really imagine he's ng her?

Between ourselves, without a shadow of doubt.

ESMER. It's monstrous, Hugo; humiliating.

Utterly monstrous, but, between ourselves, umiliating?

SMER. She is a FitzHenry! And through me, a rmortes. If only your uncle Antony were alive it kill him. Hugo, people are so unkind; they will invited Dorothy and this nabob at the same time ose. They'll say I'm a party to it. So should I.

Everyone knows you invited Mr. Messerschmann daughter because Frederic asked you to. is going to announce his engagement to Diana w.

MER. Yes. There's another puppy-witted piece Fancy becoming so infatuated with that girl he to ask her to marry him! When he was little he oked so sad and resigned when he came to kiss ristmas morning. I used to call him St. Pancras. the poor lamb's to be sacrificed. Can you bear to im being delivered over, gagged and bound, in ng coat and gardenia, to this Diana Mes-n and her millions?

Aunt.

R. No, I should think not. If it had been ld have been different. I love it when the lamb

18

FREDERIC. I love you.

DIANA. I love you, too, Frederic.

*They kiss.*

I suppose you're quite sure you're not Hugo? He's capable of absolutely anything.

*They go.*

*Enter* LADY INDIA *and* PATRICE BOMBELLES.

PATRICE. Anything! Anything! He's capable of absolutely anything.

LADY INDIA. But, dear heart, how could he suspect us? We've been so careful.

PATRICE. I tell you, I wouldn't trust that fellow Hugo an inch. Yesterday he giggled at me. Quite noticeably, as I went past him. Why should he have giggled if he didn't know all about us?

LADY INDIA. When did he giggle?

PATRICE. Last night, on the terrace, after dinner.

LADY INDIA. Last night? We were all there together. He choked himself with cigar smoke. He was coughing.

PATRICE. He was coughing to disguise his giggle, but that didn't deceive me for a moment.

LADY INDIA. Anyway, why should this young man, who has nothing to do with me, giggle because he's found out we're having an affair?

PATRICE. Never mind why; mistrust him. To begin with there's this fantastic likeness to his brother.

LADY INDIA. He can't help that.

PATRICE. My dear Dorothy! If he had any sense of propriety, he would never allow it to go on. He revels in it; he copies his brother's clothes.

LADY INDIA. No, dear, Frederic copies his.

PATRICE. Well, it's the same thing. Now, I have eight brothers——

15

LADY INDIA.   And they all look exactly like you?

PATRICE.   Not at all.

LADY INDIA.   I see; then it doesn't help to convince me that this boy would say anything to Messerschmann.

PATRICE. *Say* anything, no; but little jokes and innuendoes when we're all in the drawing-room, yes; a mysterious chuckle in the middle of a meal, or a giggle like the one you thought was choking him with cigar-smoke; yes, most certainly.

LADY INDIA.   Little jokes and chuckles will pass right over Messerschmann's head. He suffers from terribly poor reception.

PATRICE.   It's we who would have a poor reception if once he knew. Don't forget, you're his mistress and I'm his private secretary. We're both completely dependent on your magnate.

LADY INDIA (*reproachfully*).   Dearest heart, you use the most curious words.

PATRICE.   Magnate?

LADY INDIA.   No.

PATRICE.   Private secretary?

LADY INDIA.   No. (*She leans against him.*) Patrice, darling, I know I give him the pleasure of paying my bills, and every night I let him trail along to my room to kiss my hand; but that means nothing, and you mean everything.

PATRICE (*desperately*).   Dorothy! We're in the winter-garden——

LADY INDIA.   On a lovely spring morning.

PATRICE.   The season is immaterial! All this glass! Everyone can see us! We're completely exposed.

LADY INDIA.   Danger! Oh, that's wonderful; I love it; I like being mad more than anything. Did I ever tell you about the evening in Monte Carlo when I went to a little

16

dockside café, absolutely nake
diamonds? Quite alone, too,
brutes.

PATRICE.   At Monte Carlo?

LADY INDIA.   A little café wh
a secret Bock between sessi
their hands shook when the
let him come, let him catch
drive him off with a lash
magnificent!

PATRICE.   Yes.

LADY INDIA.   Don't forg
guished family, Patrice,
He should be very grat
infuriate him. Money i

*Enter* MME. DESME
*by her companion*

MME. DESMER.   Mon
oodles? Whatever d
serschmann has ood

HUGO.   He's as rich

MME. DESMER.   Oh
it all?

HUGO.   Eats noodl

MME. DESMER.   Y
Hugo.

HUGO.   It's quite
salt, and drinks

MME. DESMER.
that Dorothy I

HUGO.   She wo
much of it ev

turns round and eats up the high priest. But with poor little Frederic it won't even be funny.

HUGO. If the marriage takes place, Aunt.

MME. DESMER (*with a sigh*). And who can prevent it now?

HUGO. Who knows who?

CAPULAT *returns.*

CAPULAT. Here is your handkerchief, madam.

MME. DESMER. Thank you, my dear. Trundle me into the sun, if you will.

*Enter* MESSERSCHMANN *and* ROMAINVILLE.

Good morning, dear Romainville! Good morning, Mr. Messerschmann. Have you had a good night's rest?

MESSER. I never sleep, madam.

MME. DESMER. Neither do I. We must make an appointment with one another some time, and gossip while the rest of them snore. We can say the most terrible things about them; it will help to kill time. He takes such a lot of killing, that animal, don't you think? I'm a wicked person, Mr. Messerschmann. Are you?

MESSER. I told you so, madam.

MME. DESMER. How nice. We can be wicked together. That will amuse me very much. Push, dear, trundle me away. I told you I wanted to be in the sun. Oh, Mr. Messerschmann, my butler tells me you only eat noodles?

MESSER. That is so, without butter and without salt.

MME. DESMER. And I believe you're a great friend of my niece, Dorothy?

MESSER. Yes, I have the pleasure of Lady India's friendship.

MME. DESMER. Insomnia, Dorothy, and nothing but noodles! What a *very* interesting life . . .

*They go.*

ROMAINVILLE *tries to escape to avoid* HUGO.

19

HUGO (*catching him*).  Her train gets in at twelve-thirty.

ROMAINVILLE.  No!

HUGO.  It certainly does.

ROMAINVILLE.  I'm convinced it's all a great mistake. It's making me ill with nerves. Are you sure you're not mad?

HUGO.  Quite sure.  How about you?

ROMAINVILLE.  Not at all sure. Suppose I don't co-operate?

HUGO.  A scandal, Romainville.

ROMAINVILLE (*losing his temper*). What scandal, for God's sake? My relationship with this girl is absolutely irreproachable.

HUGO.  Suppose I say to my aunt, "Our dear Romainville, feeling the approach of springtime in the air, and in order to make his visit to you a cheerful one, has fetched his little friend over to stay at the inn at St. Fleur: he goes to see her secretly three times a week." What do you say then?

ROMAINVILLE.  That it isn't true! That I'm only interested in this girl as I'm interested in butterflies and old furniture. Is it my fault if I'm known as a patron of the arts?

HUGO.  No.

ROMAINVILLE.  The child needed a holiday before she goes back into the ballet. She was rather pale—do understand that, Hugo—she was extremely pale. Anybody would have done the same thing. It's entirely a question of common humanity. I said to her: Come and spend a few days at Auvergne with your mother. Who, for God's sake, is going to make trouble because I give a holiday to a poor girl who needs one? Certainly not your good Aunt, who buttonholes me every year for her local charities.

HUGO.  To a poor girl who needs a holiday, no. But to your mistress, Romainville—well, you know my Aunt.

20

ROMAINVILLE.   For God's sake, she isn't my mistress! I
assure you she isn't, not the least bit.

HUGO.   Who's going to believe you?

ROMAINVILLE.   Everybody—because it's true.

HUGO.   That's no help. It doesn't seem likely.

ROMAINVILLE.   So according to you the truth means
nothing.

HUGO.   Nothing, dear boy, if no one believes it.

*The sound of a dinner gong.*

Let's go amiably in to lunch. They'll be here any minute
now. I've warned Joshua and he'll let me know. I shall
come out and have a word with them, and then, during
coffee, Joshua can tell my Aunt that your niece has
arrived.

ROMAINVILLE.   But suppose my real niece comes on the
same train?

HUGO.   That's all right. I sent her a telegram from you;
you told her that my Aunt's invitation had been cancelled
for the time being.

ROMAINVILLE.   It's a trap!  And all because you found
me drinking an innocent orangeade with this little girl, in
a cakeshop at St. Fleur!

HUGO.   Exactly.

ROMAINVILLE.   You're the devil!

HUGO.   Almost.

ROMAINVILLE.   Would you just tell me what you're up to?

HUGO.   A huge and dark design.

*The gong sounds again.*

There's the second gong. So in to luncheon, Romainville.
You shall know everything before you're much older.

*They go.*

*The stage is empty for a moment, then* JOSHUA *shows in*
ISABELLE *and her* MOTHER *with their suitcases.*

21

JOSHUA.   If the ladies would be so good as to take a seat, I will go and inform Mr. Hugo of their arrival.
*He exits.*

THE MOTHER.   Isn't it luxurious, Isabelle? Such taste! Such grandeur! Now this is the kind of atmosphere where I really feel myself.

ISABELLE.   Yes, Mother.

THE MOTHER.   Some people, you know, can only breathe where there's beauty and luxury. Take luxury away from them and they go quite limp.

ISABELLE.   Yes, Mother.

THE MOTHER.   Always remember, Isabelle, your grandfather was the biggest wallpaper dealer in the town. We've even had two servants at the same time, not counting the shop-assistants, of course. When I was your age your grandmother would never have let me go out alone.

ISABELLE.   No, Mother.

THE MOTHER.   No. The maid always followed three steps behind me. Three steps. It was wonderful.

ISABELLE.   Yes, Mother.

THE MOTHER.   Did you see the butler?

ISABELLE.   Yes, Mother.

THE MOTHER.   That dignity, that sort of quilted voice, extremely polite but also slightly scornful, such a perfect manner. (*She mimics him, delightedly.*) "If the ladies would be so good as to take a seat." "To take a seat!" You see how beautifully he chose his words! . . . You know, dear, in my dreams of you, there's always a butler like that in the background.

ISABELLE.   Oh, Mother, you know it's not——

THE MOTHER.   Ah yes, there is. It's been a dream of mine that you shall have everything I've missed. I don't say very much, I know, but there are times when I suffer. For instance, when I see your hands getting rough and red from washing-up . . .

ISABELLE. Now, please, Mother——

THE MOTHER. I know it means nothing to you, because you haven't my sensitive nature. And I know I don't help you as much as I should. If only I were a little stronger; but even so I have to think of my art, I have to preserve my hands for my piano. And then I never knew what it was to want for anything when I was a girl, so different from you, my poor child, so I mustn't expect you to understand me. You roll up your sleeves, you sing something, and abracadabra everything's done; you think no more about it.

ISABELLE. It's the best way, Mother.

THE MOTHER. I admire you for it. But with my upbringing, and all my dreams which came to nothing, I could never do it. I still have dreams, but now they're for you, Isabelle: a quite different future for you, a future of luxury and beauty, with a little corner somewhere for your Mother. You're artistic, you're pretty, a little more commonplace than I was, perhaps—that's owing to your Father—but interesting and attractive. You will certainly please someone, I'm sure you will. What do you suppose the young man wants you here for?

*Enter* HUGO.

HUGO. Thank you for being so punctual.

THE MOTHER. Not at all. Punctuality is the politeness of princes, I always think. And I'm sure you'll agree with me.

HUGO. Oh yes, indeed. And this is Miss Isabelle? . . . I wasn't mistaken.

THE MOTHER. She's a charming child.

HUGO. More than charming.

23

THE MOTHER. Mr. Romainville must have spoken about her to you.

HUGO (*not taking his eyes from* ISABELLE). He has indeed.

THE MOTHER. He is one of our dear Parisian friends.

HUGO (*rather coldly*). Yes, I know. How do you feel about this adventure, Miss Isabelle? The most essential thing is for you to enjoy it.

THE MOTHER. She is thrilled about it!

ISABELLE. All Mr. Romainville said was that you had asked us up to your house this evening.

HUGO. Nothing else?

ISABELLE. No, nothing.

THE MOTHER. I expect our friend meant it all to be a surprise.

HUGO. And why should you think I would ask you to come here?

ISABELLE. I don't know. To dance, I expect. I am a dancer.

HUGO. Not only to dance.

THE MOTHER. Not only to dance? Now you're beginning to make me really inquisitive.

HUGO. There's a ball being held in this house tonight. I need you here to be very beautiful, more beautiful, indeed, than anyone else.

ISABELLE. I?

HUGO. Yes. Are you afraid?

ISABELLE. A little. I'm not very beautiful, and so I wonder——

HUGO. I rang up Paris this morning. Roeseda Soeurs are sending some dresses to choose from, and their best fitters. At the first note of the violins, you will be ready.

ISABELLE. But what am I supposed to do?

HUGO. Only to go serenely through the night like a butter-fly venturing on moonlight. With the first light of day

24

we'll set you free. (*To* THE MOTHER.) The engagement will be paid for in the usual way, and the dress will be hers.

THE MOTHER (*simpering*).    Oh, but we didn't think for one moment——

HUGO.    But I thought. Now I must go back to the dining-room or they'll begin to wonder where I am. I'm sorry I can't make it less of a mystery for you. Here is Joshua to show you to your rooms. He will bring you your lunch. No one must know you're in the house. As soon as I can I shall come and tell you what I want you to do.

*He goes.*

JOSHUA *takes the suitcases.*

JOSHUA.    If the ladies will be so good as to follow me.

THE MOTHER.    Thank you very much. What a distinguished boy, such beautiful manners. Did you not notice, dear, how he kissed my hand? Wake up, dear, are you dreaming?

ISABELLE.    No, Mother. Is he the one they call Hugo? Is he the one who asked us here?

THE MOTHER.    Well, of course. So handsome, don't you think? Now come along, we're keeping the butler waiting. Where are you, my dear, in the moon?

ISABELLE (*in a strange voice, following*).    Yes, Mother.

THE CURTAIN FALLS


SCENE 2

*The same scene. The same evening.*

MADAME DESMERMORTES *alone.*

MME. DESMER.    Capulat! Capulat! What on earth can she be up to? Capulat! Really, how marooned one is away from a bell-rope. I might be Robinson Crusoe, and

25

31833

without any of his initiative. If only one's governess, when one was a girl, had taught one something practical like running up a flag of distress or firing a gun.

JOSHUA *enters.*

Thank heaven I'm on some sort of navigation route! Joshua! Joshua! . . . Ah, Cap Gris-Nez! Joshua! Put into land for a moment, my dear man, and rescue me. I was washed up here fifteen minutes ago, and I haven't seen a living creature since.

JOSHUA. Not one, madam?

MME. DESMER. Not one, and they say the world is over-populated. I sent Mlle. Capulat to fetch the list of guests out of my bureau. You would think I'd asked her to restock the lake with carp, the time it's taking her.

CAPULAT *enters.*

Oh, there you are at last, Capulat. You left me here with a broken brake, and I've had nothing to do but to think over all my shortcomings, *twice*. If you'd been away any longer I should have started to regret them. Where have you been?

CAPULAT. You said the list was in the left-hand bottom drawer, madam, but it was the right-hand top drawer.

MME. DESMER. That's just another way of looking at it. (*She takes the list from* CAPULAT.) Now . . . well, get to work. . . . I must try and remember who all these names belong to. It is so difficult. Nowadays no one has any proper sense of family; people have perfectly good names and then go and produce the most unpredictable faces to go with them. I don't know how they expect to be recognized; and, worse still, it encourages all those terrible people who go to parties without being asked. I remember an evening at the Baroness Grave-Toureau's . . . where is

26

everybody? Capulat, are you listening? . . . I was saying, I remember an evening at the Baroness Grave-Toureau's when . . . well, mend me—mend me! . . . Joshua, I remember an evening at the Baroness Grave-Toureau's when there were so many uninivited guests the Baroness imagined she must be at someone else's party, and spent most of the evening looking for her hostess to say goodbye. Now . . . must you do that? Oh! Deliverance! . . . Now, Joshua, did you hear what I was saying to Capulat? We don't want an unfortunate episode like that. Do you understand, Joshua, we don't want any mistakes.

JOSHUA.  Certainly not, madam; though as madam says, faces these days have taken a haphazard turn, most inconsiderate.

MME. DESMER.  You will have to look into them very carefully, Joshua, and so shall I. If one stares fixedly at an interloper's frontal bone, fixedly, Joshua, for a count of nine, a look of guilt will steal over it at once. Remember that, Joshua. I intend to stare myself, with great penetration, whenever the occasion offers.

JOSHUA.  I hope and trust, madam, that no such occasional offering will ensue. It would be a cloud on an otherwise evening of nice and aristocratic joy, which none of us would like to have to denounce, madam.

MME. DESMER.  You're crumbling into a benevolent old man, Joshua. Denouncing—that's delicious; and I depend on you to see that we have no trespassers. Come with me now, and we'll make a last inspection of the battlefield. Well, Capulat, well, my dear.

CAPULAT.  I feel so excited, madam, like a little yeasty bun in a good oven, really I do.

MME. DESMER.  How splendid! And no doubt the buns feel like little Capulats. . . . Now, the Prince of Palenge, what on earth does he look like, Joshua? Oh, yes, yes, I remember; like a rather half-hearted resolution with a Balaclava beard. . . .

*The chair starts suddenly and—*

MADAME DESMER MORTES *rolls out followed by* CAPULAT *and* JOSHUA.

*After a moment,* HUGO *and* ISABELLE *enter.*

HUGO.  All right; now just walk a few steps towards me. Turn. Walk away again. You're perfect. What on earth are you trembling for?

ISABELLE.  Scared.

HUGO.  Scared of what? Of going to a party?

ISABELLE.  Yes, I suppose so. The violins tuning up, a house full of strange people all at this moment dressing for the great occasion; and scared of the mystery you're making of it.

HUGO.  And scared of me?

ISABELLE.  Very much.

HUGO.  You think I'm going to drag you into some shameful scene or other. Romainville has been maligning me.

ISABELLE.  He said——

HUGO.  And of course you believed him?

ISABELLE (*gently*).  No.

HUGO.  You should have believed him. When you discover what I've planned for this evening, you'll think I'm even worse than Romainville imagines. But you don't have to be afraid of bad people; they're just poor complicated devils like everyone else. It's only the fools who are formidable.

*Enter* ROMAINVILLE.

And here he is. We were talking about you. How are you this evening?

ROMAINVILLE.  Very poorly, very poorly indeed. I'd been looking forward to this party very much, but I feel now

28

as though I were going to an execution. I can't see why you want to go on with it.

HUGO. He's afraid you'll lose your head among the knives and forks, or use a dessert-spoon on the foie-gras, and they'll leap to their feet and say, "This can't be his niece at all! She's an imposter!" . . . Just walk away a little; now turn. Look at that, Romainville. There's a niece for you! Between ourselves, old man, what's your niece really like?

ROMAINVILLE (*stiffly*). She's a rather plain girl. Her nose is perhaps not as small as others. But she has an extremely nice character.

HUGO. It's clearly high time you replaced her. Look at this girl in a dress like the smoke of bonfires. You'll never see a niece more transparent, less of this world, or so entirely fashioned for a singular night of dancing in the early summer.

ROMAINVILLE (*solemnly inspecting her*). Hold yourself upright. When you're presented to people don't address them by their titles. Always wait for an older person to speak to you.

HUGO. Dear me, you're wasting your breath. Isabelle was waiting for older people to speak to her in the womb. My aunt has an infallible instinct for quality, and she's given her a room looking out on to the garden. If she hadn't had the highest opinion of her, she would have put her facing the park.

ROMAINVILLE. Not at all; I'm facing the park.

HUGO (*laughing*). So you see what I mean!

THE MOTHER *enters.*

THE MOTHER. May I come in? May I come in? I couldn't keep away for another minute; I simply had to come and see the dress.

29

HUGO (*going to her, vexed*). I thought it was agreed you should stay in your room. We don't want people asking who you are.

THE MOTHER. I came on tiptoe the whole way; you would have thought I was a shadow. I'm dying of curiosity. Oh, how charming! Oh, how wonderfully elegant! Hold yourself up straight, dear. What good taste! I'm quite sure Mr. Hugo chose it himself.

HUGO. Not at all. Your daughter chose it.

THE MOTHER. Then I'm sure you had something to do with it. Or else the child guessed your taste and chose it to please you.

ISABELLE. Mother!

THE MOTHER. Turn round, dear. Once again. Hold yourself up. She's a constant surprise to me. Dressed, you would think she's *such* a skinnygalee; undressed, she's almost plump. Raspoutini her ballet-master said it's quite simply because she is well-built. As a matter of fact, and I don't say it just because I'm her mother, she has very good legs. This dear gentleman can bear me out, can't you?

ROMAINVILLE (*embarrassed*). Hm! I still thinks she looks extremely pale. We should give her a tonic. That's it, a splendid tonic.

THE MOTHER. Pale! How can you say so? Look at her, she's as pink as a strawberry.

ROMAINVILLE. Hm! The country-air has done some good already, you see. There's nothing like the country, nothing like it.

THE MOTHER. How can you say so? The country is death to her. And to me. We're just hothouse flowers, two Parisians, two artists. In the countryside we just wait to be eaten by sheep. Only our dear friend insisted we should come.

ROMAINVILLE. Her health comes first, her health comes first!

30

THE MOTHER. Isn't he domineering? His friends must do what he says; he can't bear not to have them with him. When he knew he was coming here, he wouldn't rest until the child came too.

ROMAINVILLE. She looked extremely pale. I said to myself——

THE MOTHER. Yes, yes; and we forgive you because we know you do it out of friendship, just as you did when you made her learn to swim.

ROMAINVILLE (*increasingly embarrassed*). Everybody should learn to swim.

THE MOTHER. He came to the baths himself to watch her, and one day he fell in without taking his clothes off!

ROMAINVILLE (*beside himself*). Didn't I say so, doesn't that prove everybody should learn to swim? We've chattered quite enough; Hugo must be wanting to give Isabelle her instructions. And I know you'd like to see the carriages arriving. You can come up to my room; it faces north, but you can see everyone who comes to the door.

THE MOTHER. Yes, that's it, we'll leave together. Of course I'm burning with curiosity to know what the mystery's about, but Isabelle will tell me tomorrow. Come along, then. I shall hide away like a dilapidated old moth who's been told not to dance round the candles.

ROMAINVILLE (*hurrying her off*). That's right. Like a dilapidated old moth. Off we go. I can hear the first carriages arriving already.

HUGO. And you shall have supper brought up to you.

THE MOTHER. Just a crust, a crust and a glass of water for poor little Cinders. Enjoy yourself, you fortunate girl. I was twenty once; and not so long ago either. . . . She looks charming, charming!

*She goes, dragged off by* ROMAINVILLE.

HUGO. And she's blushing.

ISABELLE. With embarrassment.

HUGO. Needlessly.

ISABELLE. It's easy enough to talk. My cheeks burn, my eyes are stinging, I've a lump in my throat, and I should like to be dead.

HUGO. She amuses me.

ISABELLE. She might amuse me, too, if only—— (*She stops herself.*)

HUGO. If you had ever listened to what they call a society woman trying to put up the bidding for her daughter, you wouldn't be indignant any more. Your mother's discretion itself.

ISABELLE. I'm not plump, nor a skinnygalee; I've not got very good legs. I don't want to stay here.

HUGO. You can't go yet.

ISABELLE. I feel so ashamed.

HUGO. Why should you be? Because this party and the slight air of mystery has kindled your mother's imagination? Because she likes to think I'm in love with you and tries to throw you at my head? It's most natural. I'm rich, I belong to an old family, and ever since I was marriageable I've heard mothers hammering out that old tune. If you're ashamed because of me, forget your blushes. I've heard the tune so often, I'm deaf to it.

ISABELLE. But I can still hear it.

HUGO. Yes, I can see it must be unpleasant for you. I'm sorry.

ISABELLE (*suddenly*). Have you considered Romainville?

HUGO. Oh no, I never do that. Romainville is scrupulous and considerate, but not considerable. I met you with him in a cakeshop at St. Fleur. I thought you were charming, and it occurred to me you might be very useful this evening. That's all.

ISABELLE. But I think you should know . . .

HUGO. I don't want to know anything else at all.

ISABELLE (*softly, flatly*). I see. I only wanted to—to tell you. . . . Oh dear, I'm silly! I've been crying, and now I shall have to begin my face all over again. Will you excuse me for a little while?

HUGO. Of course.

*She goes.*

HUGO *signals to* JOSHUA *who is crossing the stage.*

Joshua!

JOSHUA. Mr. Hugo?

HUGO. Does anyone suspect anything?

JOSHUA. No one, sir. The dress-shop people and the shoe-shop person have went, sir, unobserved. So many outside individuals here to-night, in any case, making the preparations. . . .

HUGO. You'll keep your eye on the Mother.

JOSHUA. As far as the human eye can be kept, sir. I beg your pardon, but she escaped my notice just now. What with all the responsibility for the Ball as well, sir. . . .

HUGO. If only she'll content herself with trotting between here and her room, it may be all right. But she'll worry me considerably once the evening has really begun. (*He locks an imaginary door with a key.*) Click, click!

JOSHUA. Very good, sir. But if the lady starts to scream? We have to look all eventualities in the face, sir.

HUGO. Tell her I told you to shut her in, and promise her two hundred francs extra.

JOSHUA. Certainly, sir. . . . Excuse me, sir, but . . . you think that will be sufficient to—to quench this particular individual, sir?

HUGO.  Quite sufficient.

JOSHUA.  Very good, sir.

> *To* ISABELLE *who re-enters*
> *as* JOSHUA *goes.*

HUGO.  Everything all right again?

ISABELLE.  Yes; no sign of tears now.

HUGO.  It's very useful to be able to disappear and come back with new eyes and a fresh smile, ready to pick up the conversation where you left off. The poor naked face of the male has to fight for a façade as best it can. (*He looks at his watch.*) It's almost ten o'clock: your dress makes you look like Helen of Troy: the first carriages are grinding the gravel in the drive: the fiddlers are rubbing rosin on their bows: and it's time I explained things to you.

ISABELLE.  High time!

HUGO.  I had to get to know you a little first. If you had been a fool I should have thought up a story for you, something picturesque and sentimental, a snip for a house-wife's magazine. I'd begun to invent something like that when I asked you to come here. Something conventional; that's always the easiest. But, once in a very great while, something conventional is too threadbare for the circumstances, and a man's left standing stupidly with his intelligence on his arm, like a rolled umbrella he hadn't expected to use. So much the worse for me. Now I shall have to talk without preparation.

ISABELLE.  I'm so sorry.

HUGO.  Not at all. It's my fault for being such a poor judge of character. I ought to have been able to tell at a glance. You're not a fool, you have simplicity; you're not romantic, you're tender; you're not hard, you're exacting. Each one is almost like the other, but in fact they're opposites.

34

This will teach me to look carelessly at girls in cake-shops! I'd thought of everything except one. I didn't expect you to look at me with such penetrating eyes.

ISABELLE. If it upsets you I can shut them.

HUGO. No, it's all right; your penetration will save time. I can cut the preamble and get to the point. Now, listen. I have a brother who is addled with love for a rich, young, beautiful girl. This party is in her honour.

ISABELLE. And she doesn't love him?

HUGO. She's engaged to him, which means that she gives him her lips two or three times a day, and no doubt lets him have contact occasionally with her pretty, lukewarm hand, while she turns her mind to something else. She makes all the loving gestures expected of her, she even tells him she loves him, but she doesn't.

ISABELLE. Does she love someone else?

HUGO. I should say she's quite incapable of loving anybody. But as she's a little multi-millionairess, and badly spoilt, blown skyhigh by every breeze of a whim, she's made herself believe—yes, that she loves someone else.

ISABELLE. And that person is . . .

HUGO. As you've so quickly guessed, myself. You'll tell me she must be extremely stupid, because my brother is at least a thousand times nicer than I am.

ISABELLE. What does he look like?

HUGO. You see, that's the devil of preparing speeches in advance. I've forgotten to tell you the most important thing. We're twins.

ISABELLE. You look like each other.

HUGO. Physically, we're so alike it's neither permissible nor proper. But morally—morally, we're as different as day and night. My brother is good, sensible, kind, and intelligent, and I'm the reverse. But nevertheless she loves me and not him.

35

ISABELLE. And you?

HUGO. I?

ISABELLE. You love her, perhaps?

HUGO. I love nobody. That's why I can organize this evening's little comedy with complete serenity. I'm acting providence tonight. I deflect the influence of the stars! The stars, twinkling up there, without an inkling of what's going to happen tonight. Now this is what I want you to do.

ISABELLE. Tell me.

HUGO. To begin with, unquestioning obedience, and keep your eye on me all the time. I can only give you the broad outline; the details will have to be worked out as the evening goes on. Don't be afraid, you'll never be alone. I shall appear from behind a screen; I shall be behind the sofa where you go to sit with your partner, or under the tablecloth, or lurking in a shadow in the garden. I shall be everywhere, always watching you and whispering my orders to you. It's very simple. All you've got to do is to become the centre of interest; the party must revolve round you and no one else.

ISABELLE. You're expecting too much of me. I can never do it!

HUGO. I can do it. Don't worry, be yourself. Say whatever you want to say. Laugh whenever you want to laugh. If you suddenly feel like being alone, be alone. I shall expound you brilliantly; I shall make everything you say or do seem enchantingly extravagant and witty. I shall make them all think I'm in love with you.

ISABELLE (happily). Will you?

HUGO. And you will make them all think you're in love with my brother.

ISABELLE. But if your brother is in love with this other girl, he won't even look at me!

36

HUGO.  Being a fool, perhaps he won't. But even if he never takes his eyes off Diana *her* eyes will tell him that you're the beauty of the evening. She will be *so* jealous.

ISABELLE.  It will make your brother love her more than ever.

HUGO.  You think so? What a pretty idea of love you have in the theatre! No, put your mind at rest; I have everything nicely worked out. My brother is going to love you. It's all a question of waking him up. Diana isn't remotely the sort of girl he would want to love. He's suffering in his sleep, walking along a parapet of infatuation, and we're going to waken him.

ISABELLE.  Suppose he should die of it?

HUGO.  Whoever died of love?

ROMAINVILLE *enters, full spate.*

ROMAINVILLE.  There you are, there you are! I've been looking everywhere for you! Catastrophe!

HUGO.  What do you mean, catastrophe?

ROMAINVILLE.  My dear boy, the whole idea's exploded. Thank God!

HUGO.  What are you talking about?

ROMAINVILLE.  I was shepherding your mother back to her room, relying on the corridors being fairly dark, and we turned a corner slap into the Capulat!

ISABELLE.  Capulat?

ROMAINVILLE.  His aunt's companion.

HUGO.  Well, you could pass that off all right.

ROMAINVILLE.  I passed right on. But what did they do? They threw themselves like a pair of idiots into each other's arms, and burst into tears. It seems that they took piano-lessons together at the Mauberge Conservatoire. They've been thinking each other dead for twenty years, but, astonishing as it may be, they're alive! I was completely helpless. They're there still, looped around each

37

other's necks, telling their life-stories. Thank God they're both talking at once, and neither knows what the other one's talking about. Whatever happens, there's only one thing for it: flight! (*To* ISABELLE) Go up and change. I shall say you've been taken ill, you've had a telegram, your grandmother's had a stroke; I'll say something or other. I've got an imagination too. There's not a minute to lose. Go up and change!

HUGO.   Stay down here. I forbid you to go.

   THE MOTHER *knocks and enters.*

THE MOTHER.   Coo-ee! Have you heard *my* little piece of excitement?

HUGO (*going to her*).   Yes. What have you been saying to her?

THE MOTHER.   Oh, my dears, what bliss there can be in a friendship! You've often heard me speak of Geraldine Capulat, haven't you, Isabelle? I thought she was dead: but she's alive, the dear sweet soul. What have I been saying to her? Why, everything, everything, you know: my unhappy marriage, the end of my artistic career: in fact, all my disappointments. You don't *know* what Geraldine has been to me! Both of us with golden hair; we were always taken for sisters.

HUGO.   How did you explain your being in this house?

THE MOTHER.   Quite simply. Did you think I should be taken off my guard? I told her I was one of the orchestra.

HUGO
ROMAINVILLE } Ouf!

THE MOTHER.   But she didn't believe me. It wasn't a fortunate choice. It appears they are all negroes. So then do you know what I did? I have complete confidence in Geraldine. I made her swear on our long friendship that she wouldn't say a word to anybody, and I told her everything.

38

HUGO  
ROMAINVILLE } (*in a panic*). Everything?

THE MOTHER. Everything!

HUGO. How could you have told her everything? You know nothing about it.

THE MOTHER. No, but you know I'm quick with my little romances; like a big child, really; I'm incorrigible. I embroidered something to suit the case, a little figment!

ROMAINVILLE. A little figment?

HUGO. What little figment?

THE MOTHER. A little rosy-coloured figment! Oh dear, I believe you're going to scold me.

HUGO. Let's get to the point: what exactly have you said?

THE MOTHER. Nothing; just foolishness, words, day-dreams. I said you were in love with my little girl, and you wanted to bring her here without a lot of to-do, so you were pretending she was Mr. Romainville's niece.

ISABELLE (*distressed*). What right had you to say so?

ROMAINVILLE. Good heavens! My dear Hugo, by now your aunt knows the whole thing. I don't know what you're going to do, but I'm leaving. It's a great pity, I shall never be able to come here again. Our whole life gets altered by accidents! Go upstairs and change, for goodness sake!

HUGO (*starting for the door*). I shall have to find Capulat. We must make sure she keeps her mouth shut.

> *At the door he runs into* MME. DESMERMORTES *pushed in her wheelchair by* CAPULAT. ROMAINVILLE *and* ISABELLE *hide* THE MOTHER *as well as they can.*

MME. DESMER. Where are you off to, Hugo, dear?

HUGO. Nowhere in particular.

39

MME. DESMER.  Then stop behaving like a cul-de-sac. I've come to see my young guest. Why hide her away in this hole and corner? I congratulate you, my dear friend.

ROMAINVILLE (*with a start, suspiciously*).  Congratulate me? Why congratulate me?

MME. DESMER.  She's very charming.

ROMAINVILLE.  No!

MME. DESMER.  No?

ROMAINVILLE.  Yes!

MME. DESMER.  Is she well and happy?

ROMAINVILLE.  No—not just now. Rather faint.

MME. DESMER.  What nonsense are you talking? Her cheeks are like roses. One dance will put her on top of the world.

ROMAINVILLE (*not knowing what he's saying*).  She's afraid of getting a telegram.

MME. DESMER.  That's a curious anxiety. She's wearing such a pretty dress. Is that your present to her, you generous man?

ROMAINVILLE.  Certainly not!

MME. DESMER.  I hope you like your room, my dear. Tomorrow morning you'll get the very first of the sunshine. Do you mean to enjoy yourself this evening?

ISABELLE.  Oh yes!

MME. DESMER.  Who was it told me it was your first ball?

ROMAINVILLE.  It wasn't I!

MME. DESMER.  Was it you, Hugo? No, it couldn't have been; you don't know her. I hope someone has introduced you?

HUGO.  Yes, Aunt, someone has introduced us.

MME. DESMER.  She's entrancing, isn't she?

HUGO.  Entrancing.

MME. DESMER.  Why don't you ask her to dance? They're playing the first waltz.

40

HUGO.  I was about to. (*To* ISABELLE) Will you give me the pleasure of this waltz, mademoiselle?

*They waltz away together.* HUGO *drops a word to* ROMAINVILLE *as he goes past him.*

She's bluffing. She doesn't know a thing.

ROMAINVILLE.  She knows everything.

MME. DESMER (*watching them go*).  She is exquisite, she is pretty, and she's well-bred. How is it, Romainville, you've never talked about her to me?

ROMAINVILLE (*unhappily*).  I don't know. . . . I can't explain it at all . . . not even—not even to myself.

MME. DESMER (*signing to* CAPULAT *to push her towards the ball*).  Let me think, now: on her mother's side, if my memory serves, she is a Dandinet-Dandaine?

ROMAINVILLE.  Yes, but . . .

MME. DESMER.  Then she's connected with the Roche-marsouins?

ROMAINVILLE.  Perhaps, perhaps, but . . .

MME. DESMER.  If she's connected with the Rochemar-souins, she must also be a Cazaubon.

ROMAINVILLE.  Yes, I suppose she must, but . . .

MME. DESMER.  My poor Antony was a Cazaubon through the Marsusses and the Villevilles, so he would have been as it were a slight relation of hers if he had lived.

ROMAINVILLE.  As it were . . . but as it is, he is dead!

MME. DESMER.  But I'm still alive, Romainville, and I like to be quite clear about relationships. It's very important I should see exactly how this girl fits in. Now, let me see: you said her mother, who was a Fripont-Minet, is dead.

ROMAINVILLE.  Dead!

MME. DESMER.  Her mother's cousin, then, one of the Laboulasses. . . .

41

ROMAINVILLE (*interrupting*).  Also dead.

MME. DESMER.  The elder? The one I went to school with? I don't mean the younger one.

ROMAINVILLE.  Dead, dead!

MME. DESMER.  What, both of them?

ROMAINVILLE.  Both of them.

MME. DESMER.  And on her father's side: the Dupont-Pitard family?

ROMAINVILLE.  All dead.

MME. DESMER.  Poor little thing! Why, she's living in a morgue!

ROMAINVILLE.  A charnel-house!

*They go.*

*As* CAPULAT *goes she drops her long mauve scarf.* THE MOTHER *comes out of hiding as cautiously as a great mouse. Re-enter* CAPULAT. *She rushes to* THE MOTHER.

CAPULAT.  I told them I had lost my scarf!

*They fall into each other's arms.*

THE MOTHER.  To see you! To think that I really see you! It's like a dream!

CAPULAT.  It is, isn't it, it really is? The whole thing, the whole thing's such a romance, it really is.

THE MOTHER.  He worships her; you could see it in every look he gave!

CAPULAT.  He's absurdly rich. It really is a romance!

THE MOTHER.  And handsome as a lion! You must help me, my dear, or my little girl will die of it.

CAPULAT.  I'll do anything and everything. The whole thing's such a romance, it really is. Ah, dear! Our little wild whirling days at Mauberge, can you remember them? The cake shop Marius Laubonne!

THE MOTHER.  And the ice creams at Pinteau's!

CAPULAT. And the first duet we played together, at the Charity Concert for the Mauberge Widows' Fund! (*She listens to the music.*) The "Invitation Waltz."

THE MOTHER. The "Invitation Waltz." (*She starts to sing the music.*) La, si, do, re, do, la, sol, la, sol, fa, mi, re, do.

> *The orchestra takes up the waltz during the final bar and continues playing.* THE MOTHER *and* CAPULAT *stand for a moment rocking to and fro, with their heads together, then* CAPULAT *breaks away and creeps furtively off, blowing kisses with her scarf.*
>
> THE MOTHER, *her eyes half closed, her head leaning on her hands, starts to waltz herself.* JOSHUA *appears, moves towards her like a man stalking a butterfly.*
>
> *She goes out waltzing without seeing him. He follows her.*

THE CURTAIN FALLS ON ACT ONE

# ACT TWO

*Behind the lowered curtain, gay music of the dance.*
*As the curtain rises, couples are whirling round the stage;*
*the music comes to an end. and they drift away.*
MME. DESMERMORTES *enters in her wheel-chair,*
*pushed by* CAPULAT.

CAPULAT (*after a pause*).   Well, the ball has really got
going now, hasn't it, madam?

MME. DESMER (*peevishly*).   It can get going and go, for all
I care. It bores me until I don't know whether to yawn
or yelp. I was never fond of dancing, and since I've been
screwed to this chair, it looks more than ever like the
hopping of kangaroos. You've never liked it either, have
you?

CAPULAT (*simpering*).   I was a girl of twenty, you know,
once upon a time.

MME. DESMER.   When, for goodness' sake? You've never
looked any different to me.

CAPULAT.   Oh yes, I was, madam. I was young when
I was with the Baron and Baroness, before I came
here.

MME. DESMER.   Ah, well, you may have thought so.
You're a nice girl, Capulat, but . . . you know this as well
as I do . . . you're plain. No one who is plain can ever
have been twenty.

CAPULAT.   But a heart beats in my breast all the same,
madam.

MME. DESMER.   My good soul, a heart with no face is
more bother than everything else put together. Let's talk

45

no more about it . . . you've been quite happy, Capulat, without a face; you've been respected, and you've been appreciated. What could be nicer than that?

CAPULAT. On evenings like this, when there's music and the young people dancing under the chandeliers, I feel something indescribable in the air.

MME. DESMER. Then don't attempt to describe it. It's much too late. You really have nothing to grumble about. And there's always the life to come. A dull life in this world is a splendid recommendation for the next.

CAPULAT. Oh, madam.

MME. DESMER. You will be hobnobbing with the Blessed while I'm roasting over a slow fire for two or three thousand years. Well, perhaps it won't seem so long.

CAPULAT. God's mercy is infinite, madam.

MME. DESMER. Certainly; but He must abide by what He says, you know, otherwise the Just like you, who've staked everything on it, are going to feel very badly let down. Suppose a rumour started circulating among the Sheep that the Goats were going to be pardoned as well? They would use such bad language that they'd get themselves damned on the spot. Don't you think it would be rather comic?

CAPULAT. Oh, you can't really think that, madam!

MME. DESMER. Why not? I can think anything I like, it's all I have left to do. . . . Push me nearer the doors where I can see the frisking of little fools. Isn't that Romainville's niece dancing with my nephew?

CAPULAT. Yes, madam.

MME. DESMER. She has a very unusual grace; the only woman who is being herself. Why didn't Romainville bring her here before?

CAPULAT. She's so graceful, really she is, isn't she? She has such . . . what shall I say . . .?

46

MME. DESMER. Whatever you care to, dear; I'm not listening. Do you know what I think? I think you'll need amusing this evening. Now, what can we think of to liven ourselves up?

CAPULAT. A cotillion?

MME. DESMER. A cotillion! That is so like you! You couldn't have suggested anything sillier. Except the ball itself. . . . Look at them twirling and twiddling! They think they're enjoying themselves, but all they're doing is twizzling their vain little heads. The world isn't amusing any more; it's time I left it. The fabulous evenings I've known in my time. In 1902, for instance, at Biarritz, the Duke of Medino-Solar was out-of-this-world in love with the Countess Funela. You won't guess what he did. They were giving a public assembly—a ridotto, it used to be called—and everyone had to be dressed in yellow. Well, the Duke came in green! It was the colour of his mistress's eyes, but of course nobody understood that. The rules of a ridotto were always very strict, and they refused to let him in. The Duke was a Spaniard of the hottest and bluest blood. Without any attempt to explain, he killed the footman. Of course, the ball went on. Their Highnesses the Infantas were there, so it was decided that anonymity should still be respected. The police were brought in, wearing yellow dominoes, and if you happened to dance with them you could see their beady eyes and really horrible moustaches under their masks. But, as they could only dance with the ladies, they weren't able to spot the Duke! The next day he crossed the frontier and a bull killed him in Madrid. That's what living used to be!

CAPULAT. Yes, of course, but one doesn't know, really one doesn't; romantic things may be going on here, at this very moment.

47

MME. DESMER. At this ball? Dear Capulat, you should go and lie down.

CAPULAT. Perhaps so, but perhaps not so. Suppose there was a young, rich, handsome man, spellbound with love, who had smuggled his loved one into the ball. . . . But I've said too much. I promised I wouldn't breathe a word.

MME. DESMER. Why should I suppose there was?

CAPULAT. And, as well as the young man, an old friend, a dear, dear friend given up for dead, suddenly coming back like the bluebells in May! It's really wonderful, it really is, suddenly to take part in a fairy story!

MME. DESMER. Bluebells? Fairy story? Capulat, I don't know what you're talking about.

CAPULAT. To think the world is still so colourful, madam, it really is! Love can still be stronger than social barriers, careless of scandal, as pure as death. There can still be the desperate plot, the impersonation, madam. And the poor apprehensive mother, hiding herself away and watching her child's triumph without ever . . . ever . . . Oh, I really can't stop the tears, madam, I can't really. I'm so sorry!

MME. DESMER. Suppose you explain yourself, Capulat, instead of watering my hair? What apprehensive mother, what impersonations?

CAPULAT. Oh, I've said too much! I promised I wouldn't breathe a word!

MME. DESMER. A word about what?

CAPULAT. It's a secret, madam; the diamond at the bottom of a mine. She loves him, he worships her, she is poor, he brings her here disguised. It's really like a fairy story, really it is, isn't it?

MME. DESMER. She? He? Who are these people?

CAPULAT. Everyone is either whispering her name or asking who she is. She moves among them like a queen. Her evening of triumph! And her mother played the treble and I played the bass, all those years ago. . . . I'm so sorry; do forgive me; it's all too much!

MME. DESMER. Capulat, you've been my companion for twenty years, and though you've never said anything that amused me I've always been able to understand you. At last you interest me and I can't understand a word. Either you explain, or you leave my service.

CAPULAT. Oh, I've said too much! I promised not to breathe a word. I'd rather die in poverty; I'd rather you killed me!

MME. DESMER. I wouldn't dream of it. I'm used to being obeyed without having to kill people. And you know I always give you my old clothes. Don't I deserve a little consideration?

CAPULAT. I know, I know that, madam! I'm being nearly torn apart by the two duties. Oh, madam, we were such friends, we both played on the same piano! Such happy days! I thought she was dead and I found her again. She told me she belonged to the orchestra, but they were all negroes. I was astonished. Then she confided in me, and swore me to secrecy. All about the mad love of this young man for her daughter, and the stratagem of the good kind friend.

MME. DESMER. What good kind friend?

CAPULAT. M. Guy-Charles Romainville, such a good kind man!

MME. DESMER. What has he done?

CAPULAT. His niece is not his niece. Love snaps its fingers! A young man who is very close to you. But I've said too much. I promised not to breathe a word.

MME. DESMER. Promised whom?

49

CAPULAT. My dearest friend. I promised on the days of our duets. So better to die! . . . Oh, madam, the violins! They're like strong wine to me!

MME. DESMER. So I've noticed, mon amie! Push me to my room where we shan't hear them, and tell me the rest of it.

CAPULAT. You're so good, madam; there's nothing you can't do! A word from you, and all the obstacles will evaporate.

MME. DESMER. Well, we shall see about that. Trundle me off and explain things without falling over yourself. You were saying that Romainville's niece . . .

CAPULAT. Is not his niece, madam. She's your nephew's loved one. He wanted her to be the belle of the ball. So he had a dress brought from Paris for her, and he begged her mother, my dear, sweet friend . . .

MME. DESMER. My nephew? Which nephew? Frederic?

CAPULAT. No, madam. Mr. Hugo. But, oh dear, I'm sure I've said too much! I promised not to breathe a word. . . .
*They go.*

*The music wells up again. Enter* LADY INDIA *and* PATRICE BOMBELLES, *dancing a Mexican tango.*

PATRICE. They've put me in a room looking out on the park, facing direct north . . . it's most unkind . . . and they've moved all my things, in the middle of the afternoon, without telling me. They said they couldn't find me, but they're not going to make me believe that. I never left the billiard-room. They couldn't find me because they didn't want to find me.

LADY INDIA. Then who has got your room?

PATRICE. Romainville's niece. The girl with the lovely eyes. But that's only the excuse. The real reason is that he saw us together yesterday, and wants to have me further away from your room.

50

LADY INDIA. Nonsense! He would have to explain it all to my aunt. You mustn't be idiotic. And how do you know she has lovely eyes?

PATRICE. Who, dear heart?

LADY INDIA. This niece of Romainville's.

PATRICE. Have I said so?

LADY INDIA. Now be careful, Patrice. I don't like competitors. And if Messerschmann *has* seen us together and feels like braining you, I shall quite understand. Frankly, Patrice, I should be very disappointed if he didn't. Don't you agree?

PATRICE. Well, I suppose . . . I don't know . . . I suppose so.

LADY INDIA. I may deceive Messerschmann, but I like to think well of him. The man I love must be noble and courageous, and the man I deceive must be noble and courageous too. It gives life a kind of dignity which is most pleasing. Surely, Patrice, you, so proud and susceptible, would be terribly upset if he didn't give a savage cry of uncontrollable jealousy?

PATRICE. I—well, Dorothy, I——

LADY INDIA. Exactly! Men of your calibre wouldn't want a woman who wasn't fiercely loved already. Creatures such as ourselves have no patience with the lukewarm. We blaze! Other people may be born to live, but we're on earth to blaze.

PATRICE. Yes, Dorothy.

LADY INDIA. And it's very nice of us to bother about him at all. Suppose he does ruin us? What fun it would be to be poor, as long as one was *excessively* poor! Anything in excess is most exhilarating.

PATRICE. Yes, Dorothy!

LADY INDIA. Our squalor would seem like a great dark poem, wouldn't it, Patrice?

51

PATRICE.  Very dark!

LADY INDIA.  How amusing it would be! I should wash the dishes and clean the flues, whatever that may be, and bake and brew. How beautifully I should brew! I must ask Roeseda Soeurs to make me some affecting little aprons. There's no one else, you know, who so well understands my style. What miracles she will do with a scrap of muslin and a ruche! And then I shall set to work with my tiny dustbin and my tiny broom. And you will work in a factory. I know so many people on the Steel Board; they'll find you a job as a metal-worker easily. You will come home in the evening, nearly dead with fatigue, and smelling dreadfully. It will be absolutely delicious! And I shall wash you down, my dear, from head to foot with a tiny sponge. It's beautiful to be poor, Patrice.

PATRICE.  Beautiful?

LADY INDIA,  Let him come. What is he waiting for? His money is burning my fingers. I shall give it all back, immediately, everything except the pearls.

MESSERSCHMANN *enters and stops, not daring to approach.*

PATRICE (*terrified*).  Do be careful—he's here! Do be careful!

LADY INDIA.  Don't be such a coward, Patrice!

PATRICE.  I don't like you. I've never liked you. I'm never likely to like you.

LADY INDIA.  What?

PATRICE.  I'm only with you out of sheer necessity. It's quite obvious you bore me. Anyone can see that I'm yawning. (*He yawns.*)

LADY INDIA.  Patrice, don't dare to yawn! Take my arm. We'll go away, dancing as ostentatiously as possible.

52

PATRICE. You're crazy!

LADY INDIA. When the bull is drowsy, one stirs it up with a banderilla. (*Aloud, as they dance off.*) Have you ever seen a bull-fight, dear friend?

PATRICE (*aloud*). Yes, dear friend, but I didn't like it.

LADY INDIA (*aside to him*). Hold your head up. Don't look as though we've seen him. He needn't know yet we know he knows.

PATRICE (*stumbling in tongue and foot*). Yes, but perhaps he doesn't know, Dorothy. Don't you think that by seeming to know we know he knows we run the risk of making him know?

*They go.*

MESSERSCHMANN *makes to follow them. He calls* JOSHUA, *who is crossing the stage.*

MESSER. Come here, my friend!

JOSHUA. Sir?

MESSER. The two people walking along the terrace there; they'd be making for the greenhouses, I suppose?

JOSHUA. Yes, sir. Would you care to give me your order for supper, sir?

MESSER. Noodles.

JOSHUA. Without butter, sir?

MESSER. And without salt.

JOSHUA. Very good, sir.

MESSER (*makes to go, then hesitates*). Tell me, my friend. . . .

JOSHUA. Sir?

MESSER. If I go down those steps, I get to the greenhouses through the orchard, do I not?

JOSHUA. Yes, sir. But if you are hoping to catch up with the lady and gentleman, sir, I take the liberty to say that I've been watching the lady and gentleman, sir, while you were giving me your order, and they've come back into the house by the small door at the end of the terrace. The lady and gentleman have no doubt gone upstairs by the little staircase, sir.

MESSER. I see!

JOSHUA. No doubt they wish to tidy their persons up, as it were, sir.

MESSER (*sighing*). No doubt yes. Thank you.

(*He is going out when* JOSHUA *bows and says:*

JOSHUA. Without butter?

MESSER (*sighing, sombrely*). And without salt.

*He goes,* JOSHUA *also.*
*Couples, waltzing, fill the stage again.* FREDERIC *crosses thoughtfully among the crowd of dancers.* ISABELLE *enters. At the end of the dance* FREDERIC *re-enters, still searching, through another door. He sees* ISABELLE. *They stand, looking at one another, a little uncomfortably, on the now empty stage.*

ISABELLE. I hope you'll forgive me?

FREDERIC. For what, mademoiselle?

ISABELLE. I must seem to be following you. I happened to come in here and . . . and found you were here before me.

FREDERIC. Yes, of course.

ISABELLE. I'm enjoying . . . enjoying the evening very much.

FREDERIC. Yes, it's splendid.

*A silence. We hear the orchestra playing. They don't know what to say to one another.*

That's a very pretty dress you're wearing.

ISABELLE. Yes, it is pretty. (*Another silence, and then she suddenly asks*) Do you believe in them, I wonder?

FREDERIC.  Believe in them?

ISABELLE.  In ghosts.

FREDERIC.  A little. Why?

ISABELLE.  You look as though you might be your brother's ghost, made very sad by something.

FREDERIC.  It's what I am.

ISABELLE.  You're young, you're handsome, and you're rich. What can possibly have made you sad?

FREDERIC.  Being handsome, as you call it, being young and rich, and nothing to be gained by it. Will you excuse me if I leave you now?

ISABELLE.  Yes, certainly.

> FREDERIC *goes into the garden.*
>
> *A snatch from the orchestra, perhaps.* HUGO *bursts in through another door.*

HUGO.  That was perfect!

ISABELLE.  I didn't know what to say. I feel very shy with him.

HUGO.  Excellent!

ISABELLE.  He'll wonder why I'm always at his elbow, and why I keep trying to speak to him.

HUGO.  That's what I want.

ISABELLE (*sinking into a chair*).  I can't do it any more.

HUGO (*sternly*).  We're not yet past midnight, and you have a duty till dawn. Up you get! You're a kindly creature, and this is a kindly action you're doing. I can promise you won't regret it. That's right; look at him just as you're looking now. You're an astonishing actress. Where did you learn that look of deep regard?

ISABELLE.  It's my own.

HUGO.  Congratulations. Turn it on Frederic from now till morning. He couldn't help being moved by it.

ISABELLE (*softly*).  It may be different when it turns on him.

HUGO. Well, something in the same line will do. Dear little brother; he's not used to being given pretty looks. Look out, he's coming back. He wants to talk to you after all, you see. Now, compose yourself and use your imagination. I shall be listening.

*He disappears.*

FREDERIC *returns.*

FREDERIC. My brother was looking for you just now.

ISABELLE. Oh, was he?

FREDERIC. Usually, when my brother is looking for a girl, she knows it.

ISABELLE. Oh. I . . . I didn't know.

FREDERIC. He's very good-looking; don't you think so?

ISABELLE. Yes—very.

FREDERIC. We're as alike as two blades of grass, but it's only men who get us confused. Women always know which is my brother? How do they do it?

ISABELLE. I don't know.

FREDERIC. It's because he doesn't look at them, maybe. That's a very pretty dress you're wearing.

ISABELLE. Isn't it? He's not only good-looking.

FREDERIC. Who?

ISABELLE. Your brother.

FREDERIC. No. He's very intelligent; much more intelligent than I am. Very brave, too; completely fearless; always ready to shoot the rapids or put his hand in the fire. But there's one thing he couldn't ever do, not every day for any length of time. He couldn't be in love; and perhaps that's why they love him. He's very hard, but he's also very kind.

ISABELLE. He's very fond of you. He wouldn't like to see you hurt.

FREDERIC. It would irritate him. It's not so much that

56

he's very fond of me. It annoys him to see me unhappy. He doesn't like people to be unhappy. Particularly unhappy in love. (*He gets up.*) Honestly, he's looking for you. I'm looking for someone, too. If I come across him during my search shall I tell him where you are?

ISABELLE. Really, no. Thank you, but don't tell him.

FREDERIC. He's good company; much more so than I am.

ISABELLE. I like being with you. Please stay!

> FREDERIC *looks at her in astonishment and sits beside her with a sigh.*

FREDERIC. Oh! How sad it all is!

ISABELLE. How sad all what is?

FREDERIC. I'm sorry. What I'm going to say isn't very polite. Perhaps it's impolite, though I don't want to be impolite. But if the girl I'm looking for so unsuccessfully had said what you have just said I might very well have died of happiness.

ISABELLE (*smiling nicely at him*). Then it's as well that it was I who said it. (*She gets up.*) And it wasn't in the least impolite. I understand how you feel only too well.

FREDERIC (*also rising*). Thank you for understanding, but forgive me all the same, and forgive me if I go now.

ISABELLE. Of course.

FREDERIC. Good-bye.

> *He goes.*

> HUGO *enters immediately, by the same door, in a bad temper.*

HUGO. No, no, no! I didn't bring you here for that!

ISABELLE. What have I done?

HUGO. Sighing and hinting that you'd rather be with someone else! No more of that! You're paid to act a part, my dear, so act it. And without being ashamed of it. It's a serious job, and you should try to do it well.

ISABELLE (*gently*).   Please don't go on.

HUGO.   Why?

ISABELLE.   If you went on talking to me in that voice, I should cry.

HUGO.   Now that really would be a good idea. I wouldn't have suggested it myself. Manufactured tears always look a bit grotesque; but if you'll cry naturally, excellent! My dear little brother will founder at once!

ISABELLE.   Why haven't you a heart?

HUGO.   Because my brother has too much. We were born at the same time, and things were divided between us, this and that to me, a heart to him.

ISABELLE.   But you must be able to see that I'm unhappy?

HUGO.   Splendidly. You have a way of being unhappy that would fetch tears out of a rock. Have you a twin-sister, by any chance, without a heart?

ISABELLE.   I can't bear you!

HUGO.   It's a very good thing you can't. Tell my brother so, and swim away with him in a flood of sympathy. That's just what I want.

ISABELLE.   You don't suppose I'm doing what I'm told this evening just for the sake of this dress and a fee for dancing?

HUGO.   My pretty one, I thought nothing so unpleasant.

ISABELLE.   I'm not interested in your brother, or in curing him, or in looking well-dressed, or in having everyone looking at me. Men have looked at me before even when I wasn't dressed well. Do you think that's amusing?

HUGO.   Don't fight back the tears any more, let yourself go. Cry, cry, cry, my dear. That's better. You see how easy it is.

ISABELLE (*crying*).   Now my eyes will be red. Isn't that rather clever of me?

58

HUGO. Superbly! (*He throws himself suddenly on his knees and declaims theatrically.*) Ah! Isabelle, dear Isabelle! I suffer too, I die as well!

ISABELLE (*stopping crying*). What are you doing?

HUGO. He's coming back. Stay just as you are. I want him to find me at your feet.

ISABELLE. Oh, no; this is dreadful!

HUGO (*on his knees*). Yes, my darling. My heart is over-flowing! I'm drowning in it! A heart in full flood! Is he coming towards us?

ISABELLE. Yes. Oh, please get up!

HUGO. Now's the time; all or nothing. Ah well; I suppose I'd better kiss you.

> *He takes her in his arms and kisses her. She relaxes with a little cry—then she suddenly asks:*

ISABELLE. Why did you say 'Ah well'?

HUGO (*bowing coldly*). You must excuse me. A kiss was necessary.

> *He makes his escape.*
> *She drops to the sofa, crying.*

FREDERIC (*entering*). Are you crying?

ISABELLE. Yes.

FREDERIC. You ought to be happy; my brother kissed you. Usually when that happens, the girl is blushing and dancing like fire. But you're pale and you're crying.

ISABELLE. Yes.

FREDERIC. I'm sorry. Perhaps he went away because he saw me coming.

ISABELLE. No.

FREDERIC. Don't be unhappy. One unhappy person at a party is enough. I don't know how it is, but I should hate it if you were unhappy too.

59

ISABELLE. Please let me alone.

FREDERIC. I want to tell you something; I realize it's no consolation to hear other people's troubles, but even so. It's something I've been almost certain about since yesterday. She chose to be engaged to me because she couldn't be engaged to my brother. She said to herself, "If the other one won't have me I'll take his double".

ISABELLE. If that were true it would be shameful.

FREDERIC. No; very lucky, really. Otherwise she would never have chosen me at all. Anyway, I'm used to it. When we were small, if my brother was naughty and the governess couldn't find him, she punished me. It was a sort of alternative. Life only comes to me absentmindedly.

ISABELLE. You, as well.

FREDERIC. Why do you say "You as well"? You can't know what it feels like. I don't mean to pay you an empty compliment, this is hardly the moment; but I'm certain no one could mistake you for anyone else.

*ISABELLE is looking off-stage, suddenly tense. She shakes her head to someone in the wings. Then:*

ISABELLE. It wasn't because of your brother that I was crying.

FREDERIC. No?

ISABELLE. It was because of you.

FREDERIC. Because of me?

ISABELLE. Yes—Frederic, it's you I love.

FREDERIC. Oh!

*He goes.*

*ISABELLE runs across the stage; HUGO returns, dragging her by the hand.*

HUGO. Very good! But you needn't have run away! That's the first time anyone has told him they loved him. You

60

see, you've made him walk with quite a swagger! Let's make things even brisker. A pinch of jealousy while the blood's on the simmer. A third young man is in love with you.

ISABELLE.  What young man?

HUGO.  That's my business; I'll find one. Furious because I never leave your side, he challenges me to fight, and we choose our weapons.

ISABELLE.  You're mad!

HUGO.  Imagine it—a duel by moonlight, in the spinney, during supper. Conversation disrupted by the sound of pistol shots. They stop the orchestra, and all troop into the park with lanterns and hurricane lamps to look for the corpse. And then you, your wits crazed with love (you do understand you're crazed with love, don't you, Isabelle?)—you throw yourself into the lake. You swim, I imagine? Well, anyway, it doesn't matter; you've got feet, the lake's no depth, and I shall be there. I shall fish you out, carry you back to land, lay you streaming with water on the grass at my brother's feet, and say to him, "There! You did this!" And if he doesn't love you after that he's got more resistance than I have. . . . You're looking rather dubious. Don't you enjoy batling? I'll treble your fee. I'll buy you another dress. (*He takes her in his arms before she can draw back; he suddenly speaks like a little spoilt boy.*) Be a nice girl, agree to it, to please me. I'm enjoying myself so much tonight, and it's not often that I do.

ISABELLE (*breaking away and running off with the same hurt cry as before*).  Oh!

DIANA (*entering suddenly*).  Frederic!

HUGO (*turning with a smile*).  Hugo, if you please.

DIANA.  Oh! I beg your pardon.

HUGO.  I'm not blushing. The one who doesn't blush is

61

Hugo. Remember that: you may find it useful. Are you looking for him?

DIANA.   I thought it was Frederic with that girl in his arms. As it was you, it's different. I apologize. Have you seen him?

HUGO.   Of course. Everybody except you has seen him. He wanders like a soul in pain through this desert of gaiety. Why? Are you wanting to satisfy yourself that you've well and truly broken his heart this evening?

DIANA.   I don't want to break anyone's heart. It wouldn't amuse me. (*She takes a step and stops.*) By the way, when I was in the park yesterday, one of you kissed me, and Frederic swears it wasn't him. I lied so that he shouldn't be upset. But it must have been you. It's the kind of joke I detest.

HUGO.   Yesterday? In the park? At what time?

DIANA. Don't pretend not to remember, Hugo. After dinner.

HUGO.   After dinner? You've made a mistake, my dear. I was playing billiards with Patrice Bombelles.

DIANA.   Frederic swears it wasn't him.

HUGO.   I can only suppose it was yet another son of Adam, making the most of some vague resemblance to us.

DIANA.   You're wrong to play with your brother's feelings, Hugo; it's too cruel. Even if you loved me, even if your love for me were too strong to control. But it isn't too strong to control, is it?

HUGO.   You put me in an impossible situation, Diana. I'm obliged to say No.

DIANA.   I hate you!

HUGO.   You, as well? I'm not very popular this evening. Have you seen Patrice Bombelles? I gather he's looking everywhere for me. It's funny, but he didn't take to finding me in that little girl's arms, either. It seems he's mad about her. I didn't know, though I suppose I might have guessed, because everybody seems to be. And I admit

62

she's enchanting, and she's wearing a very pretty dress, moreover. Don't you find it so? Well, good-bye. Shall I send Frederic to you?

DIANA.   Thank you all the same. I'll find him myself.

*He goes.*

DIANA *remains alone, unable to relax. Suddenly she calls for her father.*

DIANA.   Father!

MESSER.   Well, dear?

DIANA.   Did you hear him? Did you hear how he was mocking me?

MESSER.   No, dear.

DIANA.   Why not?

MESSER.   Because I wasn't there.

DIANA.   Things are going so wrong you'd think we had no money at all. Would you be so good as to make me happy again, at once?

MESSER.   But what is the matter, my darling girl? You wanted this boy Frederic and I bought him for you. Is he trying to get out of it?

DIANA.   You didn't buy him for me; he loves me. But his brother is laughing at me.

MESSER.   I can't give you both of them; not because I'm not rich enough, but it isn't the custom. Marry whichever you prefer.

DIANA.   You're not rich enough to buy me the one I prefer. That's why I took the other one.

MESSER.   Not rich enough! Don't put me in a rage!

DIANA.   Well, look what's happening to me, and it's Hugo who's making it happen, deliberately, I'm certain. I'm certain he brought this girl here, and she's trying to make Frederic lose interest in me; and Hugo, who never looks at anybody, the cold impersonal Hugo, never takes his eyes off her. I should begin to think I wasn't here, except that everyone has such an air of *not* looking at me that I know I must be. It's bad enough to be looked at as though you weren't there, but it's terrible, terrible, *not* to be looked at as though you were. So please set about making me happy again.

MESSER (*thoughtfully*). Who is this girl? I can do almost nothing with a young girl.

DIANA.   Romainville's niece.

MESSER.   Which is Romainville?

DIANA.   He's the one who looks as though he has gone on a horse to catch butterflies.

MESSER.   But where does his money come from?

DIANA.   He's a director of one of your companies, like all the rest of the men here.

MESSER.   What does Romainville seem to be on? Steel, cement, potash, sulphates, zinc, aluminium, creosote, nuts, nickel, emulsion, tyres, bijouterie, sewing machines, tunnels, racquets . . .

DIANA.   I think he said something about pig-iron.

MESSER.   Pig-iron! Lead me to him. What do you want this Romainville to do, my darling girl? Do you want me to make him send her away at the height of the ball?

DIANA.   Oh—do you think you can?

MESSER.   I've got them all in the palm of my hand. I lift a finger and their incomes are only half as much.

DIANA.   I'm afraid it's impossible, Father.

MESSER (*calmly*).   If he has a ha'penny in pig-iron, nothing is impossible.

*He takes her by the hand and*
*They go.*

*Enter* PATRICE *and* HUGO *from opposite sides. The orchestra plays a heroic, warlike tune.*

64

HUGO. Sir?

PATRICE. Sir?

HUGO. I was looking for you.

PATRICE. For me?

HUGO. Yes. I want to speak to you.

PATRICE. About what?

HUGO. You were in the park yesterday, I think, with Lady Dorothy India, my cousin?

PATRICE. Possibly.

HUGO. I noticed you. You seemed to be having a rather heated discussion.

PATRICE. On quite general matters, if I remember.

HUGO. I don't doubt it. But at one moment you must have outgeneralled yourself; the lady slapped your face.

PATRICE. Mine, sir?

HUGO. This one.

PATRICE. ·You're mistaken, sir.

HUGO. No, sir.

PATRICE. That is to say, the lady may have struck me, but that's no reason for you to think what you appear to be thinking, sir!

HUGO. What do I appear to be thinking?

PATRICE. After all, damn it, a slap on the cheek isn't always the sign of an understanding between a man and a woman.

HUGO. Certainly not.

PATRICE. One slaps the most casual acquaintances, even complete strangers. It proves absolutely nothing. For instance, if I suddenly struck you now, would you deduce from this that we were on amorous terms?

HUGO. I'd protect myself from that to the death!

PATRICE. Then, may I ask, why you're trying to provoke

me? Winks, sighs, hints, unpleasant chuckles, which you try to camouflage with cigar-smoke? You didn't fool me yesterday on the terrace; oh no, I wasn't fooled for a moment.

HUGO. You're very clairvoyant.

PATRICE. I can't go on, I can't go on another hour!

HUGO. This is just what I wanted to make you say. (*He takes his arm.*) Let's talk it over quietly, like the nice fellows we are. I need your help. Between you and me and the bed-post, this long-drawn-out affair with my mad cousin is boring you to desperation—admit it!

PATRICE. I've never said so.

HUGO. Naturally not. But let's speak frankly, shall we? You're in the hell of a cleft stick. If Messerschmann gets to know she's your mistress . . .

PATRICE (*terrified*). Don't say that, don't mention it!

HUGO. He'll break your neck!

PATRICE (*in a terrible state*). I've been enduring this for two years, twenty-four months—a hundred and four nerve-racking weeks, seven hundred and twenty-eight days. . . .

HUGO. Never mind, dear man; it will be all over this evening.

PATRICE. What do you mean?

HUGO. In the simplest possible way. Imagine you're on a visit to the dentist. You've rung the bell, flickered over the pages of the magazines in the waiting-room, and now you're sitting in the dentist's chair. You've shown him the bad tooth; the dentist has seized the forceps. You're a big boy now; it's too late to run off home.

PATRICE. Do you know my dentist?

HUGO. No.

PATRICE. What are you talking about?

HUGO. This! Either you fall in with my plans this

66

evening, or else, to be honest with you, I make quite sure that your employer knows how you employ yourself.

PATRICE. No!

HUGO. Now I wonder what you mean when you say no?

PATRICE. You're a gentleman, you wouldn't do it.

HUGO. Not by an anonymous letter or by bribing a servant; but though I do things like a gentleman, I do them.

PATRICE. You're contemptible!

HUGO. I see.

PATRICE. And you're not ashamed?

HUGO. Not at all.

PATRICE. Oh. Then there's nothing more to discuss. What do you want me to do?

HUGO. I want you to choose the alternative way of having your neck broken. There's a very charming girl here tonight. It's a matter of the greatest importance, which I can't explain, that you should pretend you're desperately in love with her.

PATRICE. I?

HUGO. You. But that's not all. You've seen me in the arms of this girl, and in a fit of ungovernable jealousy you box my ears.

PATRICE. I?

HUGO. You. Come with me. We put the incident on a proper footing. We fight by moonlight, in the spinney, with pistols. Don't be afraid; I'm a very good shot. I promise I shan't hit you.

*They go.*

*Enter* CAPULAT, *followed by* THE MOTHER, *magnificently dressed and plumed.*

67

CAPULAT. Oh! Oh! You look like the best in the land, you do really, really you do!

THE MOTHER. Do I, Capulat?

CAPULAT. Really you do! You couldn't look nicer in that dress if you'd been born in it!

THE MOTHER. It's my dreams come true, isn't it? I feel as if I'd been born in it.

CAPULAT. No one could doubt it. But wait, wait! I'll go and find madam.

*As she goes,* JOSHUA *enters. He stops suddenly, rooted to the spot, when he sees* THE MOTHER *in her finery.*

JOSHUA. Oh!

THE MOTHER. My man, would you kindly announce me? The Countess Funela.

JOSHUA. The Countess . . .?

THE MOTHER (*magnificently*). Funela!

JOSHUA. (*goes out, shouting*). Mr. Hugo! Help me Mr. Hugo, sir . . .!

JOSHUA *goes out.*

*Enter* MME. DESMERMORTES, *pushed by* CAPULAT. JOSHUA *goes past without seeing her.*

MME. DESMER. Where's he running? What is it? Fire? That would be most diverting. . . . Let me see you, ma chérie! Mille tonnerres! Why, she's a great success! Now we'll go in and make a sensation.

*Enter* HUGO *with* JOSHUA.

My dear Hugo, I know you will be delighted to be presented to one of my oldest and dearest friends. The Countess Funela. We knew one another in Italy. My nephew, Hugo, Countess.

THE MOTHER.  I'm so charmed to meet you!

HUGO.  Madam!

MME. DESMER.  Come along, my dear; wheel me, Capulat. I'm so happy to see you again after such a desolation of separation. We can talk about Venice. Such days! Do you remember Palestrini? Such a madman! Jaundice made an end of him. Now I shall introduce you to all my other guests. Tell me, my dear, you have a daughter, isn't that so? What has become of her?

THE MOTHER.  Oh, it's a very long story indeed.

MME. DESMER.  Well, you must let me hear it. We have all the night before us. . . .

*They have gone.*

JOSHUA (*badly shaken*).  Here's the key, Mr. Hugo. So she can only have got out through the window, unless madam opened the door herself. The Countess Funela! When she said that, I could have knocked myself down with one of her feathers. (*He so far forgets himself as to sit down and quickly jumps up again.*) Oh, I beg your pardon, sir.

HUGO.  What for?

JOSHUA.  I sat down. Quite an accident, sir. That hasn't happened to me before in thirty years.

ROMAINVILLE (*entering*).  Stop! Oh, stop! Stop!

HUGO.  Stop what?

ROMAINVILLE.  Everything, stop everything! This time it's altogether calamitous! We've fallen into a trap, we're caught by the avalanche! High finance at its worst! Don't say a word about it! Isabelle must be got away this instant, this very moment, or else I'm ruined!

HUGO.  What in the world are you raving about? Everybody's out of their minds tonight!

ROMAINVILLE.  I'm a director of several sulphate companies, and one pig-iron company.

HUGO. Yes, we know that. But what's that got to do with it?

ROMAINVILLE. That's why Isabelle must leave this house at once! Yes: powerful financial interests make it essential! Not a word! I can't explain. Manœuvres at the Stock Exchange. If you won't help me, your aunt can go to the devil. I'd sooner have the scandal. I'd sooner upset her for life. I'd sooner any damn thing! I'm going to tell her the whole truth immediately!

HUGO. Tell my aunt? Just take a look at who she's introducing to everybody, in the middle of the ballroom!

ROMAINVILLE. I'm too short-sighted. I can't see at this distance.

HUGO. Put your glasses on; it's worth it.

ROMAINVILLE (*putting them on*). Good heavens! What on earth is she doing? Am I dreaming or is that . . .

HUGO. Yes. The Countess Funela. She used to revolve in the best Italian circles.

ROMAINVILLE. Is this you up to your tricks again?

HUGO. No. But my aunt is up to hers.

ROMAINVILLE. But why?

HUGO. No reason, which is what makes it serious.

PATRICE (*entering aggressively*). Sir!

HUGO (*who has entirely forgotten*). Sir?

PATRICE. This state of affairs cannot go on, and as you refuse to give the girl up——(*He tries to box* HUGO'S *ears.*)

HUGO (*pushing him tetchily away*). No, no, no! Another time! You're being a nuisance! Later on, later on! Come on, Romainville, we've got to go and stop her jumping in the lake.

*He goes, dragging* ROMAINVILLE *in a flurry after him.*

PATRICE.   All right. I'll come back.

*He goes, jostled by the couples who fill the stage wildly dancing the polka.*

THE CURTAIN FALLS ON ACT TWO

# ACT THREE

## SCENE I

*The same.* (ISABELLE *sits in the centre of the stage.* HUGO *walks about.*)

ISABELLE.  And so?

HUGO.  And so it doesn't amuse me any more. And, anyway, that moronic mother of yours is going to drop every brick in the hod any moment now. Look at her: cooing and clucking and crowing, all our feathered friends rolled into one. She makes me shiver. She told General de Saint-Mouton that she's the Pope's god-daughter. He's delighted; he can see his catholicism becoming profitable at last; he imagines he's Ambassador to the Vatican already!

ISABELLE.  Am I still to throw myself into the lake?

HUGO.  That's no good now; think of something better, and think quickly, or else my respectable undelectable aunt is quite likely to spoil the whole thing. I know! I've got it!

ISABELLE.  You frighten me when you say that.

HUGO.  There's no doubt you're still the attraction of the evening, in spite of your mother behaving like a circus. You've made a sensation: distinction, poise, reserve. Even the dowagers are on your side.

"What birdwings rocked her cradle, what swift grace
     Caught her and taught her limbs to move
  Gravely as shadows in a sunlit place,
     Or branches in a grove?"

73

I walk behind you, gleaning the whispers, as flattered as if I were an impresario. Your effect on the men needs no comment. But all the mothers with marriageable daughters have shot their lorgnettes at you; and you emerge unscathed! You return triumphant from the underworld of undertones. And the daughters are white with fury. Where Diana fell they tumble after. But all this is only a curtain-raiser, an appetiser, good enough to revive poor Frederic. Now I'm ready for better things! I'm going to start a rumour that you're not Romainville's niece at all, nor can your mother possibly be your mother. Better still, you're the wonderfully wealthy side-issue of a Portuguese princess and an Admiral, an Admiral who wrote Byronic poetry and was drowned at sea (I shall think of one; there must have been several): and this is your coming-out party, incognito. And in the small hours, when my little puffball of a story has been blown sufficiently from mouth to mouth, when my cuckoo-history has laid its eggs in the well-washed ears of all the little ladies, when Diana is withered with jealousy, when my abstracted brother, vaguely flattered by your smiling on him, has begun to look not quite so submissively at his executioner, I shall step from the wings, climb on a chair as though to announce the cotillion, crave silence and say to them more or less: "My lords, ladies and gentlemen, you've been cuckooed!" And, making the most of the confusion, I shall continue: "Dear asses! Tonight has been all a gullery; a fiction, all of it! Conceived, and planned, and carried out to the letter! During these few memorable hours you've been able to see (I shall say, calling on Diana to witness it) into the hearts of these young ladies: the rocks that lie there, the sediment, the dead flowers. . . . And you have also been able to see (and my gesture will light on you) something too like an angel to be true! You've been made dupes of, ladies and gentlemen! What you have called distinction, breeding, poise, are only pretences. This angel, this girl who made your evening dazzle, is a lay-figure hired by me, a poor little ballet dancer from the Opera brought here to play the part. She's not Romainville's niece, and she's not the daughter of any Byronic admiral: she is nothing at all. And no one would have more than barely noticed her if I'd brought her here to do her usual turn. But her turn tonight has been to represent yourselves. I've thrown her amongst you, dressed by your own dressmaker, using the words of your own kind, and this has been enough to knock sideways for a whole evening the prestige of your society beauty. "Vanity, vanity, all is vanity." I hope at least that my brother Frederic now sees the light. As for me, I find you unutterably dreary. I should be glad to have looked my last on the whole lot of you! Tomorrow I set off by the first train to hunt big game in Africa." . . . How do you like that, Isabelle?

ISABELLE (*softly*, *after a pause*).   What happens to me?

HUGO.   You! What do you mean?

ISABELLE.   I mean, what becomes of me?

HUGO.   What do you want to become of you? You go off home, with the present you well deserve, with your mother on your arm and you on Romainville's; and you have a nice dress and a happy memory. Nothing more than that ever remains of a night's dancing.

ISABELLE.   You haven't thought I might be ashamed?

HUGO.   Of what? You're a free spirit, and intelligent. You must loathe all these people as much as I do. Together we're going to have a good laugh at them. What better entertainment? You wouldn't want to be *like* them, would you?

75

ISABELLE.   No, but . . . give the dress to someone else and let me go home! I'll call my mother; you can send us back to St. Fleur *now*, and I promise no one will hear of me again.

HUGO.   Nonsense!

ISABELLE.   It may be, but . . . Not in front of your brother, then! Nor in front of you! Not just yet!

HUGO.   (*breaking free and going*). Yes, now! This moment!

ISABELLE (*calling after him*).   It's wrong to think only of how it's going to amuse you!

HUGO.   It's all there's time for, before we laugh on the other side of our graves.

*He goes.*

ISABELLE *sinks on to the sofa again with a little hurt cry. Enter* DIANA. *She stands for a moment looking at* ISABELLE, *who raises her head and sees her.*

DIANA.   It's quite true; you're wearing a most attractive dress.

ISABELLE.   Yes, it is.

DIANA.   And you're looking beautiful; that's true, too.

ISABELLE.   Thank you.

DIANA.   Perhaps not perfectly groomed, still a little too close to nature; and certainly not a very good powder, nor a very good perfume.

ISABELLE (*she has got up*).   That must be why I find yours a little too good, and you a little too far . . .

DIANA.   Well? Too far what?

ISABELLE.   From nature.

DIANA.   You've managed quite well; but if one hasn't a maid who understands these things it's almost fatal; with the best will in the world one neglects oneself. No woman

76

can tend herself and altogether survive. Do you get up early in the morning?

ISABELLE.  Yes.

DIANA.  Yes, one can see.

ISABELLE.  Do you go late to bed?

DIANA.  Yes.

ISABELLE.  Yes, one can see.

DIANA.  Thank you. Tell me, do you mind very much?

ISABELLE.  Mind what?

DIANA.  Wearing something you haven't made yourself?

ISABELLE.  As a compensation, my eyelashes are my own.

DIANA.  Happily for you. You'll need them tomorrow, without the help you get from the dress.

ISABELLE.  I take it away with me. It was given me.

DIANA.  That's very nice, isn't it? You'll be able to be a beauty all over again. I believe there's going to be a jolly dance on the fourteenth day of July at St. Fleur. You'll turn all the bumpkins' heads. Do you like my dress?

ISABELLE.  Yes, it's most beautiful.

DIANA.  Would you like it? I shall never wear it again. I hardly ever wear a dress more than once. Besides, I can't really tell myself I like petunia. Tomorrow I shall dine in rose-pink, rather a miracle dress, a harass of little pleats, twenty yards of them. If you come up to my room I'll show it to you. Come and see it; I'm sure it'll give you pleasure.

ISABELLE.  No.

DIANA.  Why not? Do you envy me? That's one of the sins, you know. (*She goes to her.*) You'd love to be rich, wouldn't you? If this evening were only a true story, and you had as many dresses as I have!

ISABELLE.  Naturally.

77

DIANA. But you'll never have more than one, isn't that so? And if I put my foot on your train, in this way, and tug it a little, you'll not even have one.

ISABELLE. Take your foot away!

DIANA. No.

ISABELLE. Take your foot away or else I shall hit you!

DIANA. Don't squirm, you little fury; you'll do some damage!

*The dress tears.*

ISABELLE (*with a sorrowful cry*). Oh! My dress!

DIANA. You did it yourself. A few tacks, it will still do very nicely for St. Fleur. It's exciting, I expect, to have such a triumphant evening with a borrowed dress on your back. The pity is, it's over so soon. Tomorrow morning you have to pack your cardboard box, and I shall still be here, and that's the difference between us.

ISABELLE (*looks at her without dislike, and suddenly says*): Is it so pleasant to be unpleasant?

DIANA (*changing her tone, sitting and sighing*). No, not at all. But one can't always be pleased.

ISABELLE. Can you be unhappy as well? That's very strange. Why?

DIANA. I have too much money.

ISABELLE. But Frederic loves you.

DIANA. I don't love him. I love Hugo, and he dislikes my money, and I think he's right.

ISABELLE. Become poor, then.

DIANA. Do you think it is so easy?

ISABELLE. I make no effort.

DIANA. You don't know how lucky you are. I suppose this is a lovely party—but all my friends give parties like it. I shall never again know the excitement of being "invited up to the great house"—and that's so sad.

ISABELLE. So sad.

DIANA. I tell you, money is only worth something to the poor!

ISABELLE. Which proves there is something the matter with the world. (*She moves towards* DIANA.) I have been humiliated and hurt this evening, and my only dress has been torn, because I'm one of the poor ones. I'm going to do what the poor ones always do. I'm leaving words for deeds, and asking you to go away.

DIANA. Go away? Do you think you're in your own home, you little adventuress?

ISABELLE. Go and cry over your millions somewhere a long way off! I'm pretty stupid and very ashamed to have spent so many minutes trying to understand you. So now I shall use the arguments of the poor. If you don't go I shall throw you out.

DIANA. Throw me out? Let me see you try!

ISABELLE. You're going to see me try! And as you wouldn't care if I tore your dress, I shall tear your face instead: God has been unusually impartial, giving us one face each.

DIANA. You're a common little slut. Do you think I'm afraid?

ISABELLE. Not yet. But I think you may be.

ISABELLE *leaps on* DIANA. *They fight.*

DIANA. Oh! You'll ruin my hair!

ISABELLE. You have a maid to put it right! What does it matter?

DIANE (*fighting*). I've got claws as well as you!

ISABELLE. Then use them!

*They fight.* DIANA *suddenly stops and cries out:*

DIANA. I was poor once, myself! When I was ten I fought all the little toughs on the docks at Istamboul!

79

*They throw themselves at each other again and roll on the ground. Enter* JOSHUA, *who gives a yell of terror when he sees them and—*
*goes off shouting for* MR. HUGO.
FREDERIC *enters immediately and stands speechless. The* GIRLS *see him and loose each other.* ISABELLE *rises first, scratched and dishevelled. She goes to him.*

ISABELLE. Well, are you satisfied now? Don't you think you've had a great success? You wanted entertainment, and no one can now say you haven't had it. How is this for your scandal? You stood up on your chair and told them who I was: or if you haven't yet, you have no need to. I'm going to show myself to them, looking as I am. A common little slut, as this lady called me. You can watch your bit of fun get funnier. They'll have no doubts about me now; they'll know exactly where I come from! Do you want me to tell you the climax of the ball? To begin with, I insult my mother: I pluck her feathers in front of them all: and I take her away, back to her piano lessons. Down the wind goes the Countess Funela! Her father sold wallpaper; he carried the rolls on his back and a paste-pot in his hand. They used to give him five francs a time, which kept him happy because it meant he could buy himself a drink without telling his wife. That's the poor for you! You wanted to play with them tonight because you were bored, but you'll see what a mistake it was, and how right your nurses were when you were little and told you not to play with the common children in the park. They don't know how to play, and I haven't played for one moment since I came here. I've been unhappy: isn't that vulgar of me? I've been unhappy. And all because you didn't understand, or wouldn't understand,

80

that I love you. It's because I love you that I've done my
best to dazzle them this evening; it's because I love you
that I've pretended to love your brother; it's because I
love you that I was ready to throw myself in the lake, like
a baby and a fool, to finish it all! If I hadn't loved you,
and loved you from the moment we met, do you think I
should have agreed to be in your mad puppet show? . . .
Well, won't you say something? It's tiresome, of course,
this poor girl standing here saying she loves you. But
please say *something*. You usually say so much. What's
the matter?

FREDERIC (*stammering*). But . . . I'm afraid . . . none of
this was me.

ISABELLE. What do you mean, not me?

DIANA. Certainly it wasn't. Look at him. He's blushing:
it's his brother!

ISABELLE (*suddenly confused*). Oh, I'm so sorry. . . . I'm so
very sorry.

FREDERIC. No, no, no. It's I who should be sorry. I should
have . . .

DIANA. Come away, Frederic. There's nothing you need
say to this girl. Hugo will send Joshua along to pay her,
and she can go home.

FREDERIC. Don't talk like that, Diana.

DIANA. You will come with me now, Frederic, at once, or
from now on you can stay away from me.

   *She goes.*

FREDERIC. I came to tell you how distressed I am by what
you've been made to go through this evening, how
unpleasant and cruel I know it has been. May I ask you
to accept my most sincere apologies for all the rest of
them here?

ISABELLE (*gently*). You must go. If you don't follow her
quickly she going to make you very wretched.

81

FREDERIC (*bowing*). Will you excuse me, then? (*He takes a step.*) Shall I explain to my brother that you've told me you love him?

ISABELLE. No; there's no need.

> FREDERIC *makes a sorrowful gesture—and goes.*
> THE MOTHER *sweeps in.*

THE MOTHER. Oh, my dear child! Such mortification!

ISABELLE. I was coming to find you.

THE MOTHER (*sinking into a chair*). Everything has collapsed! The young man has gone mad. He got up on to a chair, and said simply terrible things. There must be something really very wrong with his head. It's most unfortunate. If he had only waited for another hour I should have been spending the autumn with a General, a very nice one. But now everybody will turn their backs on me, I know they will.

ISABELLE (*rising*). We're leaving now, Mother. Take off your finery. You have to give your piano lessons again next week.

THE MOTHER. You're quite extraordinary. There's not an ounce of poetry in you. All our brilliant dreams vanish, and you go on as usual. You're so insensitive. He couldn't have loved you, I suppose, and I was so convinced. . . . Well, why, why should he have asked you here if he wasn't in love with you?

ISABELLE. You've talked quite enough. Go and take off your feathers.

THE MOTHER (*going to her*). Now just listen to me. I've had a long conversation with Romainville. All this business this evening has nudged him awake, and he's spoken up at last. You've seen yourself this evening how the high-flown young men behave. Romainville is middle-aged, steady, and a gentleman. He has had his eye on you for a long time, he told me so himself: he knows just what he can expect. He isn't going into it with his eyes shut. So there you are. He'll see we're both taken good care of; moreover, he hasn't actually said, but I know he means, that when he has talked his family round he may even make a promise to marry you. Isn't that a nice surprise, dear?

ISABELLE. Now go upstairs.

THE MOTHER (*getting up, furious*). All right then; go your own way; never think of me and all I've done for you! Lose a good chance, you stupid little ninny, and lose your looks, too, before they get you anywhere!

MESSERSCHMANN *enters.*

(*Suddenly all smiles*) Oh, I'm so happy to see you! How do you do?

MESSER (*coldly*). Well, madam.

THE MOTHER. The Countess Funela. We were introdduced just now, but in such a hub-bub. . . .

MESSER. Madam, I must ask you to let me have a few moments alone with your daughter.

THE MOTHER. But of course you may. I give you my permission without any hesitation at all. . . . I'm leaving you with Mr. Messerschmann now, Isabelle. I'm going upstairs for a little rest. These social occasions, you know, are so tiring. One comes to wish for a little peace and quiet. We go out too much, I'm afraid, a great deal too much. I'll leave you. . . . Don't forget about our good friend, Isabelle. We must give him an answer tonight, you know, to his charming invitation for the summer. . . . Dear sir, I'm delighted to have seen you again!

*She flounces away.*

MESSER (*speaking straight out*). Now, young lady, I'm going to be rather brutal. I know who you are, and in half an hour's time everybody will know. The party's over, as far as you're concerned. You've had a great success, everybody's been charmed by you, but it was a little adventure which couldn't last. I've come to ask you to cut it even shorter. Go up to your room and disappear without seeing anyone again. And I shall be most grateful to you.

ISABELLE. How can it affect you whether I go or stay?

MESSER. It's a little present I should like to give my daughter. You see, I make no bones about it. I've never deceived anyone in my business affairs, and I've always succeeded. How much do you want?

ISABELLE. Nothing. I had decided to go before you asked me.

MESSER. I know. But it isn't fair that you should go without being paid. How much did Hugo promise you?

ISABELLE. My usual dancing fee, and this dress, which someone has torn.

MESSER. Who tore it?

ISABELLE. Your daughter.

MESSER. Then that's my business, too. As well as what you were going to ask me, I'll pay for two more dresses.

ISABELLE. Thank you, but I'm happy with this one, with the tear.

MESSER. Let's get the situation clear. I don't want you to see Hugo again, even to get your fee. How much do I pay you to go without seeing him?

ISABELLE. Nothing at all. I didn't expect to see him.

MESSER. But how about the money he promised you?

ISABELLE. I don't intend to take it. I can be said to have danced here this evening for my own pleasure.

MESSERSCHMANN *looks at her for a moment, in silence, then weightily and powerfully moves towards her.*

84

MESSER.   I don't like it when things don't cost anything, young lady.

ISABELLE.   Does it disturb you?

MESSER.   It's too expensive. Why are you refusing Hugo's money?

ISABELLE.   Because I'm glad not to take it.

MESSER.   And mine?

ISABELLE.   Because you haven't any reason to give it to me. I was asked to act in a comedy here this evening. My performance is over, the curtain is down, and I'm going home.

MESSER.   But not with nothing to show for it?

ISABELLE.   Why not?

MESSER.   It's not as it should be.

ISABELLE.   I'm sorry, but it's what I'm going to do. You will excuse me. (*She starts to go.*)

MESSER (*suddenly furious*).   No, no, no! Don't be like Ossowitch!

ISABELLE (*stops, astonished*).   Like Ossowitch?

MESSER.   Yes. He was a banker of a rival group, and I had to have important discussions with him. I never met such a man for getting up and going. Whenever we disagreed, which was pretty often, he got up and went. Every time I had to catch up with him in the vestibule or in the lift or somewhere. And the further I had to go to catch him, the more it cost me. In the end I had to invite him to come out in a canoe, when I'd first made quite sure he couldn't swim. After that we were wonderfully good friends: but now he has learnt to swim and things are not so nice. So don't you start this getting up and going, my dear child, it isn't a good way to talk. Nobody ever agrees with anybody in a business discussion, but we stay sitting, or else business is no good. Now, come along, my dear young lady, be reasonable. Strike a good bargain with me before it's too late. What do you want?

85

ISABELLE. Nothing.

MESSER. It's too much. Now, look, I'm going to be foolish. I'm going to offer you twice what you expect. I've the notes on me here. (*He brings a bundle of notes from his pocket.*) Look at this bundle here, such virgins and so clean, such a pretty little bunch! It would be very nice, you will agree with me, to carry about a sprig or two of these little papers?

ISABELLE. How should I carry them?

MESSER (*suddenly like a shopkeeper*). Would you like me to wrap them up for you? I could make you a nice little parcel of them.

ISABELLE. Listen. I don't want to have to walk out like Mr. Ossowitch; I don't want to bring back unhappy memories to you; but I insist that you believe me. I don't want your money.

MESSER (*pocketing the notes, furious*). You're being very exorbitant.

ISABELLE (*looks at him and says*): Is it really possible to be a great power in the world without being very intelligent?

MESSER. I am intelligent! I'm very intelligent! It's because I'm very intelligent and experienced that I tell you I don't believe you!

ISABELLE (*taking him gently by the arm*). Then, if you're intelligent, let's talk intelligently. If you hadn't kept me here I should have been gone already. So you see I have nothing to sell.

MESSER (*angrily*). There's always something to sell! Anyway, even if you haven't, I've got to buy something now we've started bargaining.

ISABELLE. Why?

MESSER. Why? Because I should lose all faith in myself if I didn't.

86

ISABELLE (*with a slight smile*).　If it takes so little to make you lose faith, I must write to Mr. Ossowitch.

MESSER (*calmer*).　Ossowitch was a baby. But you're an opponent who interests me. What I'm buying from you now isn't my daughter's peace of mind any more, it's my own peace of mind. And I put no limit whatsoever on that. How much do you want?

ISABELLE.　Do men become masters of the world by continually repeating themselves?

MESSER.　You're as rich as any girl in the house tonight. And if I want it, Romainville shall adopt you: you really will be his niece!

ISABELLE.　Thank you.

MESSER.　Listen. I'll make you so rich, the grandest and handsomest young fellow here will ask you to marry him immediately.

ISABELLE.　I'm sorry. But none of that will please me as much as saying No to you.

MESSER (*suddenly howling*).　Whatever shall I do? I don't believe in money any more either! All it gives me is dust, smoke, nausea, and indigestion. I eat noodles and I drink water, and I get no pleasure at all from my frozen snow-queen mistress: I don't even suffer when she deceives me, because I don't really want her: I want nothing at all! I'm a poor little tailor from Cracow, and my only really pleasant memory is the first suit I made when I was sixteen: a jacket for a priest, and it turned out very well. My father said to me: "This time you have done it well: you know now what your calling is." And I was happy . . . but since then I've succeeded at nothing, except at making money, more and more money, and money has never made anybody love me, not even my own daughter. Please be sympathetic. Do stand by me this evening. Take my money!

ISABELLE. No.

MESSER. No? Ah well: now you can see what I'll do with these beautiful little bundles which can't do anything: I'll bite them and tear them with my teeth and spit them on the ground!

*He has taken the bundle of notes and starts tearing them with his own teeth; then, soon, for the sake of speed, with his hands.*

ISABELLE (*joyfully*). What a good idea! Give me some, I'll help you. This will make me feel much better!

*She takes some of the bundles and starts happily and quietly tearing them up. They throw the scraps of paper into the air. They both work feverishly in a rain of paper.*

MESSER (*in a kind of fury*). There! So! So! There! So! That's a country house: the dream of all the small householders!

ISABELLE (*tearing away merrily*). With the garden, the pond, the goldfish, the roses!

MESSER. Everything! There goes a business. A millinery business: the one I was going to give you, like the fool I was!

ISABELLE (*tearing*). Hooray! That was a hat!

MESSER (*annoyed, but not stopping*). Why only one hat?

ISABELLE. It was very expensive!

MESSER. There go the dresses, and still more dresses, rolls and folds and billows of material, what they're all dying to put on their backs. There go the cloaks and the coats and the wraps and the furs!

ISABELLE (*tearing*). Not too many: it's nearly summertime!

MESSER. Away goes the beautiful linen, the satin sheets, petticoats as light as cobwebs, embroidered handkerchiefs!

ISABELLE (*tearing*). There goes a trunk!

MESSER (*stopping in surprise*). Why a trunk?

ISABELLE. To put everything into!

MESSER (*starting again*). There go the necklaces, the bracelets, the rings—all the rings!

ISABELLE (*tearing*). Oh! Such a beautiful pearl!

MESSER. You'll regret that!

ISABELLE (*taking more to tear*). No, not a bit!

MESSER. Away go the holidays abroad, the servants, the racehorses, the beautiful ladies ready and willing, away go the consciences of honest men, and all the prosperity of this lamentable world! There! There! There! There! (*He tears the last of the notes and turns to her.*) Are you happy now?

ISABELLE (*softly*). No. Are you?

MESSER. Not at all.

*They are kneeling side by side, exhausted.* ISABELLE *finds one untorn note on the ground and tears it up.*

ISABELLE. There go the poor! We'd forgotten them. (*A pause. She looks at the exhausted* MESSERSCHMANN *and asks him gently*): I bet it wasn't so exhausting to get it all!

MESSER. I'm very unhappy.

ISABELLE (*with a wry smile*). Me, too.

MESSER. I understand very well how you feel. And I'm the only person in this house this evening who does understand. For a long time, such a long time, I was humiliated, until I became stronger than they were. Then I could turn the tables. Every man is quite alone. That's definite. No one can help anyone else: he can only go on.

89

*They both look straight in front of them, squatting on the ground in the middle of the torn notes.* JOSHUA *enters and finds them so, to his surprise.*

(*Seeing him*) What do you want?

JOSHUA. It's Mr. Hugo, sir: he wishes to speak to the young lady in the little drawing-room, to settle her account.

ISABELLE (*getting up*). Tell him he doesn't owe me anything. Mr. Messerschmann has paid me.

*She goes.*

MESSERSCHMANN *watches her go, then rises with difficulty, with* JOSHUA's *help.*

MESSER. My friend.

JOSHUA. Sir?

MESSER. You seem to have a pleasant face.

JOSHUA (*after the first astonishment*). I belong to a generation of old servants who could never permit themselves to have such a thing while on duty, sir. But on Sundays, and particularly on holidays, my friends tell me I have an amiable face, sir, almost jovial, what I hope I may call a nice face, very French and very homely, sir.

MESSER. Then listen to me. You must have read your Bible when you were a little boy?

JOSHUA. Here and there, sir, like everybody else.

MESSER. Did you ever come across Samson?

JOSHUA. The gentleman who had his hair cut, sir?

MESSER. Yes; and he was very unhappy. Jeered at, my friend, always jeered at by everybody. They had put his eyes out. They thought he was blind, but I'm sure he could see.

JOSHUA. Quite possible, sir. . . .

90

MESSER. And then, one fine day, unable to stand it any more, he got them to lead him between the pillars of the temple. He was very strong, terribly strong, you understand? He twined his arms round the pillars . . . (*He puts his arms round the dismayed* JOSHUA.) Like this!

JOSHUA. Oh, sir! Do take care, sir, someone will see us!

MESSER. And then he shook them with all his might. (*He shakes* JOSHUA.)

JOSHUA (*being shaken*). Yes, sir! Do be careful, sir! I'm the one who will get into trouble!

MESSER (*letting him go with a sigh, his feelings relieved*). There!

JOSHUA (*putting himself to rights*). Well, there, sir. (*He adds, for something to say*): It wasn't at all the thing to do in a church. . . .

MESSER (*with a dark chuckle*). You might well say so. He was so strong the entire temple crumbled down on to the two thousand Philistines who were there praying to their false gods, and thinking Samson no better than a fool!

JOSHUA. But it fell on him, too, sir.

MESSER. It fell on him, too. But that wasn't of any kind of importance. How could being poor hurt him!

JOSHUA. If you say so, sir.

*A pause.* JOSHUA *starts to go.*

MESSER. My friend.

JOSHUA. Sir?

MESSER. I'm putting through an overseas telephone call from my room tonight.

JOSHUA. Certainly, sir.

MESSER. That's all. Like Samson. With my eyes tight shut.

91

JOSHUA (*going*).　Quite so, sir.

MESSER.　And all at once there's a frightful uproar, a telephone ringing in the small hours. And that is the temple starting to crumble. Do you understand?

JOSHUA.　No, sir.

MESSER.　It doesn't matter. (*He finds a forgotten note in his pocket and gives it to* JOSHUA.) Here's a thousand francs. Forget everything I've said. (*As he goes out, he turns and says*): And for supper, you remember . . . without butter.

JOSHUA (*bowing*).　And without salt.


### THE CURTAIN FALLS


## SCENE 2


*As the lights begin to fade in,* ISABELLE *is seen wandering across the stage. She drifts across the bridge and away into the park towards the lake.*

MADAME DESMERMORTES *wheels herself in, watching* ISABELLE *through her opera glasses.*

CAPULAT *enters in a terrible state.*


CAPULAT.　Madam, madam! Everyone's searching the place for Isabelle. Her mother is out of her mind!

MME. DESMER.　Why?

CAPULAT.　She has left her ring, the only valuable thing she has, wrapped up in a piece of paper on her dressing-table. Oh, madam, madam, we're all to blame! Mr. Hugo didn't love her!

MME. DESMER.　You can cry later on, Capulat. Look out there, down to the lake; I can't see. Is there a white figure there?

CAPULAT. There is, you're quite right. And it's Isabelle, it really is, it is really! Oh dear, oh dear, unhappy girl! Oh, madam, she's leaning over the water. Oh, madam, madam, madam, she has jumped! Rescue her! Rescue her! She'll be drowned, really she will, she will really!

MME. DESMER. No, she won't. Hugo is down there, and there isn't enough water. But she might quite well catch cold, and so might he. Run and get some blankets.

CAPULAT. Mr. Hugo is there, you're quite right, he's there. He has plunged into the water—oh, hero! It's all right, I think, madam, it's all right. He'll save her.

MME. DESMER. It could hardly be less difficult.

CAPULAT. He has picked her up in his arms, he has really, and they're coming glittering across the grass in an armour of moisture, madam, as you might say.

MME. DESMER. As I certainly wouldn't say. Stop talking nonsense, you stupid woman, and go at once and find some blankets.

CAPULAT *hurries off*.

Joshua! Joshua! Someone! Quickly!

JOSHUA (*appearing*). Madam?

MME. DESMER. I'm afraid we're having a little drama here this evening, Joshua: heartbreak and attempted death by water. I'm so sorry. Do go down to the kitchens and make some very hot punch.

JOSHUA. Yes, madam. Nothing serious, I hope?

MME. DESMER. Not at all. What a blessing you are, Joshua. Do try never to break *your* heart, won't you?

JOSHUA. I handle it with as much care, madam, as if it was yours. It's quite safe with me, madam.

MME. DESMER. The punch, Joshua.

JOSHUA (*bowing*). Hot and very soon, madam.

*As he goes—*

*Enter* HUGO *and* ISABELLE *wrapped in blankets, and followed by* CAPULAT.

CAPULAT. They're safe, madam, they're safe, but they're wet!

MME. DESMER. I can show almost no surprise. Go and tell your friend that her daughter is well.

CAPULAT. I will. She was out of her mind!
*She goes.*

MME. DESMER. Are you cold, my dear?

ISABELLE. No, thanks; no, no, I'm not.

MME. DESMER. Joshua has gone to fetch you some punch. Are you cold, Hugo?

HUGO. Frozen, thank you, aunt.

MME. DESMER. Then let's make the most of being alone for a few minutes. Stay as you are. Sit down. Sit down, Hugo. Now, look at me, my dear.

ISABELLE *looks at her.*

She looks even prettier with her hair down. Why do you ever wear it up?

ISABELLE. It's the usual way.

MME. DESMER. Is it also the usual way, at the first crossing of love, to walk into a lake? You can swim, I imagine?

ISABELLE. Yes, I can swim.

MME. DESMER. You see how absurd you are!

HUGO. I suppose it was my fault. I asked her to pretend to drown herself for love of Frederic; but I cancelled the arrangement immediately afterwards. I simply don't know what she thought she was doing.

MME. DESMER. Why should you want to drown yourself?

ISABELLE. For my own reasons.

HUGO. It wasn't in our agreement. You were supposed to do what you were told.

94

ISABELLE. My working-day was over. You had already sent the butler to pay me; and I think I'm allowed to kill myself in my own free time, if I want to.

MME. DESMER. Certainly she is! And it's very nearly morning, and Sunday morning, too. If a working-man can't kill himself on a Sunday morning we can have the revolution at once.

> "For pity, pretty eyes, surcease
>     To give me war! and grant me peace."

You know you're a madman, don't you, Hugo?

HUGO. Yes, aunt.

MME. DESMER. He doesn't love you, my dear, and he'll never love you. He'll never love anyone, I think, if that's any consolation to you. He'll be amorous, perhaps, like a cat with a mouse, from time to time; but you're too delicate a mouse: he would eat you too soon, which he wouldn't like at all. And I'm going to tell you a splendid thing: he's not your sort of cat, either. You think you're in love with him. In fact, you're not in love with him at all. Look at him. Look at him. Look at this sulky Red Indian. Isn't he comic?

ISABELLE *looks at* HUGO.

You find him so handsome? Well, so he is, tolerably, when he's not thinking of anything. Clear eyes, straight nose, an interesting mouth. But let even the smallest of his wicked little thoughts creep into him—look at him now, for instance: we're irritating him: he wants to strangle us—and the change is quite terrifying. The nose is getting pinched, there's an angry little crease tugging the mouth, the eyes are turning themselves into gimlets. . . . And this chin! It suddenly makes him, wouldn't you say, into a fairly pretty but entirely wicked old woman?

95

No one's altogether handsome who isn't altogether human.

HUGO (*getting up in a rage*). That's quite enough! If you want to analyze faces I'll go and send Frederic to you.

MME. DESMER. That's a very good idea.

HUGO *goes*.

No, my dear, it's the appearance of Hugo you love, not Hugo.

ISABELLE (*hiding her eyes and crying*). Oh, it's terrible!

MME. DESMER. It would be terrible, if we only had one specimen; but fortunately we have two.

FREDERIC *enters*.

(*To* FREDERIC) Come here, my nephew. You can look at him, Isabelle; it's the same picture as before. Here is a young woman who was going to drown herself, and we can't get her to tell us why.

FREDERIC (*to* ISABELLE). I know why. I wish I could help you, but there's nothing I can do. There's something I want to tell you. When I left you just now I was being a coward for the last time. I followed Diana when she told me to. But when I caught her up I couldn't help telling her how wickedly she had treated you. And it's all over now: our engagement is broken off.

ISABELLE. Oh, no, no! Do you think it does any good for us both to be unhappy at once?

FREDERIC. I don't know, but I do know I couldn't love someone who could be so cruel.

MME. DESMER. Neither can Isabelle. She's beginning to see she could never love Hugo.

FREDERIC. I've finished with love altogether. I saw down to the sea-bed of a woman's heart.

96

ISABELLE (*smiling gently*).  The rocks that lie there, the sediment, the dead flowers, as your brother said.

FREDERIC.  It's the worst plunge I ever took.

MME. DESMER.  Come up to the surface again; there's still some dry land in places.

FREDERIC.  I'm going to find a desert island, out of the way of it all.

MME. DESMER.  And so is Isabelle. Make sure that your desert islands aren't too far apart. You can have visiting days, hermit to hermit.

FREDERIC.  I could have forgiven her for being unkind . . .

ISABELLE.  I saw from the first I had to take him as he was, and forgave him for that, but . . .

FREDERIC.  I could have forgiven her for being hard, egotistical and hot-tempered . . .

ISABELLE.  I could have forgiven him . . .

MME. DESMER.  The only thing you could never forgive them was not loving you. We're terrible tailors! We cut the cloth, take no measurements, and when it doesn't fit we cry for help.

FREDERIC.  And no one comes.

MME. DESMER.  Or so we think. Not content with being blind we have to be deaf as well. We all go howling along together, never seeing or hearing who's beside us, and then we say we're in a wilderness! Luckily there are certain old women who have begun to see more clearly, just at the time, alas, when they're having to take to spectacles. Didn't you hear anything, young lady? This young gentleman called for help.

ISABELLE.  How can I help him?

MME. DESMER.  You can take him into the park and tell him why you feel so unhappy. And he'll tell you why his life seems over. Go along; be as sad as you possibly can;

97

give her your arm, Frederic. You're quite alone in the world. No one is more hopeless than you are.

FREDERIC (*going with* ISABELLE). It's my own fault for being such a fool. I imagined women could be warm-hearted and have sincerity.

ISABELLE. And, of course, they can't. I imagined men could be honest and good and faithful.

FREDERIC. Faithful! We're faithful to ourselves, that's all. We dance the dance of the heart obstinately in front of a mirror. But I expected the dance to be with a partner.

ISABELLE. And there are no partners . . .

*They have gone.*

MME. DESMERMORTES *watches them off.*

MME. DESMER. Good. Those two only need another five minutes. Now for the others. (*She calls.*) Hugo!

HUGO *enters by another door.*

HUGO. Yes, Aunt?

MME. DESMER. That's as good as done. Now what have you decided?

HUGO. What do you want me to decide?

MME. DESMER. Either I'm a dense and myopic old woman, my dearest Hugo, or you're in love with Diana, and she with you, and you have been since the first day you met.

HUGO. Absolutely ludicrous! And even if it were true, I'd rather die of jaundice, like your friend Palestrini you were talking about, than give her the pleasure of hearing me say so.

MME. DESMER. You can't die of jaundice—Palestrini's as well as you or I. Only last year he threw himself into a lagoon because he was in love with an Austrian swimming champion. She rescued him, and they have a baby.

*Enter* PATRICE BOMBELLES.

98

PATRICE. Oh, there you are, I've been looking for you everywhere.

MME. DESMER. What does this madman want?

PATRICE. Sir, as you will not give this young woman up of your own accord . . . (*He slaps* HUGO'S *face.*)

HUGO (*slapping back*). Go away, for heaven's sake. I won't have you making such a confounded nuisance of yourself.

PATRICE. Well, may you be forgiven . . .

HUGO. May I be forgiven. . . . Are you insulting me?

PATRICE. Yes, I am insulting you. You told me to insult you.

HUGO. Well, now I'm telling you to stop insulting me. Go away for goodness sake. . . .

PATRICE. I demand satisfaction. . . .

HUGO. If you don't go I shall knock you down.

PATRICE. The arrangement was pistols—the arrangement was pistols.

> HUGO *leaps on* PATRICE. *They fight in spite of* MME. DESMERMORTES *trying to separate them with her stick. Enter* LADY INDIA, *terrified.*

LADY INDIA. Patrice!

PATRICE (*freeing himself at once*). Oh, my goodness, look, she's here! Do try to seem friendly. (*He puts his arm round* HUGO'S *shoulder.*) We were playing, my dear! We love playing together! A little early morning exercise, you know.

LADY INDIA. This is no time to be taking exercise, Patrice! Do you know what has happened? I've had a call from Paris. Messerschmann is out of his mind. He is selling in London, he is selling in New York, he is selling in Paris. He's ruining himself!

99

PATRICE.   I don't believe it. I'll go and ring up his agent!
*He rushes out.*

DIANA *enters.*

DIANA.   Have you heard the news? Within six hours my father will be a poor man.

HUGO.   What are you going to do about it?

DIANA.   Be poor. What do you expect me to do?

HUGO.   Marry Frederic, who is rich.

DIANA.   I don't want him. And now he doesn't want me. Look at him, down there in the park with the little adventuress. She hasn't lost much time tonight. Was it you, Hugo, who taught her how to find a rich husband in one evening? You will have to teach me. I need one now.

HUGO.   Let's be quite clear about this: it's a lesson that wouldn't help you in the least.

*He starts to go.* MME. DESMERMORTES *stops him.*

MME. DESMER.   Hugo, where are you going?

HUGO.   I'm going to find Frederic. It's no good his thinking he can break the engagement now. Diana's ruined, and the honourable thing is to make her his wife.

DIANA (*in tears*).   But I don't want him!

HUGO.   We can't help that.

*He goes.*

MME. DESMER.   Mille tonnerres! He's going to mix everything up again!

*Enter* CAPULAT *and* THE MOTHER.

CAPULAT.   Madam! News! Extraordinary news! It really is!

MME. DESMER.   I think we have heard it.

THE MOTHER.   You've heard it? Now how could that possibly be? But news travels so fast these days. Here he is, to tell you himself.

100

*Wedding March from the orchestra. Enter* ROMAIN-
VILLE *in morning coat and white gloves, carrying a
bouquet. He goes to* MME. DESMERMORTES.

ROMAINVILLE.   My dear friend. In the first place, please
excuse my clothes, but as dawn is about to break I
changed into a morning coat: I felt it to be the correct
wear for the present occasion. I'm going to give you some
interesting news: my niece, dear friend, is not my niece—
that was an entirely imaginary relationship spun from
your nephew's fancy. But she is about to become even
more nearly related. After extremely careful thought, I've
decided to marry her.

MME. DESMER.   My good man, I would be the first to
congratulate you, but I have an idea that you're too late.

ROMAINVILLE.   Too late? What can you mean? It's five
o'clock in the morning.

> ISABELLE *and* FREDERIC *come in with their arms round
> one another.*

MME. DESMER.   (*To* ISABELLE *and* FREDERIC.) Well, my
dears, what news have you for us? Have you altered the
fit of the coat?

ISABELLE.   There wasn't any need to alter it! It fitted
perfectly!

FREDERIC.   Aunt, I must have been out of my mind. I
don't love you any more, Diana; do forgive me.

ISABELLE.   Why couldn't I have known it before? It was
Frederic, just as you said.

MME. DESMER.   Romainville, you'll have to get some
other niece. This is the one you have to give away!

ROMAINVILLE.   It's appalling! I had just begun to like
the idea!

> JOSHUA *enters, carrying a tray.*

MME. DESMER (*to* JOSHUA). Joshua, give him some of the punch.

ROMAINVILLE *drinks the punch.*

But where is Hugo? Someone go and find him at once. He has made this girl unhappy for quite long enough. (*To* DIANA.) Don't be too dismayed; he loves you, he told me so.

LADY INDIA. Why, look! He's down there in the park, escaping!

MME. DESMER. Escaping? Joshua, catch him before he goes, and bring him here.

JOSHUA *goes.*

(*To* DIANA.) He's a thoroughly crack-brained boy, but he knows he's cornered; he's certain to come back.

DIANA. But suppose he doesn't love me?

MME. DESMER. Impossible. Everything has to end happily, it's only decent. Besides, here he is. Well, Hugo?

*They all look at the door through which* HUGO *should come. A pause. It is* JOSHUA *who enters.*

FREDERIC. I knew he wouldn't come!

JOSHUA. Mr. Hugo has given me this note for you, madam.

MME. DESMER. Read it aloud, Joshua.

JOSHUA (*puts on his glasses and reads*). "Dear Aunt,—For reasons which you all know, I'm not able to appear among you to take part in the general rejoicing. There's nothing I've ever regretted more. But now Diana is poor I know I love her. Nothing will separate us again. I shall marry her. Tell her to look for me in the park."

102

MME. DESMER (*to the happy* DIANA).   Off you go!

DIANA.   Yes, I will! Oh, Hugo! Hugo!

DIANA *goes.*

*Enter* MESSERSCHMANN *with a little overcoat, a little hat, and a little suitcase. Mocking music from the orchestra.*

MME. DESMER.   What's this, will someone tell me?

MESSER.   It is I, madam. I've come to say good bye.

MME. DESMER.   But the suitcase, the hat, the coat?

MESSER.   I borrowed them from your butler. I've nothing of my own to put on. I'm ruined. I shall return them in a few years' time. I'm going back to Cracow, on foot, to start a small tailoring business.

LADY INDIA (*running into his arms*).   Oh, my darling boy, what a great, great man you are after all! You must love me so much, so beautifully. It was for me, wasn't it, that you ruined yourself? I'll follow you: barefooted to the bottom of the Steppes of Siberia!

MME. DESMER (*to the others*).   She gets so muddled.

LADY INDIA.   I'll cook for you, my darling, in your dark, dingy igloo, ever your faithful squaw.

MME. DESMER.   She hasn't even a working idea of geography.

*A frightful racket suddenly, flashes and bangs. Everybody turns round. Enter* PATRICE BOMBELLES.

PATRICE.   There they go! They've started!

LADY INDIA.   What is it? The fire from heaven already?

MME. DESMER.   No. We haven't deserved that, not quite, not yet. It's my firework display, which all the upset tonight has made a little late. Come along, come and watch: the gardener will be so disappointed if we don't.

It will feel rather odd, in broad daylight. We shall hardly be able to see them.

*As they all go out—*

*Enter* JOSHUA *with a telegram. He plucks* MESSERSCHMANN *by the sleeve.*

JOSHUA. Sir, a telegram for you, sir.

MESSER (*opening it*). Who is still sufficiently interested in me to send me a telegram? A letter would have done just as well. (*He reads it and sighs.*) How funny it all is. . . .

JOSHUA (*compassionately*). All over, sir, is it? If you should still need anything, sir . . . I've got a small amount in the savings-bank. . . .

MESSER. What? No, thank you. It's not so easy to ruin yourself as you'd think. It was believed to be a manœuvre on the stock exchange. They bought everything, and now I'm twice as rich as I was before! . . . But I do beg of you: don't let anyone know.

JOSHUA. I must say, I'm very happy for you, sir. I should have felt very sad, sir, not to have brought you your breakfast. (*He has taken up his butler's stance, and says*): Without butter?

MESSER. Yes, my friend. But this morning, as a special celebration, you may add a little salt.

JOSHUA (*following him*). Ah, it's a happy day for me, sir, to see you taking such a pleasure in life again. . . .

*They go.*

### THE CURTAIN FALLS

104